STARK

ABITUR 2015

Prüfungsaufgaben mit Lösungen

2015

Englisch

Leistungskurs
Gymnasium
Sachsen

2009–2014

STARK

ISBN 978-3-8490-0988-5

© 2014 by Stark Verlagsgesellschaft mbH & Co. KG
20. ergänzte Auflage
www.stark-verlag.de

Inhalt

Fortsetzung siehe nächste Seite

Abiturprüfungsaufgaben

Jeweils im Herbst erscheinen die neuen Ausgaben
der Abiturprüfungsaufgaben mit Lösungen.

Autoren

Klimmt, Robert: Hinweise und Tipps,
                      Lösungen zu den Abiturprüfungsaufgaben
Redaktion: Kurzgrammatik

Vorwort

Liebe Schülerin, lieber Schüler,

bald werden Sie Ihre Abiturprüfung im Fach Englisch ablegen. Wir begleiten Sie auf Ihrem Weg zu einem guten Abschluss und helfen Ihnen, sich mit den Anforderungen des Abiturs in Sachsen vertraut zu machen.

Im vorliegenden Band finden Sie verschiedene Möglichkeiten, sich auf die **schriftliche Prüfung** vorzubereiten:

* Das Kapitel **Hinweise und Tipps** enthät alle wichtigen Informationen zu Aufbau und Gestaltung der Abiturprüfung. **Hinweise zur Bearbeitung der verschiedenen Aufgabenstellungen**, ergänzt durch **hilfreiche Redewendungen**, ermöglichen es Ihnen, Ihre Herangehensweise an einzelne Aufgaben zu verbessern. Auch die wichtigsten **Stilmittel** für die Analyse von Texten sind ausführlich und unter Berücksichtigung ihrer jeweiligen Funktion dargestellt.
* In der **Kurzgrammatik** können Sie noch einmal die wichtigsten Phänomene der englischen Grammatik nachschlagen (z. B. die *tenses*).
* Um die Prüfungssituation zu simulieren und die verschiedenen Aufgabenstellungen einzuüben, eignen sich die **Original-Prüfungen** der letzten Jahre. Neben der schriftlichen Prüfung finden Sie für jeden Jahrgang auch eine Auswahl von Prüfungen des praktischen Prüfungsteils. Zu jeder Aufgabe wurden vollständig auf Englisch ausformulierte **Lösungen** erstellt. Die grau gerauteten **Bearbeitungshinweise** helfen Ihnen bei der Erstellung und Überprüfung von eigenen Lösungen.

Sollten nach Erscheinen dieses Bandes noch wichtige Änderungen in der Abiturprüfung 2015 vom Kultusministerium bekannt gegeben werden, finden Sie aktuelle Informationen dazu im Internet unter:
www.stark-verlag.de/pruefung-aktuell

Viel Erfolg bei Ihrer Abiturprüfung!

Stichwortverzeichnis

Hinweise und Tipps

Allgemeine Hinweise und Tipps

Dieses Buch soll Ihnen helfen, sich auf die schriftliche und mündliche (praktische) Abiturprüfung vorzubereiten. Die vorliegenden Originalprüfungen helfen Ihnen, eine Vorstellung von Umfang und Niveau des sächsischen Abiturs zu bekommen.

Aufbau der Prüfung

Die Schüler in Sachsen schreiben ein Zentralabitur, d. h., die schriftlichen Aufgaben werden, für alle Schüler gleich, vom Kultusministerium erstellt. Das schriftliche Abitur im Leistungskurs Englisch beinhaltet neben der schriftlichen Prüfung, die 270 Minuten dauert, auch einen praktischen Prüfungsteil von ca. 20 Minuten.

Schriftliche Abiturprüfung

Die zu bearbeitende Textvorlage umfasst etwa 750 bis ca. 900 Wörter. Es können Ihnen literarische, aber auch komplexe Sachtexte vorgelegt werden. Neben Fragen zum Text gehört zu diesem Prüfungsteil eine *composition*. Im Prüfungsteil B sollen Sie eine Sprachmittlungsaufgabe (Mediation) bearbeiten. Als Hilfsmittel sind ein- und zweisprachige Wörterbücher sowie ein Nachschlagewerk der deutschen Rechtschreibung zugelassen.

Praktischer Prüfungsteil

Der praktische Teil wird als Partnergespräch zwischen zwei (in Ausnahmefällen drei) Prüfungsteilnehmern gestaltet. Die Prüflinge haben keinen Einfluss auf die Auswahl des Partners. Es gibt keine Vorbereitungszeit. Hilfsmittel sind nicht erlaubt.

Bewertungsmaßstab

Teil A

Textproduktion
- Textverständnis *(comprehension)* — 10 BE
- Stellungnahme *(comment o. Ä., auch creative writing)* — 10 BE

Sprachliche Leistung
- Sprachliche Korrektheit — 20 BE
- Ausdrucksvermögen — 10 BE

Teil B
- Mediation — 20 BE

Praktischer Prüfungsteil — 20 BE

gesamt 90 BE

Kriterien für die Bewertung sind

- **Inhalt**
  - Vollständiges Erfassen und Lösen der Aufgabe
  - Sachlich richtige, klar dargestellte Aussagen ohne unnötige Abschweifungen und Wiederholungen
  - Themenbezogene Einbeziehung von Kenntnissen aus der Landeskunde sowie Fachtermini
- **Sprachliche Korrektheit**
  Sprachrichtigkeit und Ausdrucksvermögen werden ganzheitlich, mithilfe einer Bewertungsmatrix bewertet.
- **Ausdrucksvermögen**
  Hier wird bewertet, wie reichhaltig, treffsicher, logisch und selbstständig der Prüfling sprachliche Mittel einsetzt. Die Bereiche Lexik, Syntax und Textgestaltung sind dabei die wichtigsten Kategorien.

Tipps zur Vorbereitung: Wie arbeite ich mit diesem Buch?

Es gibt verschiedene Möglichkeiten, wie Sie mit dem vorliegenden Buch arbeiten können. Entscheidend ist, dass es Ihnen nützt, z. B. indem Sie Ihre sprachlichen Leistungen verbessern, die Prüfungssituation trainieren, ein Gefühl für die Zeiteinteilung in der Prüfung bekommen und damit Ihre Kompetenz und Ihr Selbstvertrauen stärken.

Variante 1: Vergleich Ihrer Lösungen mit den „Musterlösungen"

Sie bearbeiten die Aufgaben zunächst selbst und schreiben z. B. eine *composition* zu einem Thema, mit dem Sie etwas anfangen können. In der Abiturprüfung haben Sie in diesem Prüfungsteil die Wahl zwischen drei Aufgaben, d. h., auch hier können Sie sich für eine Aufgabe entscheiden. Im vorliegenden Buch finden Sie zu den Themen, die in den letzten Jahren zur Wahl standen, jeweils eine ausformulierte Musterlösung. Vorangestellt sind einige *key points,* also Aspekte, die Sie in Ihrer Lösung berücksichtigen sollten. Falls Sie einmal nicht weiterkommen, lesen Sie zunächst nur die *key points* im Lösungsteil. Danach vergleichen Sie Ihre Ausarbeitung mit der Musterlösung.

Achtung: Beachten Sie bitte, dass die Musterlösung natürlich nicht die Gesamtmöglichkeiten einer Aufgabe abbilden kann, d. h., die vorgestellten Lösungen können von Ihren eigenen Ergebnissen erheblich abweichen. Vergleichen Sie daher, ob Sie ähnliche (oder ähnlich viele) Fakten, Argumente, Textstellen usw. integriert haben bzw. ob Sie Ihren Text vergleichbar strukturiert haben. Dazu gehören die Gliederung und die sprachliche Gestaltung, z. B. der Einsatz von Satzverknüpfungsmitteln, komplexen Strukturen und thematisch angemessenem Vokabular.

Tipp

Nehmen Sie zu Beginn die Formulierungshilfen *(useful phrases)* aus dem Kapitel „Tipps zu den einzelnen Aufgabenformen" zu Hilfe, indem Sie die entsprechenden Seiten aufgeschlagen neben Ihren Text legen und für Sie geeignete Formulierungen in Ihren Text einbauen. So erweitern Sie Ihren Wortschatz und verinnerlichen gelungene sprachliche Hinführungen und Überleitungen.

Variante 2: Die *key points* als Strukturierungshilfe

Da Sie wahrscheinlich nicht alle Aufgaben im Buch bearbeiten werden, können Sie einige Aufgaben auch einfach „nur" in Stichworten oder Mindmaps skizzieren und anschließend mit den *key points* vergleichen. Haben Sie ähnliche Schwerpunkte gesetzt?

Variante 3: Die Musterlösungen als „Steinbruch"

Nach dem Vergleich Ihrer Stichpunkte und der *key points* im Buch können Sie die Musterlösungen genau lesen. Unterstreichen Sie hilfreiche Passagen, z. B. in Bezug auf sprachliche Mittel, und schreiben Sie eventuell Abschnitte, die Sie in Ihrer Prüfung verwenden könnten, heraus. Hier fungieren die Musterlösungen sozusagen als „Steinbruch", aus dem Sie sich nützliche Formulierungen „herausbrechen" können.

Variante 4: Das vorliegende Buch als „Lesebuch"

Lesen bildet. Und das Lesen in der Fremdsprache hilft, neben der Stärkung Ihrer Lesekompetenz, Ihren Wortschatz zu erweitern. So können Sie – als Ergänzung zu den Varianten 1 bis 3 – Teile des Buchs ganz entspannt (soweit vor der Prüfung möglich) lesen, ganz nach Interesse, „einfach so". Auch hier wird bei Ihnen „etwas hängen bleiben".

Weitere Tipps zur Vorbereitung:
- **Hören und lesen Sie Texte**, die Sie interessieren und/oder die von unterrichtlicher Relevanz sind, z. B. im Internet. Dazu gehören Zeitungsartikel, Sprachportale, Blogs, Websites, Radiosendungen, Filme usw. So setzen Sie sich im Sinne einer Immersion („Eintauchen") der englischen Sprache aus und lernen automatisch dazu.

Tipp

> Für englischsprachige DVDs: Schalten Sie ab und an die englischen (nicht die deutschen) Untertitel dazu. Das hilft Ihnen beim „Festhalten" neuer oder für Sie nützlicher Sprachmittel, da Sie diese auf zwei Kanälen (auditiv und optisch) präsentiert bekommen. Zusätzlich erleichtert es bei vielen Filmen den Filmgenuss.

- **Sprechen Sie** mit Ihren Freunden und Bekannten Englisch, sooft Sie können. Verabreden Sie Zeiträume (z. B. eine Stunde am Tag), in denen Sie Englisch sprechen. Das wirkt am Anfang etwas komisch, man gewöhnt sich aber daran, vor allem wenn man den Trainingseffekt voranstellt.
- **Schreiben Sie** eigene Texte in der „realen Welt". Warum nicht an einer Internetdiskussion teilnehmen oder über Facebook auf Englisch kommunizieren?
- **Zeitmanagement:**
  - **In der Schule:** Ihre Zeit ist nicht unerschöpflich und Sie legen Ihr Abitur nicht nur in Englisch ab. Nutzen Sie daher die Zeit im Englischunterricht, so gut es geht. Beteiligen Sie sich intensiv und nehmen Sie konzentriert auf, was an Sprache und Inhalten im Kursraum besprochen wird. Achten Sie auf die Sprache der Lehrkraft und besonders guter Mitschüler, die Ihnen als Sprachvorbilder dienen können. Schreiben Sie mit, was Ihre Sprachvorbilder sagen und wie sie es sagen. Sie nehmen dadurch wertvolle Sprachmittel in Form von treffenden Formulierungen und Gedanken (Inhalt) mit und erweitern so Ihren Wortschatz.
  - **Außerhalb der Schule:** Es ist nicht leicht, neben dem Schulalltag noch Texte in der Fremdsprache zu schreiben. Sie müssen daher nicht gleich Texte in Abiturlänge verfassen. Das Training für einen Marathon besteht ja auch nicht aus dem Absolvieren der gesamten Strecke, sondern geschieht in kleineren, aber regelmäßigen Einheiten. Vorschlag: Setzen Sie sich ein Limit (z. B. mindestens 30 Minuten schreiben, dreimal pro Woche), innerhalb dessen Sie Texte verfassen. Steigern Sie die Länge der Texte (und damit die Zeit), bis Sie ungefähr die Textlänge der Musterlösungen erreicht haben. Dafür brauchen Sie natürlich mehr Zeit, was heißt, dass die Anzahl der Übungseinheiten heruntergefahren werden kann. Statt dreimal pro Woche Training hätten Sie dann nur noch einen Termin, sodass aus den drei 30-minütigen Einheiten 90 Minuten intensiver Arbeit werden.

- **Sozialform der Vorbereitung: Partnerarbeit**
  Geteiltes Leid ist halbes Leid. Bilden Sie mit „Gleichgesinnten" eine Arbeitsgruppe. Nachweislich arbeiten Gruppen mit maximal drei Mitgliedern am effektivsten. Erarbeiten Sie Aufgaben gemeinsam, z. B. in Form von *brainstorming* und *mindmaps*. Dies ist der erste und vielleicht wichtigste Schritt zur Aufgabenlösung, denn hier legen Sie fest, was Sie schreiben wollen. Oft wird in dieser Phase auch das Vokabular (z. B. Fachausdrücke, treffende Wendungen) geklärt.
  Dann können Sie in Stillarbeit eine Lösung erarbeiten, also einen Text schreiben. Die Texte könnten Sie miteinander besprechen und anschließend mit der Musterlösung vergleichen.
  Für die praktische Prüfung (mündlicher Teil) eignet sich Gruppen- oder Partnerarbeit natürlich besonders gut, da sie darauf angelegt ist, neben der Sprachkompetenz auch die allgemeinen Kommunikationsfähigkeiten (dazu gehören auch non-verbale Elemente wie Sitzhaltung, Augenkontakt mit dem Prüfungspartner, Körpersprache allgemein) zu bewerten.

Tipp
Wenn Sie die Möglichkeit haben, nehmen Sie einen „Spezialisten" in die Gruppe auf, z. B. einen Muttersprachler oder jemanden mit besonders guten Englischkenntnissen (Auslandsaufenthalt). Dieser kann Ihnen als Vorbild und Korrektiv dienen.
Anmerkung (aus eigener Erfahrung): Das gemeinsame Erarbeiten und Trainieren macht Spaß!

- **Motivation und Durchhaltevermögen:**
  Idealerweise beschäftigen Sie sich in der Vorbereitung (auch) mit Aspekten des Faches Englisch, die Ihnen Spaß machen bzw. die Sie interessieren (intrinsische Motivation bzw. „Motivation von innen"), z. B. Sport, Musik, Naturwissenschaften, Technik oder Filme.
  Darüber hinaus hilft es, sich nach einem guten „Arbeitstag" mit einer schönen Aktion, z. B. einem leckeren Essen, einem (englischsprachigen) Film usw. zu belohnen (extrinsische Motivation, also „Motivation von außen").

Allgemeine Tipps für den Tag der Prüfung

Vorbereitung

Gehen Sie frühzeitig ins Bett, sodass Sie an den Prüfungstagen ausgeruht sind. Seien Sie rechtzeitig am Prüfungsort. Nehmen Sie ausreichend Essen und Trinken für die Prüfung mit. Versichern Sie sich, dass Ihr Schreibzeug in Ordnung ist (Ersatzfüller, Marker usw.).

Nach Erhalt der Prüfungsaufgaben

Sie haben 270 Minuten Zeit: Das sind 4,5 Stunden.
Jeder Mensch ist anders, und Menschen arbeiten unterschiedlich schnell. Daher können die folgenden Tipps nur von allgemeiner Natur sein.

- Erstens: Verschaffen Sie sich zunächst einen Überblick. Was kommt auf Sie zu?

- Zweitens: Erstellen Sie dann eine Reihenfolge, in der Sie die Aufgaben bearbeiten wollen. Planen Sie grundsätzlich mit einer ca. 30-minütigen Kontrollphase am Ende der Prüfung, in der Sie Ihre Ergebnisse noch einmal Korrektur lesen. Das Korrekturlesen am Schluss hat den Vorteil, dass Sie einen gewissen „Abstand" zu Ihren Texten gewonnen haben. Dies schärft den Blick und macht den Korrekturprozess effektiver.

- Notieren Sie die Reihenfolge bzw. einen Zeit- bzw. Arbeitsplan, z. B.
  1. *Working with the text* (ca. 90–120 Min.)
     (Hier müssen Sie bedenken, dass Sie einen relativ komplexen Text lesen und gründlich verstehen müssen.)
  2. *Composition* (ca. 60–70 Min.)
  3. Sprachmittlung (ca. 60 Min.)
     (Auch hier müssen Sie eine Textvorlage bearbeiten.)
  4. Korrekturlesen/Puffer (ca. 30 Min.)
- Strategie: Es ist wichtig, dass Sie **alle** Aufgaben vollständig erarbeiten. Achten Sie also darauf, keine „Romane" zu schreiben bzw. sich nicht zu verlieren.
  Konzentrieren Sie sich auf die Aufgabenstellung und vergewissern Sie sich, dass Sie diese verstanden haben (alle geforderten Aspekte berücksichtigen!). Erstellen Sie ein Konzept bzw. eine Gliederung, in der Sie Ihre Gedanken strukturieren, bevor Sie mit der Erstellung der Reinschrift beginnen. Gehen Sie dabei aber nicht zu ausführlich vor, damit Sie genug Zeit für die eigentliche Texterstellung haben. Verzichten Sie auf das „Vorschreiben" einer Aufgabe. Das kostet unnötig Zeit, die Ihnen später fehlt.

Die Bearbeitung der verschiedenen Aufgabenformen in der schriftlichen Prüfung

Working with the text

Verschaffen Sie sich zunächst einen Überblick, indem Sie den Text einmal ganz durchlesen, und klären Sie lexikalische Verständnisprobleme mithilfe Ihres Wörterbuchs.

Tipp
> Schlagen Sie nur nach, was für das Gesamtverständnis bzw. die **Aufgabenstellung** relevant ist. Ansonsten haben Sie „Mut zur Lücke".

Markieren Sie für die Aufgabenstellung relevante Stellen im Text. Für verschiedene Aspekte (z. B. Inhalt, Stil) können Sie je nach Aufgabenstellung unterschiedliche Farben verwenden. Einzelne Argumente oder andere Aspekte im Text können auch am Rand nummeriert werden.
Nehmen Sie die relevanten Gesichtspunkte in Ihr Konzept auf und ordnen Sie diese entsprechend (je nach Anforderung: chronologisch, kontrastierend usw.); notieren Sie auch die Zeilennummern, damit Sie korrekt zitieren bzw. Ihre Ideen am Text belegen können.
Ganz wichtig: Bleiben Sie beim Thema. Auch wenn es andere für Sie interessante Aspekte im Text gibt, vergewissern Sie sich in regelmäßigen Abständen, dass Sie (noch) der Aufgabenstellung folgen.
Achten Sie beim Erstellen der Reinschrift darauf, dass Sie Ihren Text sprachlich angemessen, flüssig und kohärent (also in sich logisch) gestalten. Sprich: Er muss sich gut lesen lassen.

Composition

Beachten Sie die Aufgabenstellung und – wenn vorgegeben – auch die Textform, die von Ihnen erwartet wird. Strukturieren Sie Ihre Gedanken und Argumente und bleiben Sie am Thema *("Don't get carried away.")*. Belegen Sie Ihre Argumente mit Fakten und/oder Beispielen. Schreiben Sie einen flüssigen, nachvollziehbaren bzw. gut lesbaren Text.

Sprachmittlung

Versuchen Sie nicht, den Text (oder Teile daraus) zu übersetzen. Dies entspricht nicht der Aufgabenstellung und ist zudem schwierig und zeitaufwendig.

Fassen Sie das Geforderte in Ihren eigenen (englischen) Worten zusammen. Es wird nicht erwartet, dass Sie im Englischen genauso geschliffen bzw. anspruchsvoll formulieren können, wie dies im deutschen Ausgangstext der Fall sein könnte.

Achten Sie bei der Aufgabenstellung darauf, ob eine allgemeine Zusammenfassung oder aber eine Zusammenfassung von Teilaspekten verlangt wird.

Tipps zum Korrekturlesen

Achten Sie auf folgende sprachliche Problemfelder, die in Abiturarbeiten immer wieder auftauchen, obwohl die meisten Prüfungsteilnehmer die Regeln eigentlich kennen. Es handelt sich um vermeidbare Flüchtigkeitsfehler *(unforced errors)*. Wenn Sie sich in einem der Bereiche unsicher fühlen, können Sie die Regeln noch einmal in der Kurzgrammatik in diesem Band nachschlagen.

- *Tenses* (allg.): z. B. Analysen/Zusammenfassungen im Präsens, im Normalfall kein Zeitenwechsel *(present tense/past tense)* in einem Text
- *Present perfect vs. simple past*
- *Past perfect* („Vorvergangenheit")
- *If-clauses ("if + would: no good")*
- *Adjectives vs. adverbs*
- *Prepositions*
- *Reported Speech (backshift!)*
- *Apostrophe: My daughter's dog – my parents' bikes – My brothers like ice-cream.*
- *Inverted commas:* Anführungsstriche kommen im Englischen beide nach oben: *She said, she "grew up in Mississippi."*
- Klein- und Großschreibung: The <u>American</u> car industry

Praktischer Teil (mündlich)

Kleiden Sie sich zur Prüfung angemessen, aber verkleiden Sie sich nicht.

Achten Sie gemeinsam mit dem Partner darauf, dass Sie alle Aspekte der Aufgabenstellung berücksichtigen. Sollte Ihr Partner das Thema aus dem Blick verlieren, lenken Sie das Gespräch zurück zur Aufgabe. Auch das gehört zur kommunikativen Kompetenz!

Achten Sie auf Ihr Kommunikationsverhalten: Die Redeanteile zwischen beiden Partnern sollten ungefähr gleich sein. Sind Sie also Ihrem Partner sprachlich (und inhaltlich) überlegen, achten Sie darauf, ihn nicht „zuzuquatschen" bzw. zu monologisieren, sondern geben Sie ihm durch geeignete Gesprächsangebote die Gelegenheit, wieder zurück in die Diskussion zu kommen (zum Beispiel durch das Stellen einer Frage an den Partner, anstatt lediglich die eigenen Gedanken zum Thema vorzubringen).

Sind Sie ein mündlich eher zurückhaltender Typ, müssen Sie „aus sich herauskommen" und Ihrerseits darauf achten, dass Sie das Gespräch gleichberechtigt mit Ihrem Partner führen.

Tipps zu den einzelnen Aufgabenformen

Working with the text

Bei dem Teil *Working with the text* wird von Ihnen erwartet, dass Sie einen in sich geschlossenen Text schreiben, in dem Sie den vorliegenden Text tiefgründig, der Aufgabenstellung folgend, bearbeiten.

Als Erstes sollten Sie die Aufgabenstellung erfassen, also sichergehen, dass Sie wissen, was von Ihnen erwartet wird. Dazu benötigen Sie die Kenntnis der folgenden Operatoren (Auswahl):

1. **Analyse:** (auch: **examine**)
   Die Analyse beinhaltet die Zerlegung eines (komplexen) Ganzen in seine Einzelteile (Inhalt, Form, Funktion). Beschreiben und erklären Sie, was der Autor sagt (Inhalt), wie er es sagt (Form) und warum er es so sagt (Funktion). Anders gesagt: Worum geht es? Wie gestaltet der Autor das Ganze sprachlich (oder/und visuell)? Welche Absicht steht hinter dem Ganzen (z. B: die Parteinahme des Lesers, die Diffamierung eines politischen Gegners usw.)?

2. **Assess:** (auch: **evaluate**)
   Hier wird eine wertende Einschätzung verlangt, die auf einer Analyse basiert, also eine qualifizierte Wertung/Bewertung einer Situation oder Absicht.
   Beispiel: *Analyse and assess the way the author presents the subject ...*

3. **Describe:**
   Hier wird eine Beschreibung bzw. Schilderung eines Sachverhalts, eines Prozesses oder einer Person verlangt.
   Beispiel: *Describe how the author creates an atmosphere of suspense.* Oder: *Describe how the protagonist turns into a violent character.*

4. **Compare:**
   Beim Vergleichen kommt es darauf an, sowohl Unterschiede als auch Ähnlichkeiten von Prozessen bzw. zwischen Personen herauszuarbeiten und darzustellen.
   Beispiel: *Compare Hector's and Irwin's attitudes towards education.*

5. **Explain:**
   Hier gilt es, einen Prozess oder eine Handlungsweise zu begründen, also herauszufinden, warum etwas so ist, wie es im Text beschrieben wird. z. B. *Explain how Martin Sorrow reaches the conclusion that ...* oder *Explain why the protagonist fails to win Helena's love.*

Insgesamt wird erwartet, dass Sie Ihre Erkenntnisse am Text belegen (Zitate, Zeilenhinweise) und das entsprechende Fachvokabular bzw. die richtige Stilebene (Textformat: Analyse) verwenden, also eher formal statt umgangssprachlich schreiben.

Daher ist es sinnvoll, die Lösungstexte nicht nur inhaltlich, sondern auch nach sprachlichen Mitteln zu durchforsten.

Useful phrases: Working with the text

The author/speaker ...
- *wants the audience to adopt his views on ...*
- *tries to convince his listeners that .../of his own opinion.*
- *tries to influence his listeners to believe .../tries to exert his influence on ...*
- *tries to encourage his listeners to stand up against ...*

- *emphasizes the difference between …*
- *highlights his own ideas.*
- *employs/uses different rhetorical devices such as … to make his speech/text/article more interesting and appealing for the reader/to attract the audience's attention.*
- *uses positively/negatively connoted expressions such as … in order to …*
- *uses humour/irony to evoke/create a positive/negative image of …*
- *tries to create a sense of patriotism/togetherness/community.*
- *creates a (positive) picture/image in the reader's mind in order to …*
- *deliberately makes people appear funny/threatening/dangerous.*
- *appeals to the audience's sympathy/general fears.*
- *connects directly with his listeners/readers.*
- *confronts the listener with (the assumption that) …*

The tone of the speech/passage … /
The way the speaker treats this topic/in which he reflects on his topic …
- *is supposed to evoke/provoke an emotional response from the audience.*
- *appeals to the listeners' emotions.*

To the audience/readership this must come across like a provocation/a direct appeal to take action which …
- *helps to draw further attention to his speech/arguments.*
- *emphasizes the message/main idea of his speech.*
- *aims at undermining the opposition.*
- *aims at gathering support.*

This metaphor …
- *is meant to stimulate the imagination of the listener/reader.*
- *alludes to … by pointing out that …/by alluding to the fact that …*
- *refers to the fact/the general assumption/the widespread commonplace that …*
- *points out that … tries to convey (the idea) that …*
- *expresses/enhances the authors criticism/critique of …*
- *depicts the author's political opponent as being …*
- *aims at pushing the listener/reader to a certain conclusion.*

Tipp
Gehen Sie die Lösungen zu den Aufgaben *Working with the text* durch, und unterstreichen Sie die Ausdrücke, die Ihnen als Formulierungshilfe bzw. als Baustein geeignet erscheinen.

Composition

Allgemeines

Im Teil *composition* können Sie zwischen drei Aufgaben wählen. Die Aufgabenstellungen sind unterschiedlich. Sie reichen von „traditionellen" *comment*-Themen bis hin zu kreativen Aufgaben, z. B. dem Verfassen eines (alternativen) Schlusses zu einer Geschichte oder dem Erstellen einer Rede.

Generell wird bei der *composition* ein flüssiger, nachvollziehbar gegliederter, gut lesbarer Text erwartet, der die jeweils geforderten Textmerkmale (z. B. *comment, discussion, letter to the editor*) berücksichtigt. Dies bezieht sich sowohl auf die Struktur als auch auf die Wortwahl (Stil bzw. Ausdruck).

Tipp
Gehen Sie die entsprechenden Lösungen zu den verschiedenen Aufgaben zum Aufgabenfeld *composition* durch. Achten Sie sowohl auf die sprachliche als auch auf die formale und inhaltliche Gestaltung.

Typische Aufgabenstellungen für die *composition* sind:

1. **Comment on ...** (Kommentar)
   Hier wird erwartet, dass Sie eine begründete Meinung zu einem Sachverhalt (Text, Cartoon, Bild usw.) oder einem Standpunkt zum Ausdruck bringen. Im Gegensatz zur *discussion* (Erörterung) wird **nicht** erwartet, dass Sie das Problem von allen Seiten beleuchten. Vielmehr geht es darum, seine Meinung begründet (also mit Belegen in Form von Fakten, Argumenten) darzulegen.

   Die Grobstruktur eines *comment* ist wie folgt:
   - Einleitung: Behauptung/These:
   - Mittelteil: Argumente, Begründungen, Belege (Fakten, Beispiele)
   - Schlussteil: Schlussfolgerung, Fazit

2. **Discuss** (Erörterung)
   Wenn Sie einen Text diskutieren bzw. erörtern, beziehen Sie sich zunächst auf vorliegende (oder Ihnen bekannte) Fakten oder Aussagen zu einem Thema (Analyse). Dann wägen Sie pro und contra ab. Dabei können Sie die Argumente einander direkt gegenüberstellen *(On the one hand ... on the other hand)* oder jeweils einen Contra- und einen Pro-Teil erstellen. Wichtig ist, dass Sie mit einer auf Grundlage der vorangegangenen Argumentation begründeten Schlussfolgerung *(conclusion)* enden.
   Wie bei (fast) allen *composition*-Themen sollten Sie eine Einleitung, den argumentativ-diskursiven Mittelteil und abschließend Ihre Schlussfolgerungen als Grobstruktur verwenden.

3. **Reflect**
   Hier sollen Behauptungen im Zusammenhang geprüft und abgewogen, also anhand eigenständig gewählter Kriterien eine ausführliche Aussage über Richtigkeit, Wahrscheinlichkeit und Angemessenheit eines Textes gemacht werden.

   Useful phrases

• **Logische Ordnung/ Hinzufügen von Aspekten**	*Above all ...*
	At first sight ...
	In the beginning/In the end ...
	At the beginning of something .../At the end of something ...
	First .../First of all .../In the first place ...
	To begin with ...
	Let me begin by stating that ...
	Second .../Secondly .../In the second place ...
	Furthermore .../Moreover ...
	In addition .../There is also ...
	Apart from ...
	Similarly .../In the same way ...
	Equally important is the fact that ...
	Therefore .../Hence .../For that reason .../That is why .../
	Because of that ...
	Besides ...
	Consequently ...
	In general .../In particular ...
	Generally ...
	At last .../Eventually .../Finally ...
	In other words ...
	In a word .../Briefly ...

- **Anführung**   *For instance ...*
  von Beispielen   *For example ...*
                         e. g. ...
                         ... such as ...
                         ... like ...

- **Anführung**   *In spite of .../Despite ...*
  von Gegen-   *Whereas .../While ...*
  argumenten   *Although ...*
                         Nevertheless ...
                         However ...
                         On the other hand ...
                         On the contrary ...
                         It is true, ... but ...

- **Vergleichen/**   *The problem with ... is that ...*
  Begründen: *Compared with ..., ... is much more ... than ...*
                         You need to be good with ... for/in order to ...
                         ... might be the best option because ...
                         ... and besides/what's more/moreover ...
                         Well, in that case ...

- **Wendungen für**   *In one way or another ...*
  die Schluss-   *Both ... and ...*
  formulierung   *Taking everything into consideration/account ...*
                         All in all ...
                         You come to the conclusion that ...
                         Summing up .../To sum up ...
                         In conclusion ...

4. **Write a letter to the editor**
   Hier wird erwartet, dass Sie den formalen Kriterien eines Leserbriefes Rechnung tragen. Dazu gehört:

   - Datum: (rechts oben) *e. g. 9th May 2014*

   - Ansprache: *Sir or Madam* oder *Dear Editor*

   - Bezug: *I am writing to you with reference to your recent article on ... / With reference to your article of 22 March, I would like to object to what I consider a rather one-sided approach to ...*

   - Eigene Meinung: *In my opinion the author's arguments are highly misleading ... Consequently, I must strongly protest ... / I would like to congratulate you on your recent article on ...*

   - Argumente: *There is definite proof that ... / Nobody can deny the fact ...*

   - Schlussteil: *All in all ... / To put it all in a nutshell ... / To cut a long story short ... / In conlusion*

   - Schlussformel (kann auch weggelassen werden): *Regards/Best regards (in an email or note, rather casual) / Yours faithfully (in a formal letter to s.b. whose name you know) / Yours sincerely (in a formal letter to s.b. whose name you don't know)*
     Name *
     Wohnort* (optional)
     (*Aufgrund der Anonymität im Rahmen der Abiturprüfung sollten Sie auf Ihren echten Namen sowie den Wohnort verzichten und einen „Künstlernamen" wählen.)

Die sprachliche Gestaltung eines Leserbriefes richtet sich nach Adressatengruppe bzw. Leserschaft. So wäre ein eher formeller Ton für ein *quality paper* angemessen, während er für ein *student magazine* auch etwas umgangssprachlicher sein kann.

5. Comment on the survey (charts and statistics)

Wenn die Aufgabenstellung eine Stellungnahme zu einem Schaubild verlangt, dann sollten Sie als Erstes das Thema des Schaubildes benennen, dann die für die Aufgabenstellung relevanten Aspekte beschreiben und schließlich auf die Zusammenhänge und Relevanz der Informationen eingehen.

Useful phrases

Different kinds of charts: Bar chart (Säulendiagramm), *pie chart* (Tortendiagramm), *flow chart* (Fließdiagramm), *line graph* (Kurvendiagramm)

The chart compares/show/depicts/implies/demonstrates/proves/suggests ...
From the given figures you can conclude that ...
The most significant fact that can be deduced is ...
The given statistics support/challenge the view ...
It shows that the number of ... fell/dropped/went down/went up/rose/increased/doubled/tripled by ...
There has been a steady/sharp/dramatic/significant increase in ...
The number of ... has fallen steadily/sharply over a period of ...
The given numbers suggest only a negligible/rather insignificant rise of ...
The given statistics were compiled in 1994, which allows the conclusion that ...
All in all it can be deduced that ...

6. Discuss the message of the cartoon or picture

Wenn Sie einen Cartoon oder ein Bild kommentieren sollen, wird nicht erwartet, dass Sie die Abbildung bis ins letzte Detail beschreiben. Sie sollten Ihre Ausführungen jedoch am Bild belegen und daher auf die für die Aufgabenstellung relevanten Aspekte der Abbildung eingehen.

Useful phrases

The cartoon/picture depicts/shows ...
In the centre/foreground/background ...
In the top right-hand corner/bottom left-hand corner ...
The caption reads .../In the caption it says that ...
The drawing represents a highly exaggerated image of ...

7. Write an article

Die Gestaltung eines Artikels im Abitur richtet sich nach der Aufgabenstellung. Je nach Adressatengruppe ist die Sprache formal *(quality paper)* oder kann auch Umgangssprache enthalten *(student magazine)*.
Bezeichnend für einen Artikel ist eine Schlagzeile bzw. Überschrift *(headline)*, um die Aufmerksamkeit des Lesers zu wecken. Dazu gehört auch ein entsprechender Einstieg *(topical sentence/lead)*, der zum Weiterlesen ermutigt.
Artikel sind in der Regel eher informativ und sachlich gehalten, die eigene Person tritt zugunsten der Argumentation bzw. des Inhaltes zurück. Anderseits soll ein Artikel auch Lust am (Weiter-)lesen machen. Daher sind überraschende Fakten, Zitate oder (kurze) Anekdoten sowie literarische Stilmittel geeignete Mittel, einem Artikel die gewisse „Würze" zu geben.

8. Creative writing

Die Ausgestaltung einer kreativen Schreibaufgabe richtet sich nach der Aufgabenstellung. Wenn Sie eine Geschichte (oder eine Theaterszene) weiter schreiben sollen, dann sollten Sie auf die sprachliche Gestaltung der Vorlage eingehen bzw. sich an ihr orientieren. Ebenfalls sollte Ihre Fortsetzung inhaltlich an das Vorgegebene anknüpfen.

Bei einer nicht textgebundenen Aufgabe sind Sie relativ frei in der Auswahl literarischer Stilmittel, sollten den Text aber so gestalten, dass er sprachlich und inhaltlich nachvollziehbar und kohärent ist.

9. Write a speech

Es gibt verschiedene Formen von Reden: eher informativ gehaltene Reden *(informative speeches)*, erläuternde Reden *(explanatory speeches: How do things work?)* und meinungsbildende Reden *(persuasive speeches)*. Je nach Kontext sind in den meisten Reden alle drei Elemente enthalten. Wo Sie Ihren Schwerpunkt setzen sollten, geht aus der Aufgabenstellung hervor.

Beachten Sie in jedem Fall, dass Sie den Zuhörer erreichen wollen, seien Sie also klar strukturiert und würzen Sie Ihre Rede mit Dingen wie Humor, einer Anekdote, überraschenden Fakten, Zitaten oder Vergleichen, rhetorischen Fragen, der Verwendung des Pronomens „we" und der direkten Ansprache („you"), Alliterationen, Aufzählungen, Anaphern usw.

Wiederholen und betonen Sie wichtige Punkte, sodass Ihre Zuhörer Ihr Anliegen klar verstehen.

Tipp   Konsultieren Sie dazu noch einmal den Abschnitt *Literary terms for textual analysis* und lesen Sie sich die entsprechenden Lösungen zum Thema Rede im Aufgabenbereich durch.

Useful phrases

- **Introduction:**
  Good morning everybody ... Ladies and gentlemen ... Today I'm going to talk about ... We are all aware of the fact that ... For the great majority of people are here today to ... Today, all of us ... In today's word, no day passes without ... For generations, people all over the world/scientists have been struggling to establish an answer to this pressing question ...

- **Transition (Getting from one point to the other):**
  Let's begin with ... My first point is ... That brings us to ... Now that we have established ... Now, contrast that with ... Keeping those points in mind let us now consider ... Now let me put this into perspective ... Personally, I have never experienced any such thing ... Are we not all concerned about the future of ...

- **Addressing the audience:**
  Well, did you know that ... ? Do we not all sometimes yearn for some more ... I say don't let them confuse you and sell you this as a solution to your problems ... I don't know about you, but personally I ... Would you opt for this yourself? Well, I hear you say that ... Now let me explain one or two things about ...

- **Talking about problems:**
  As we all agree, these are serious/pressing problems ... There are no simple solutions to this rather complex issue ... Today's world has become a complex place, facing complex problems asking complex solutions ... As regards this conflict we should promote reconciliation between ... Not believing in a peaceful settlement is not a choice ...

- **Drawing conclusions and asking for action:**
  As we can see, all of this points to the conclusion that ... What conclusions can be drawn from all this?
  Let me finish by pointing out the urgency of the matter ... We are left with the conclusion that ... There isn't much left to say but ...
  Everybody must ensure that ... We should be prepared to take action right away ... As you can see we must not hesitate to act right now ... Or we will lose out. ... We ought to negotiate a compromise/peace treaty/agreement ... If we don't stop this process right now ... We must put a halt to these dreadful developments or ... For the sake of justice, action must be taken at this very moment ... High time we put foot a down in order to ...

- **Ending a speech:**
  We have arrived, now, where we began. So let me end by saying that ... As I said in the beginning, now is the time to ...
  After all we have heard, there is only one logical conclusion to draw ... This leaves us with only one conclusion ...
  Thank you for listening.

Mediation (Sprachmittlung)

Sachsen beteiligt sich seit 2014 am länderübergreifenden Abitur. Das bedeutet, dass Sie im Leistungskurs nicht wie zuvor zwischen Mediation und Übersetzung wählen können, sondern in jedem Fall eine Sprachmittlungsaufgabe bearbeiten müssen. Diese unterscheidet sich von den Vorgaben im Wesentlichen nicht von den Aufgaben, die bereits im sächsischen Abitur enthalten sind. Anders als zuvor wird die Aufgabenstellung nun auf Deutsch formuliert und es wird eine spezifische Textsorte (z. B. Artikel) verlangt.

Was ist unter einer Mediation bzw. Sprachmittlung zu verstehen?

Unter Mediation, auch Sprachmittlung genannt, versteht man das sinngemäße Übertragen oder Zusammenfassen des wesentlichen Gehalts eines oder mehrerer deutschsprachiger Texte ins Englische. Die deutschsprachige Textvorlage besteht dabei aus ca. 600 Wörtern. Bewertet werden zu je 50 %:
- Inhalt (Wurde das Wesentliche erfasst?) und Textstruktur (Ist der Text in sich „rund", also gut strukturiert und nachvollziehbar?)
- Sprache (Wie angemessen bzw. korrekt ist Ihr Englisch?)

Die Mediation ist eine Übertragung (Sprachmittlung) und keine Übersetzung. Es geht somit nicht darum, einen Text Satz für Satz zu übersetzen, sondern die wesentlichen Inhalte auf Englisch auszudrücken. Von daher ist eine Mediation wesentlich freier. Komplizierte Sätze können Sie in einfachen Worten zusammenfassen, da Sie nicht daran gebunden sind, sich an bestimmte Satzstrukturen oder Stilmittel des Ausgangstextes zu halten.
In der Regel wird von Ihnen erwartet, dass Sie einen längeren oder zwei kürzere Texte auf Englisch zusammenfassen. Die Textsorte Zusammenfassung bzw. Synopse *(summary)* mit ihren Textmerkmalen sollte Ihnen also geläufig sein. Meist wird es sich um eine themenbezogene Zusammenfassungen *("What does the text say about ...?")* handeln. Hier gilt es also, sich auf genau diese Themen(aspekte) zu konzentrieren. Die Zusammenfassung wird in einen Kontext gestellt, so dass Sie z. B. eine E-Mail oder einen Artikel für eine Internetseite oder ein Schulmagazin o. Ä. verfassen müssen. Machen Sie sich also auch mit diesen Textsorten vertraut. Sie sollten hier darauf achten, an wen Ihr Text gerichtet ist. Wenn Sie den Text beispielsweise für Ihre Klassenkameraden zusammenfassen oder für eine Schülerzeitung schreiben, muss kein allzu formaler Stil gewählt werden, gewisse umgangssprachliche Formulierungen (kein Slang) sind dann möglich.

Beachten Sie bei der Erstellung Ihrer Mediation folgende Aspekte:

- **Überschrift:** Je nach geforderter Textsorte kann eine Überschrift stehen (z. B. Artikel). Sie müssen dabei nicht den Originaltitel übersetzen, sondern können selbst eine geeignete Überschrift wählen, die das Thema bzw. die Aufgabenstellung gut widerspiegelt.

  Beispiel: *Coming to grips with unemployment in East Germany*

- **Einleitungssatz:** Beginnen Sie Ihre Mediation mit einem Einleitungssatz, der zum Thema hinführt.

- **Hauptteil:** Die Gliederung des Hauptteils ergibt sich meist aus der Aufgabenstellung, den sogenannten Leitfragen (z. B.: „Fassen Sie die wesentlichen Lösungsansätze zusammen"). Wichtig ist daher die **Auswahl der Informationen:** Was ist wirklich wichtig? Was ist Beiwerk bzw. Ausschmückung oder Wiederholung oder nicht durch die Aufgabenstellung gefragt und sollte weggelassen werden? Um dies am Originaltext zu prüfen, kann man nicht nur wichtige Textpassagen markieren, sondern eventuell auch unwichtige Textpassagen ausstreichen. Berücksichtigen Sie bei Ihrer Zusammenfassung auch, welche Intentionen der Autor hat. Will er „nur" informieren oder verfolgt er politische Absichten? Ist er für oder gegen etwas? Wie baut sich die Argumentation des Textes auf? Wird Ihnen durch die Aufgabenstellung eine Position für Ihren Text vorgegeben?

- **Textaufbau:** Hinsichtlich der Textlogik sollten Sie geradlinig und sachlich schreiben. Dabei kann es sich durchaus ergeben, dass Sie die Argumentationsstruktur des Ausgangstextes nicht eins zu eins nachvollziehen, sondern zusammenfassend wiedergeben müssen. So könnte z. B. eine vom Autor am Ende seines Textes gesetzte These bei Ihrer Mediation bereits am Anfang stehen.

  Beispiel: *The author is in favour of more subsidies being given to local employers.*

- **Zeit:** Zusammenfassungen werden im Präsens als der Ausgangszeit verfasst. Im Text vorkommende Nach- und Vorzeitigkeit bleiben erhalten.

- **Bezüge:** Zeit-, Orts- und Personenbezüge werden entsprechend umgeformt – wie bei der indirekten Rede.

  Beispiel: letzte Woche → *the week before;* hier → *there*

Tipp   Wenn Sie die Mediationen in diesem Band vergleichen, achten Sie auch auf die *key points*, die Tipps zur Herangehensweise („Strategie") enthalten und auf die wesentlichen Aspekte der Aufgabenstellung eingehen.

Praktischer Prüfungsteil

Im praktischen Teil des Abiturs sollen Sie nachweisen, dass Sie sich in einem Gespräch zu einem Thema inhaltlich sinnvoll und sprachlich angemessen äußern können. Die Prüfung wird, wie der Rest des Abiturs, zentral erstellt und dauert 20 Minuten. Sie erfolgt als Partnerprüfung bzw. im Ausnahmefall auch als Dreierprüfung (25 Minuten). Es darf kein Wörterbuch benutzt werden.

Wie läuft die Prüfung ab?

Sie werden einem Partner zugelost. Wer Ihr Partner ist, erfahren Sie einen Werktag vor der eigentlichen Prüfung. Sie haben also einen Tag Zeit, sich miteinander „anzufreunden" und sich gemeinsam vorzubereiten.

Am Tag der Prüfung erhalten Sie und Ihr Partner je eine Prüfungsaufgabe. Diese besteht aus je einem Blatt mit einem sogenannten „Impuls", z. B. in Form einer Grafik, einer Karikatur oder eines Zitats, sowie einer sich auf das Thema beziehenden weiterführenden Frage. Dabei erhalten beide Partner unterschiedliche „Impulse" zum gleichen Thema. Die Vorbereitungszeit ist kurz. Nach ca. 3 Minuten wird von Ihnen erwartet, dass Sie sich zunächst zusammenhängend zu dem „Impuls" äußern *(Comment on …)*.

Nachdem beide Partner ihre „Impulse" kommentiert haben, sollen Sie nun in Form eines Gesprächs das vorgegebene Thema diskutieren – mit jeweils gleichen Redeanteilen.

Was wird von Ihnen erwartet?

Das Augenmerk der Prüfer gilt Ihrer Argumentation und Interaktion, d. h., man erwartet von Ihnen, dass Sie sowohl zur Sache sprechen, also Fakten bzw. Argumente sinnvoll miteinander verknüpfen, als auch mit Ihrem Partner angemessen kommunizieren, d. h. miteinander reden, auf Ihren Partner eingehen – und nicht nur einfach Ihren Text abspulen. Sie sollten also, je nach Gesprächssituation, Ihren Partner ergänzen, zustimmen oder aber auch widersprechen. Zur kommunikativen Kompetenz gehört natürlich auch das nonverbale Verhalten, also den Partner anzusehen, ihm durch die Körpersprache zu verstehen zu geben, dass man ihm aufmerksam zuhört. Insgesamt ist zu beachten, dass Sie möglichst differenziert auf das Thema und Ihren Partner eingehen, also Ihre Äußerungen begründen und evtl. mit Beispielen belegen. Hier benötigen Sie Fachwissen (Geschichte, Landeskunde, Allgemeinwissen) verbunden mit dem entsprechenden Sprachwissen (Vokabular).

Auf den praktischen Prüfungsteil kann man sich gut langfristig vorbereiten. Erarbeiten Sie zunächst allein und später mit einem Partner gemeinsam die angegebenen Themen in diesem Buch. Berücksichtigen Sie die Vorbereitungstipps, bereiten Sie sich sprachlich und argumentativ gut vor und führen Sie das Gespräch mit Ihrem Partner „live". Wenn Sie können, zeichnen Sie das Gespräch auf, sodass Sie nach „Prüfungsende" das Ganze noch einmal in Ruhe nachvollziehen können: Ist das, was wir sagen, schlüssig? Gibt es Fakten, die überzeugen? Gehen wir aufeinander ein oder reden wir aneinander vorbei? Benutzen wir die entsprechenden *discourse markers?*

Als zweiten Schritt sollten Sie sich die Lösungsvorschläge in diesem Buch anschauen. Seien Sie nicht verwundert, wenn Ihre Lösungen sich von denen des vorliegenden Buches unterscheiden. Es gibt in diesem Zusammenhang nicht die eine Lösung, gerade inhaltlich bieten die Aufgabenstellungen viele Möglichkeiten. Sie können allerdings vergleichen, inwieweit Sie sprachlich und rhetorisch (stilistisch) vergleichbar gearbeitet haben.

Useful phrases

- **Meinungs-**
  äußerung:

In my opinion/view …
To my mind …
(Personally,) I think …
To be honest, …
As far as I am concerned, …
If you ask me, …
I really think that …
After all/I mean …
… is excellent/extraordinary/outstanding/very special.
Actually, I think that …
I believe …
I am convinced …
I suppose …
I assume …
I must admit that …

As far as I know ...
To my astonishment/surprise/disappointment ...
Apparently .../Obviously .../Evidently ...
It is obvious that ...
I would like to point out that ...

- **Vorschläge:** *I suggest to ...*
  My (first) choice would be ...
  Personally, I would go for ...
  We should take into consideration that ...

- **Meinungen
  erfragen:** *What do you think (about ...)?*
  Why do you think so?
  What is your opinion?
  Wouldn't you say that ...?/Don't you think that ...?
  Which one do you think would ...?
  How about ...?

- **Zustimmen:** *That's a good point/idea.*
  I (entirely) agree with that view/you.
  (Yes,) that's what I think too.
  I couldn't agree more.

- **Widersprechen:** *I'm afraid I don't agree with you (at all).*
  I'm not sure I agree with you/that notion.
  I understand what you mean, but ...
  I'm afraid we'll have to agree to differ!
  It's all right if you prefer ..., but I ...
  You may be right, but I still think ...

Die wichtigsten Stilmittel zur Textanalyse

1. **Alliteration**

   Definition: An alliteration is a figure of speech in which words start with the same consonant sound.

   Examples: Literary characters such as Tiny Tim (Dickens), Donald Duck (Disney) Peter Parker (Spiderman), brand names like Coca-Cola, Best Buy or tongue twisters like "Betty Botter bought some butter."

   "So we beat on, boats against the current, borne back ceaselessly into the past."

   F. Scott Fitzgerald: *The Great Gatsby* (1925)

   Here the repetition of the "b" sound helps to create a sense of rhythm that evokes the beating of waves against a boat.

   Function: Alliterations and assonance help to emphasize a point, attract attention and make an expression (or scene) more memorable.

2. **Allusion**

   Definition: Allusion is a reference to a character, historical or political event or a piece of art or literature the reader is likely to know or be familiar with.

   Example: "This sweltering summer of the Negro's legitimate discontent will not pass until there is an invigoration autumn of freedom and equality"

   Martin Luther King: "I have a dream speech" (1963)

   Here Martin Luther King alludes to the opening lines of Shakespeare's play *Richard III* which read as follows: "Now is the winter of our discontent". These words lay the groundwork of Shakespeare's portrayal of Richard the Third as a discontented tyrant. King's allusion to *Richard III* therefore can be interpreted as connecting the suppression of the African Americans in the 1960s with the tyrant rule of Richard the Third in 15th century England.

   Function: Allusions create a series of associations (see **connotation**) in the reader's mind and thereby either have an emotional impact or stimulate the reader' intellect.

3. **Anaphora**

   Definition: Anaphora is the **repetition** of an expression at the beginning of successive clauses.

   Example: "I still have a dream. […] I have a dream that one day this nation will rise up and live out the true meaning of its creed: 'We hold these truths to be self-evident; that all men are created equal.' I have a dream that one day on the red hills of Georgia the sons of former slaves and the sons of former slave owners will be able to sit down together at the table of brotherhood."

   Martin Luther King: "I have a dream speech" (1963)

   Function: Anaphora is used to give prominence to ideas by adding rhythm and thereby making the text more pleasurable to read/listen to and easier to remember. This way it appeals to the emotions of the audience in order to persuade, inspire, motivate and encourage.

4. **Antithesis** (contrast, opposite)

Definition: Antithesis (which literally means "opposite") is a rhetorical device in which two opposite ideas (a thesis and an opposing antithesis) are put together.

Example: "It was the <u>best</u> of times, it was the <u>worst</u> of times, it was the age of <u>wisdom</u>, it was the age of <u>foolishness</u>, it was the epoch of <u>belief</u>, it was the epoch of <u>incredulity</u>, it was the season of <u>Light</u>, it was the season of <u>Darkness</u>, it was the spring of <u>hope</u>, it was the winter of <u>despair</u>, we had <u>everything</u> before us, we had <u>nothing</u> before us, we were all going direct to <u>Heaven</u>, we were all going direct <u>the other way</u> […]."

Charles Dickens: *A Tale of Two Cities* (1859)

Function: Antithesis is used to create emphasis by exposing the reader to often stark and unexpected contrast. Thus, it conveys opinions and emotions more vividly and emphatically.

5. **Characterisation** (direct/indirect)

Definition: Characterisation refers to the presentation of characters (literary figures) in a text. There are two different ways of characterisation:

a) Direct (or explicit) characterisation: A character can be characterised directly (explicitly) which means the audience is given direct information about the character:

Example: "Oh! But he was a tight-fisted hand at the grindstone, Scrooge! a squeezing, wrenching, grasping, scraping, clutching, covetous, old sinner! Hard and sharp as flint, from which no steel had ever struck out generous fire; secret, and self-contained, and solitary as an oyster."

Charles Dickens: *A Christmas Carol* (1843)

Function: Direct characterisation provides straight forward information about a character. There is no need to "read between the lines" and draw one's own conclusion.

b) Indirect characterisation: Here the audience has to find out about the character's qualities by observing his or her actions, behaviour, thoughts, language, appearance, and his/her way of relating and responding to other characters or problems.

Function: Characterisation aims at informing the audience helping them to make sense of the events taking place. Indirect characterisation is the more subtle way of allowing and encouraging the reader to draw his or her own conclusions which makes the reading (or viewing) process more demanding and challenging but also more rewarding and pleasurable.

6. **Connotation**

Definition: Connotations (or standardized associations) are ideas or emotions associated with an expression.

Example: The term "Route 66" is often associated with ideas of freedom and adventure. The term "shark" is frequently connected with images of danger and death. The expression "life sciences" might connote (negative) concepts of genetic modification and/or the successful fight against diseases.

Function: Many expressions, but especially figurative language, generate various connotations (associations) in the reader's mind, addressing his feelings as well as his understanding.

7. **Ellipsis**

Definition: Ellipsis is the omission of one or more words which are necessary to make a complete sentence but which can be supplied by the reader.

Elliptical sentences are typical of oral communication.

Example: "Got it?", "Seen it?"

Function: Ellipsis can be used as a literary device to indicate casual speech. Thus, in a speech, ellipsis could create a sense of community or familiarity between the speaker and his or her audience or help to highlight important keywords.

8. **Euphemism**

Definition: A euphemistic expression describes a rather harsh or unpleasant fact in gentler and friendlier terms and is often used to sound more indirect and polite.

Examples: "Our cat was very ill. We had her put to sleep."

"He is between jobs." (= "He is unemployed.")

"'For the time being,' he explains, 'it had been found necessary to make a readjustment of rations.'"

George Orwell: *Animal Farm* (1945)

Here, the word "readjustment" replaces the word "reduction", but the impression given is that there is only a change taking place, with "readjustment" being a rather positively connoted expression.

Function: Euphemism helps to convey ideas which are not supposed to be mentioned directly. Euphemisms can also have an ironic (even sarcastic) effect depending on the context.

9. **Figurative/metaphorical language**

Definition: "Figurative" or "metaphorical language" are general terms to describe language that differs from everyday "literal language" in order to intensify comparison, emphasis, clarity, or originality of expression. Metaphor and simile are the two most frequently used, but figurative language also includes hyperbole and puns.

Examples: See metaphor, simile, hyperbole, pun

Function: In general, figurative language appeals to our senses as well as to our intellectual curiosity as the reader has to "decipher" its meaning and message within the given context.

10. **Hyperbole** (exaggeration/over-statement)

Definition: Hyperbole is a form of figurative/metaphorical language and involves an unreal exaggeration of ideas.

Examples: "I could eat a horse." (= "I'm very hungry")

"I will die of shame."

"I had to wait in the station for ten days – an eternity."

Joseph Conrad: *Heart of Darkness* (1899)

Function: Hyperbole can be used to either achieve a humorous effect or in order to emphasize the importance or intensity of an experience.

11. **Imagery** (figurative/metaphorical language)

Definition: Imagery involves the usage of figurative/metaphorical language such as similes and metaphors, expressions which must be "translated" by the reader to make sense.

Examples: see metaphor, simile

Function: The use of imagery aims at making expressions more colourful than every-day speech and thus raises greater awareness in the reader.

12. **Irony** (and Sarcasm)

Definition: The expressed meaning is the opposite of what the author intends to say.

Example: "Wonderful. I have just dropped my favourite cup."

Function: The contrast between what is said and what is meant, the literal and the in-tended meaning, emphasizes the point made by the speaker. The use of irony can also detect a certain detachment of the speaker from his or her subject.

Dramatic irony: describes the contrast between what the protagonist and the audi-ence knows, e. g. in the first act of Shakespeare's *Romeo and Juliet* (1597):

"Go ask his name: if he be married.
My grave is like to be my wedding bed."

In this simile, Julia says that if Romeo were already married, her wedding bed would turn out to be her grave. Here, the dramatic irony unfolds because the audience al-ready knows (from the prologue) that at the end of the play she will indeed die.

Function: Dramatic irony reflects the limited understanding of man (e. g. the limita-tions and shortcomings of Shakespeare's tragic heroes). By putting the reader in a su-perior position, dramatic irony evokes his curiosity, his hopes, and his fears concern-ing the characters' fate and therefore applies to his emotions.

13. **Metaphor**

Definition: A metaphor, a form of figurative/metaphorical language, is a comparison where something is represented by an expression that normally occurs in a very differ-ent context. Unlike similes metaphors **do not** contain direct terms such as "like" or "as".

Example:
"All the world's a stage,
And all the men and women merely players:
They have their exits and their entrances;
And one man in his time plays many parts,"
William Shakespeare: *As You Like It* (1600)

Here, the theatre ("stage"/"players") serves as a metaphor for human life and devel-opment.

Function: Metaphors appeal directly to the senses of listeners or readers. They make the language colourful and challenge our imaginations, thereby providing new and original ways of looking at the world from a different perspective.

14. **Onomatopoeia**

Definition: Onomatopoeic expressions imitate the sounds of things, animals or people.

Examples: The word "whisper", "roar" or "splash" imitate the actual sounds they stand for, e. g. the sound when something hits the water.

"He saw nothing and heard nothing but he could feel his heart pounding and then he heard the <u>clack</u> on stone and the leaping, dropping <u>clicks</u> of a small rock falling."

Ernest Hemingway: *For Whom the Bell Tolls* (1940)

Function: Onomatopoeic expressions have an emotional effect on the reader as they appeal directly to his or her senses.

15. **Personification**

Definition: Personification refers to the technique of presenting animals or objects as if they possessed human qualities.

Examples: "The stars were dancing playfully."

"All he saw was the weeping sky above him."

A genre that uses personification as a guiding principle is the **fable**, where animals take on human qualities.

Function: The use of personification helps to relate animals or things closer to human life and behaviour, appealing to our experiences and emotions.

16. **Paradox** (contradiction)

Definition: A paradox is a statement that embodies two opposing statements or ideas and therefore appears to be contradictory in itself.

Examples:
"I can resist anything except temptation."

Oscar Wilde: *Lady Windermere's Fan: A Play About a Good Woman* (1892)

"All animals are equal, but some are more equal than others".

George Orwell: *Animal Farm* (1945)

Function: The usage of paradox causes the reader to reflect on the message which is often witty, ironic, playful and therefore achieves a humorous effect which in turn makes the text more enjoyable.

17. **Pun** (word play)

Definition: Puns or word plays use language in order to create two or more meanings, or they use an expression in a different, unfamiliar context.

Examples:
"Ask for me tomorrow and you shall find me a grave man."

William Shakespeare: *Romeo and Juliet* (1597)

Here, "grave" can mean "serious and solemn", or it can be taken literally, as meaning "dead in one's grave". As Mercutio has just been fatally stabbed, this pun implies a rather sarcastic undertone, but fits Mercutio's witty character well.

Function: Puns (or word plays) make deliberate use of ambiguity, revealing the cleverness and creativity of both the writers and their characters. Puns cause the reader to think about of what is being said thus demanding more concentration but also providing more intellectual and aesthetical pleasure. As many puns create a humorous effect, word plays are also used for comic relief, for example in Shakespeare's tragedies.

18. **Rhetorical question**

Definition: A rhetorical question is a question that is raised by the author but does not require an answer as the answer is either obvious, or the question cannot/is not supposed to be answered at all.

Examples:
"How many deaths will it take till he knows
that too many people have died?"
Bob Dylan: "Blowing in the Wind" (1962)

Function: Rhetorical questions are often used as means of persuasion as the answer often corresponds with the argumentation of the speaker implying that the listener understands the intended message and agrees with it.

19. **Simile** (Comparison)

Definition: A simile is a comparison between objects, persons and ideas using "like", "as" or "as if".

Examples: "He acted like a raging bull."

Function: Like metaphors, similes appeal to our senses and imagination and therefore make a speaker's speech more colourful and memorable. Sometimes, similes also include a moment of hyperbole (like in "raging bull").

20. **Tone**

Definition: The tone reflects how the writer uses language to create a certain mood, revealing the emotional attitude towards the topic, the characters and the reader. The tone may for instance be formal, informal, ironic, sarcastic, playful, humorous, angry, emotional or neutral.

Function: The tone helps to convey the atmosphere, the mood and the intention of a text. Furthermore, it can be used for implicit characterisation.

Kurzgrammatik

Besonderheiten einiger Wortarten

1 Adjektive und Adverbien – *Adjectives and Adverbs*
Bildung und Verwendung von Adverbien – *Formation and Use of Adverbs*

Bildung
Adjektiv + -*ly*   glad   → glad<u>ly</u>

Ausnahmen:
- -*y* am Wortende wird zu -*i*   easy   → eas<u>i</u>ly
                                               funny   → funn<u>i</u>ly

- auf einen Konsonanten folgendes   sim<u>ple</u>   → simp<u>ly</u>
  -*le* wird zu -*ly*   proba<u>ble</u> → probab<u>ly</u>

- -*ic* am Wortende wird zu -*ically*   fantas<u>tic</u> → fantas<u>tically</u>
  Ausnahme: pub<u>lic</u>   → public<u>ly</u>

Beachte:
- Unregelmäßig gebildet wird: good   → well

- Endet das Adjektiv auf -*ly*, so
  kann kein Adverb gebildet werden; man verwendet deshalb:
  in a + Adjektiv + *manner/way*   friendly → in a friendly manner

- In einigen Fällen haben Adjektiv   daily, early, fast, hard, long, low,
  und Adverb dieselbe Form, z. B.:   weekly, yearly

- Manche Adjektive bilden zwei
  Adverbformen, die sich in der
  Bedeutung unterscheiden, z. B.:

Adj./Adv.	Adv. auf -*ly*	
hard	*hardly*	The task is <u>hard</u>. (adjective)
schwierig, hart	kaum	*Die Aufgabe ist schwierig.*
late	*lately*	She works <u>hard</u>. (adverb)
spät	neulich, kürzlich	*Sie arbeitet hart.*
near	*nearly*	She <u>hardly</u> works. (adverb)
nahe	beinahe	*Sie arbeitet kaum.*

G 1

Verwendung

Adverbien bestimmen

- Verben,

  She <u>easily</u> <u>found</u> her brother in the crowd.
  Sie fand ihren Bruder leicht in der Menge.

- Adjektive,

  This band is <u>extremely</u> <u>famous</u>.
  Diese Band ist sehr berühmt.

- andere Adverbien oder

  He walks <u>extremely</u> <u>quickly</u>.
  Er geht äußerst schnell.

- einen ganzen Satz
  näher.

  <u>Fortunately</u>, <u>nobody was hurt</u>.
  Glücklicherweise wurde niemand verletzt.

Beachte:

Nach bestimmten Verben steht nicht
das Adverb, sondern das Adjektiv:

- Verben, die einen **Zustand** ausdrücken, z. B.:

to be	sein
to become	werden
to get	werden
to seem	scheinen
to stay	bleiben

  Everything <u>seems</u> <u>quiet</u>.
  Alles scheint ruhig zu sein.

- Verben der **Sinneswahrnehmung**,
  z. B.:

to feel	sich anfühlen
to look	aussehen
to smell	riechen
to sound	sich anhören
to taste	schmecken

  This dress <u>looks</u> <u>fantastic</u>!
  Dieses Kleid sieht toll aus!

Steigerung des Adjektivs – *Comparison of Adjectives*

Bildung

Man unterscheidet:

- Grundform/Positiv *(positive)*

  Peter is <u>young</u>.

- Komparativ *(comparative)*

  Jane is <u>younger</u>.

- Superlativ *(superlative)*

  Paul is <u>the youngest</u>.

Steigerung auf -er, -est
- einsilbige Adjektive

old, old*er*, old*est*
alt, älter, am ältesten

- zweisilbige Adjektive, die auf
-er, -le, -ow oder -y enden

clever, cleverer, cleverest
klug, klüger, am klügsten

simple, simpler, simplest
einfach, einfacher, am einfachsten

narrow, narrower, narrowest
eng, enger, am engsten

funny, funnier, funniest
lustig, lustiger, am lustigsten

Beachte:
- stummes -e am Wortende entfällt

simple, simpler, simplest

- nach einem Konsonanten wird
-y am Wortende zu -i-

funny, funnier, funniest

- nach kurzem Vokal wird ein Konsonant am Wortende verdoppelt

fit, fitter, fittest

Steigerung mit *more ..., most ...*
- zweisilbige Adjektive, die nicht
auf -er, -le, -ow oder -y enden

useful, more useful, most useful
nützlich, nützlicher, am nützlichsten

- Adjektive mit drei und mehr
Silben

difficult, more difficult, most difficult
schwierig, schwieriger, am schwierigsten

Unregelmäßige Steigerung
Die unregelmäßig gesteigerten
Adjektive muss man auswendig
lernen. Einige sind hier angegeben:

good, better, best
gut, besser, am besten

bad, worse, worst
schlecht, schlechter, am schlechtesten

many, more, most
viele, mehr, am meisten

much, more, most
viel, mehr, am meisten

little, less, least
wenig, weniger, am wenigsten

Steigerungsformen im Satz – *Sentences with Comparisons*

Es gibt folgende Möglichkeiten,
Steigerungen im Satz zu verwenden:
- **Positiv:** Zwei oder mehr Personen
  oder Sachen sind **gleich oder
  ungleich:** *(not) as* + Grundform
  des Adjektivs + *as*

Anne is <u>as</u> tall <u>as</u> John (and Steve).
Anne ist genauso groß wie John (und Steve).

John is <u>not as</u> tall <u>as</u> Steve.
John ist nicht so groß wie Steve.

- **Komparativ:** Zwei oder mehr
  Personen/Sachen sind **verschieden** (größer/besser ...): Kompara-
  tivform des Adjektivs + *than*

Steve is <u>taller</u> <u>than</u> Anne.
Steve ist größer als Anne.

- **Superlativ:** Eine Person oder
  Sache wird besonders hervorge-
  hoben (der/die/das größte/
  beste ...): *the* + Superlativform des
  Adjektivs

Steve is <u>the</u> <u>tallest</u> boy in class.
Steve ist der größte Junge in der Klasse.

Steigerung des Adverbs – *Comparison of Adverbs*

Adverbien können wie Adjektive
auch gesteigert werden.
- Adverbien auf *-ly* werden mit
  more, most bzw. mit *less, least*
  gesteigert.

She talks <u>more</u> <u>quickly</u> than John.
Sie spricht schneller als John.

- Adverbien, die dieselbe Form wie
  das Adjektiv haben, werden mit
  -er, -est gesteigert.

fast   –   fast<u>er</u>   –   fast<u>est</u>
early –   earli<u>er</u>   –   earli<u>est</u>

- Manche Adverbien haben unregelmäßige Steigerungsformen,
  z. B.:

well   –   better   –   best
badly –   worse   –   worst
little   –   less   –   least
much –   more   –   most

Die Stellung von Adverbien im Satz

Adverbien können verschiedene
Positionen im Satz einnehmen:
- Am **Anfang des Satzes**, vor dem
  Subjekt *(front position)*

<u>Tomorrow</u> he will be in London.
Morgen [betont] wird er in London sein.
<u>Unfortunately</u>, I can't come to the party.
Leider kann ich nicht zur Party kommen.

G 4

- **Im Satz** *(mid position)*
  vor dem Vollverb,

  She <u>often</u> goes to school by bike.
  Sie fährt oft mit dem Rad in die Schule.

  nach *to be*,

  She is <u>already</u> at home.
  Sie ist schon zu Hause.

  nach dem ersten Hilfsverb.

  You can <u>even</u> go swimming there.
  Man kann dort sogar schwimmen gehen.

- Am **Ende des Satzes** *(end position)*

  He will be in London <u>tomorrow</u>.
  Er wird morgen in London sein.

  Gibt es mehrere Adverbien am Satzende, so gilt die **Reihenfolge:** Art und Weise – Ort – Zeit *(manner – place – time)*

  The snow melts <u>slowly</u> <u>in the mountains</u> <u>at springtime</u>.
  Im Frühling schmilzt der Schnee langsam in den Bergen.

2 Artikel – *Article*

Der **bestimmte Artikel** steht, wenn man von einer **ganz bestimmten Person oder Sache** spricht.

<u>The</u> cat is sleeping on the sofa.
Die Katze schläft auf dem Sofa. [nicht irgendeine Katze, sondern eine bestimmte]

Beachte: Der bestimmte Artikel steht unter anderem **immer** in folgenden Fällen:

- **abstrakte Begriffe**, die näher erläutert sind

<u>The</u> agriculture practised in the USA is very successful.
Die Landwirtschaft, wie sie in den USA praktiziert wird, ist sehr erfolgreich.

- **Gebäudebezeichnungen**, wenn man vom Gebäude und nicht von der Institution spricht

<u>The</u> university should be renovated soon.
Die Universität sollte bald renoviert werden.

- **Eigennamen im Plural** (Familiennamen, Gebirge, Inselgruppen, einige Länder etc.)

<u>the</u> Johnsons, <u>the</u> Rockies, <u>the</u> Hebrides, <u>the</u> Netherlands, <u>the</u> USA

- Namen von **Flüssen** und **Meeren**

<u>the</u> Mississippi, <u>the</u> North Sea, <u>the</u> Pacific Ocean

Der **unbestimmte Artikel** steht, wenn man von einer **nicht näher bestimmten Person oder Sache** spricht.

<u>A</u> man is walking down the road.
Ein Mann läuft gerade die Straße entlang. [irgendein Mann]

In diesen Fällen steht **kein Artikel**:

- **nicht zählbare** Nomen wie z. B.
  Stoffbezeichnungen

Gold is very valuable.
Gold ist sehr wertvoll.

- **abstrakte Nomen** ohne nähere
  Bestimmung

Buddhism is widespread in Asia.
Der Buddhismus ist in Asien weit verbreitet.

- **Kollektivbegriffe**, z. B. *man,
  youth, society*

Man is responsible for global warming.
*Der Mensch ist für die Klimaerwärmung
verantwortlich.*

- **Institutionen**, z. B. *school, church,
  university, prison*

We went to school together.
Wir gingen zusammen zur Schule.

- **Mahlzeiten**, z. B. *breakfast, lunch*

Dinner is at 8 p.m.
Das Abendessen ist um 20 Uhr.

- *by* + **Verkehrsmittel**

I went to school by bike.
Ich fuhr mit dem Fahrrad zur Schule.

- **Personennamen** (auch mit Titel),
  Verwandtschaftsbezeichnungen,
  die wie Namen verwendet werden

Tom, Mr Scott, Queen Elizabeth, Dr Hill,
Dad, Uncle Harry

- Bezeichnungen für **Straßen,
  Plätze, Brücken, Parkanlagen**

Fifth Avenue, Trafalgar Square, West-
minster Bridge, Hyde Park

- Namen von **Ländern, Kontinen-
  ten, Städten, Seen, Inseln, Bergen**

France, Asia, San Francisco, Loch Ness,
Corsica, Ben Nevis

3 Pronomen – *Pronouns*

Possessivpronomen – *Possessive Pronouns*

G 6

mit Substantiv	ohne Substantiv			
my	*mine*	This is <u>my bike</u>.	–	This is <u>mine</u>.
your	*yours*	This is <u>your bike</u>.	–	This is <u>yours</u>.
his/her/its	*his/hers/–*	This is <u>her bike</u>.	–	This is <u>hers</u>.
our	*ours*	This is <u>our bike</u>.	–	This is <u>ours</u>.
your	*yours*	This is <u>your bike</u>.	–	This is <u>yours</u>.
their	*theirs*	This is <u>their bike</u>.	–	This is <u>theirs</u>.

Reflexivpronomen – *Reflexive Pronouns*

Reflexivpronomen *(reflexive pronouns)* **beziehen sich auf das Subjekt** des Satzes **zurück**. Es handelt sich also um dieselbe Person:

myself	<u>I</u> will buy <u>myself</u> a new car.
yourself	<u>You</u> will buy <u>yourself</u> a new car.
himself / herself / itself	<u>He</u> will buy <u>himself</u> a new car.
ourselves	<u>We</u> will buy <u>ourselves</u> a new car.
yourselves	<u>You</u> will buy <u>yourselves</u> a new car.
themselves	<u>They</u> will buy <u>themselves</u> a new car.

Beachte:

- Einige Verben stehen ohne Reflexivpronomen, obwohl im Deutschen mit „mich, dich, sich etc." übersetzt wird.

  I apologize …
  Ich entschuldige mich …
  He is hiding.
  Er versteckt sich.

- Einige Verben können sowohl mit einem Objekt als auch mit einem Reflexivpronomen verwendet werden. Dabei ändert sich die Bedeutung, z. B. bei *to control, to enjoy, to help, to occupy.*

  He is enjoying <u>the party</u>.
  Er genießt die Party.
  She is enjoying <u>herself</u>.
  Sie amüsiert sich.

  He is helping <u>the child</u>.
  Er hilft dem Kind.
  Help <u>yourself</u>!
  Bedienen Sie sich!

Reziprokes Pronomen – *Reciprocal Pronoun* ("each other / one another")

each other/one another ist unveränderlich. Es bezieht sich auf **zwei oder mehr Personen** und wird mit „sich (gegenseitig)/einander" übersetzt.

Beachte:
Einige Verben stehen ohne *each other*, obwohl im Deutschen mit „sich" übersetzt wird.

They looked at <u>each other</u> and laughed.
Sie schauten sich (gegenseitig) an und lachten.
oder:
Sie schauten einander an und lachten.

to meet	*sich treffen*
to kiss	*sich küssen*
to fall in love	*sich verlieben*

4 Präpositionen – *Prepositions*

Präpositionen *(prepositions)* drücken **räumliche, zeitliche oder andere Arten von Beziehungen** aus.

The ball is <u>under</u> the table.
He came home <u>after</u> six o'clock.

Die wichtigsten Präpositionen mit Beispielen für ihre Verwendung:
- *at*
  Ortsangabe: *at home*

  I'm <u>at home</u> now. *Ich bin jetzt zu Hause.*

  Zeitangabe: *at 3 p.m.*

  He arrived <u>at 3 p.m.</u> *Er kam um 15 Uhr an.*

- *by*
  Angabe des Mittels: *by bike*

  She went to work <u>by bike</u>.
  Sie fuhr mit dem Rad zur Arbeit.

  Angabe der Ursache: *by mistake*

  He did it <u>by mistake</u>.
  Er hat es aus Versehen getan.

  Zeitangabe: *by tomorrow*

  You will get the letter <u>by tomorrow</u>.
  Du bekommst den Brief bis morgen.

- *for*
  Zeitdauer: *for hours*

  We waited for the bus <u>for hours</u>.
  Wir warteten stundenlang auf den Bus.

- *from*
  Ortsangabe: *from Dublin*

  Ian is <u>from Dublin</u>.
  Ian kommt aus Dublin.

  Zeitangabe: *from nine to five*

  We work <u>from nine to five</u>.
  Wir arbeiten von neun bis fünf Uhr.

- *in*
  Ortsangabe: *in England*

  <u>In England</u>, they drive on the left.
  In England herrscht Linksverkehr.

Zeitangabe: *in the morning*	They woke up <u>in the morning</u>. *Sie wachten am Morgen auf.*
• *of* Ortsangabe: *north of the city*	The village lies <u>north of the city</u>. *Das Dorf liegt nördlich der Stadt.*
• *on* Ortsangabe: *on the left,* *on the floor*	<u>On the left</u> you see the London Eye. *Links sehen Sie das London Eye.*
Zeitangabe: *on Monday*	<u>On Monday</u> she will buy the tickets. *(Am) Montag kauft sie die Karten.*
• *to* Richtungsangabe: *to the left*	Please turn <u>to the left</u>. *Bitte wenden Sie sich nach links.*
Angabe des Ziels: *to London*	He goes <u>to London</u> every year. *Er fährt jedes Jahr nach London.*

5 Modale Hilfsverben – *Modal Auxiliaries*

Zu den **modalen Hilfsverben** *(modal auxiliaries)* zählen z. B. *can, may* und *must.*

Bildung

- Die modalen Hilfsverben haben für alle Personen **nur eine Form**: kein *-s* in der 3. Person Singular.

I, you, he/she/it,
we, you, they $\Big\}$ must

- Auf ein modales Hilfsverb folgt der **Infinitiv ohne** *to.*

You <u>must</u> <u>listen</u> to my new CD.
Du musst dir meine neue CD anhören.

- **Frage und Verneinung** werden nicht mit *do/did* umschrieben.

<u>Can</u> you help me, please?
Kannst du mir bitte helfen?

Die modalen Hilfsverben können nicht alle Zeiten bilden. Deshalb benötigt man **Ersatzformen** (können auch im Präsens verwendet werden).

- *can* (können)
  Ersatzformen:
  (to) be able to (Fähigkeit),
  (to) be allowed to (Erlaubnis)

I <u>can</u> sing./I <u>was able to</u> sing.
Ich kann singen. / Ich konnte singen.

You <u>can't</u> go to the party./
I <u>wasn't allowed to</u> go to the party.
Du darfst nicht auf die Party gehen./
Ich durfte nicht auf die Party gehen.

Beachte: Im *simple past* und *conditional I* ist auch *could* möglich.

When I was three, I <u>could</u> already ski.
Mit drei konnte ich schon Ski fahren.

• **may** (dürfen) – sehr höflich Ersatzform: **(to) be allowed to**	You <u>may</u> go home early./ You <u>were allowed to</u> go home early. *Du darfst früh nach Hause gehen./* *Du durftest früh nach Hause gehen.*
• **must** (müssen) Ersatzform: **(to) have to**	He <u>must</u> be home by ten o'clock./ He <u>had to</u> be home by ten o'clock. *Er muss um zehn Uhr zu Hause sein./* *Er musste um zehn Uhr zu Hause sein.*
Beachte: **must not/mustn't** = „nicht dürfen"	You <u>must not</u> eat all the cake. *Du darfst nicht den ganzen Kuchen essen.*
„nicht müssen, nicht brauchen" = **not have to, needn't**	You <u>don't have to</u>/<u>needn't</u> eat all the cake. *Du musst nicht den ganzen Kuchen essen./* *Du brauchst nicht … zu essen.*

Infinitiv, Gerundium oder Partizip? – Die infiniten Verbformen

6 Infinitiv – *Infinitive*

Der **Infinitiv** (Grundform des Verbs)
mit *to* steht z. B. **nach**
• bestimmten **Verben**, z. B.:

to decide	(sich) entscheiden, beschließen
to expect	erwarten
to hope	hoffen
to manage	schaffen
to plan	planen
to promise	versprechen
to want	wollen

He <u>decided</u> <u>to wait</u>.
Er beschloss zu warten.

• bestimmten **Substantiven und Pro-nomen** (*something, anything*), z. B.:

attempt	Versuch
idea	Idee
plan	Plan
wish	Wunsch

We haven't got <u>anything</u> <u>to eat</u> at home.
Wir haben nichts zu essen zu Hause.

It was her <u>plan</u> <u>to visit</u> him in May.
Sie hatte vor, ihn im Mai zu besuchen.

• bestimmten **Adjektiven** (auch in
Verbindung mit *too/enough*) und
deren Steigerungsformen, z. B.:

certain	sicher
difficult/hard	schwer, schwierig
easy	leicht

It was <u>difficult</u> <u>to follow</u> her.
Es war schwer, ihr zu folgen.

- **Fragewörtern**, wie z. B. *what, where, which, who, when, how* und nach *whether*. Diese Konstruktion ersetzt eine indirekte Frage mit modalem Hilfsverb.

We knew <u>where</u> <u>to find</u> her. /
We knew <u>where</u> <u>we</u> <u>would find</u> her.
Wir wussten, wo wir sie finden würden.

Die Konstruktion **Objekt + Infinitiv** wird im Deutschen oft mit einem „dass"-Satz übersetzt.
Sie steht z. B. **nach**

- bestimmten **Verben**, z. B.:

to allow	erlauben
to get	veranlassen
to help	helfen
to persuade	überreden

She <u>allowed</u> <u>him</u> <u>to go</u> to the cinema.
Sie erlaubte ihm, dass er ins Kino geht. / ... ins Kino zu gehen.

- **Verb + Präposition**, z. B.:

to count on	rechnen mit
to rely on	sich verlassen auf
to wait for	warten auf

She <u>relies on</u> <u>him</u> <u>to arrive</u> in time.
Sie verlässt sich darauf, dass er rechtzeitig ankommt.

- **Adjektiv + Präposition**, z. B.:

easy for	leicht
necessary for	notwendig
nice of	nett
silly of	dumm

It is <u>necessary</u> <u>for you</u> <u>to learn</u> maths.
Es ist notwendig, dass du Mathe lernst.

- **Substantiv + Präposition**, z. B.:

opportunity for	Gelegenheit
idea for	Idee
time for	Zeit
mistake for	Fehler

Work experience is a good <u>opportunity</u> <u>for you</u> <u>to find out</u> which job suits you.
Ein Praktikum ist eine gute Gelegenheit, herauszufinden, welcher Beruf zu dir passt.

- einem **Adjektiv**, das durch ***too*** oder ***enough*** näher bestimmt wird.

The box is <u>too</u> <u>heavy</u> <u>for me</u> <u>to carry</u>.
Die Kiste ist mir zu schwer zum Tragen.

The weather is <u>good</u> <u>enough</u> <u>for us</u> <u>to go</u> for a walk. *Das Wetter ist gut genug, dass wir spazieren gehen können.*

7 Gerundium (*-ing*-Form) – *Gerund*

Bildung
Infinitiv + *-ing*

read → rea<u>ding</u>

Verwendung

Die *-ing*-Form steht nach bestimmten Ausdrücken und kann verschiedene Funktionen im Satz einnehmen, z. B.:

• als **Subjekt** des Satzes

Skiing is fun. *Skifahren macht Spaß.*

• nach bestimmten **Verben** (als **Objekt** des Satzes), z. B.:

to avoid	vermeiden
to enjoy	genießen, gern tun
to keep (on)	weitermachen
to miss	vermissen
to risk	riskieren
to suggest	vorschlagen

He enjoys reading comics.
Er liest gerne Comics.

You risk losing a friend.
Du riskierst, einen Freund zu verlieren.

• nach **Verb + Präposition**, z. B.:

to agree with	zustimmen
to believe in	glauben an
to dream of	träumen von
to look forward to	sich freuen auf
to talk about	sprechen über

She dreams of meeting a star.
Sie träumt davon, einen Star zu treffen.

• nach **Adjektiv + Präposition**, z. B.:

afraid of	sich fürchten vor
famous for	berühmt für
good/bad at	gut/schlecht in
interested in	interessiert an

He is afraid of losing his job.
Er hat Angst, seine Arbeit zu verlieren.

• nach **Substantiv + Präposition**, z. B.:

chance of	Chance, Aussicht
danger of	Gefahr
reason for	Grund
way of	Art und Weise

Do you have a chance of getting the job?
Hast du Aussicht, die Stelle zu bekommen?

- nach **Präpositionen** und **Konjunktionen der Zeit**, z. B.:

after	nachdem
before	bevor
by	indem,
	dadurch, dass
in spite of	trotz
instead of	statt

Before leaving the room he said goodbye.
Bevor er den Raum verließ, verabschiedete er sich.

8 Infinitiv oder Gerundium? – *Infinitive or Gerund?*

Einige Verben können sowohl **mit** dem **Infinitiv** als auch **mit der** *-ing*-**Form** stehen, **ohne** dass sich die **Bedeutung ändert**, z. B. *to love, to hate, to prefer, to start, to begin, to continue.*

I hate getting up early.
I hate to get up early.
Ich hasse es, früh aufzustehen.

Bei manchen Verben **ändert sich** jedoch die **Bedeutung**, je nachdem, ob sie mit Infinitiv oder mit der *-ing*-Form verwendet werden, z. B. *to remember, to forget, to stop.*

- *to remember* + Infinitiv: „daran denken, etwas zu tun"

  I must remember to post the invitations.
  Ich muss daran denken, die Einladungen einzuwerfen.

  to remember + *ing*-Form: „sich erinnern, etwas getan zu haben"

  I remember posting the invitations.
  Ich erinnere mich daran, die Einladungen eingeworfen zu haben.

- *to forget* + Infinitiv: „vergessen, etwas zu tun"

  Don't forget to water the plants.
  Vergiss nicht, die Pflanzen zu gießen.

  to forget + *ing*-Form: „vergessen, etwas getan zu haben"

  I'll never forget meeting the President.
  Ich werde nie vergessen, wie ich den Präsidenten traf.

- *to stop* + Infinitiv: „stehen bleiben, um etwas zu tun"

  I stopped to read the road sign.
  Ich hielt an, um das Verkehrsschild zu lesen.

  to stop + *ing*-Form: „aufhören, etwas zu tun"

  He stopped laughing.
  Er hörte auf zu lachen.

9 Partizipien – *Participles*

Partizip Präsens – *Present Participle*

Bildung	
Infinitiv + *ing*	talk → talking
Sonderformen: siehe *gerund*	
(S. G 11 f.)	

Verwendung

Das *present participle* verwendet man:

- zur Bildung der Verlaufsform *present progressive*,

  Peter is <u>reading</u>.
  Peter liest (gerade).

- zur Bildung der Verlaufsform *past progressive*,

  Peter was <u>reading</u> when I saw him.
  Peter las (gerade), als ich ihn sah.

- zur Bildung der Verlaufsform *present perfect progressive*,

  I have been <u>living</u> in Sydney for 5 years.
  Ich lebe seit 5 Jahren in Sydney.

- zur Bildung der Verlaufsform *future progressive*,

  This time tomorrow I will be <u>working</u>.
  Morgen um diese Zeit werde ich arbeiten.

- wie ein Adjektiv, wenn es vor einem Substantiv steht.

  The village hasn't got <u>running</u> water.
  Das Dorf hat kein fließendes Wasser.

Partizip Perfekt – *Past Participle*

Bildung		
Infinitiv + *-ed*	talk	→ talk<u>ed</u>

Beachte:

- stummes *-e* entfällt

  liv<u>e</u> → liv<u>ed</u>

- nach kurzem betontem Vokal wird der Schlusskonsonant verdoppelt

  sto<u>p</u> → stop<u>p</u>ed

- *-y* wird zu *-ie*

  cr<u>y</u> → cr<u>ie</u>d

- unregelmäßige Verben (S. G 31 f.)

  be → been

Verwendung

Das *past participle* verwendet man

- zur Bildung des *present perfect*,

  He hasn't <u>talked</u> to Tom yet.
  Er hat noch nicht mit Tom gesprochen.

G 14

• zur Bildung des *past perfect*,	Before they went biking in France, they had <u>bought</u> new bikes. *Bevor sie nach Frankreich zum Radfahren gingen, hatten sie neue Fahrräder gekauft.*
• zur Bildung des *future perfect*,	The letter will have <u>arrived</u> by then. *Der Brief wird bis dann angekommen sein.*
• zur Bildung des Passivs,	The fish was <u>eaten</u> by the cat. *Der Fisch wurde von der Katze gefressen.*
• wie ein Adjektiv, wenn es vor einem Substantiv steht.	Peter has got a well-<u>paid</u> job. *Peter hat eine gut bezahlte Stelle.*

Verkürzung eines Nebensatzes durch ein Partizip

Adverbiale Nebensätze (meist kausale oder temporale Bedeutung) und **Relativsätze** können durch ein Partizip verkürzt werden.

She watches the news, because she wants to stay informed.
<u>Wanting</u> to stay informed, she watches the news.
Sie sieht sich die Nachrichten an, weil sie informiert bleiben möchte.

Aus der Zeitform des Verbs im Nebensatz ergibt sich, welches Partizip für die Satzverkürzung verwendet wird:

• Steht das Verb im Nebensatz im *present* oder *past tense* (*simple* und *progressive form*), verwendet man das *present participle*.

he finishes
he finished $\Big\} \rightarrow$ finishing

• Steht das Verb im Nebensatz im *present perfect* oder *past perfect*, verwendet man *having + past participle*.

he has finished
he had finished $\Big\} \rightarrow$ having finished

• Das *past participle* verwendet man auch, um einen Satz im Passiv zu verkürzen.

Sally is a manager in a five-star hotel <u>which is called</u> Pacific View.
Sally is a manager in a five-star hotel <u>called</u> Pacific View.

Beachte:
• Man kann einen Temporal- oder Kausalsatz verkürzen, wenn **Haupt- und Nebensatz dasselbe Subjekt** haben.

When <u>he</u> was walking down the street, <u>he</u> saw Jo.
(When) <u>walking</u> down the street, <u>he</u> saw Jo.
Als er die Straße entlangging, sah er Jo.

- Bei **Kausalsätzen** entfallen die Konjunktionen *as, because* und *since* im verkürzten Nebensatz.

As <u>he</u> was hungry, <u>he</u> bought a sandwich.
<u>Being</u> hungry, <u>he</u> bought a sandwich.
Da er hungrig war, kaufte er ein Sandwich.

- In einem **Temporalsatz** bleibt die einleitende **Konjunktion** häufig erhalten, um dem Satz eine **eindeutige Bedeutung** zuzuweisen.

When <u>he</u> left, <u>he</u> forgot to lock the door.
<u>When</u> <u>leaving</u>, <u>he</u> forgot to lock the door.
Als er ging, vergaß er, die Tür abzuschließen.

Tara got sick <u>eating</u> too much chocolate.
Tara wurde schlecht, als/während/da sie zu viel Schokolade aß.

Die Vorzeitigkeit einer Handlung kann durch *after + present participle* oder durch *having + past participle* ausgedrückt werden.

After <u>finishing</u> / <u>Having finished</u> breakfast, he went to work.
Nachdem er sein Frühstück beendet hatte, ging er zur Arbeit.

- Bei **Relativsätzen** entfallen die Relativpronomen *who, which* und *that.*

I saw a six-year-old boy <u>who</u> <u>played</u> the piano.
I saw a six-year-old boy <u>playing</u> the piano.
Ich sah einen sechsjährigen Jungen, der gerade Klavier spielte. / ... Klavier spielen.

Verbindung von zwei Hauptsätzen durch ein Partizip

Zwei Hauptsätze können durch ein Partizip verbunden werden, wenn sie **dasselbe Subjekt** haben.

Beachte:
- Das Subjekt des zweiten Hauptsatzes und die Konjunktion *and* entfallen.
- Die Verbform des zweiten Hauptsatzes wird durch das Partizip ersetzt.

<u>He</u> did his homework and <u>he</u> listened to the radio.
<u>He</u> did his homework <u>listening</u> to the radio.
Er machte seine Hausaufgaben und hörte Radio.

Unverbundene Partizipialkonstruktionen – *Absolute Participle Constructions*

Unverbundene Partizipialkonstruktionen haben ein **eigenes Subjekt**, das nicht mit dem Subjekt des Hauptsatzes übereinstimmt. Sie werden in **gehobener Sprache** verwendet.
Mit einleitendem *with* werden sie auf allen Stilebenen verwendet.

The <u>sun</u> having come out, the ladies went for a walk in the park.
Da die Sonne herausgekommen war, gingen die Damen im Park spazieren.

With the <u>telephone</u> ringing, she jumped out of bed.
Als das Telefon klingelte, sprang sie aus dem Bett.

Bildung und Gebrauch der finiten Verbformen

10 Zeiten – *Tenses*

Simple Present

Bildung
Infinitiv, Ausnahme 3. Person Singular: Infinitiv + *-s*

stand   –   he/she/it stand<u>s</u>

Beachte:
- Bei Verben, die auf *-s, -sh, -ch, -x* und *-z* enden, wird in der 3. Person Singular *-es* angefügt.

kiss   –   he/she/it kiss<u>es</u>
rush   –   hc/she/it rush<u>es</u>
teach   –   he/she/it teach<u>es</u>
fix   –   he/she/it fix<u>es</u>

- Bei Verben, die auf Konsonant + *-y* enden, wird *-es* angefügt; *-y* wird zu *-i-*.

carry   –   he/she/it carr<u>ies</u>

Bildung von Fragen im *simple present*
(Fragewort +) *do/does* + Subjekt + Infinitiv

<u>Where</u> does he <u>live</u>? / <u>Does</u> he <u>live</u> in London?
Wo lebt er? / Lebt er in London?

Beachte:
Die Umschreibung mit *do/does* wird nicht verwendet,
- wenn nach dem Subjekt gefragt wird (mit *who, what, which*),

<u>Who</u> <u>likes</u> pizza?
Wer mag Pizza?

<u>Which</u> tree <u>has</u> more leaves?
Welcher Baum hat mehr Blätter?

- wenn die Frage mit *is/are* gebildet wird.

<u>Are</u> you happy?
Bist du glücklich?

Bildung der Verneinung im *simple present*
don't/doesn't + Infinitiv

He <u>doesn't like</u> football.
Er mag Fußball nicht.

Verwendung
Das *simple present* wird verwendet:
- bei Tätigkeiten, die man **gewohnheitsmäßig** oder häufig ausführt Signalwörter: z. B. *always, often, never, every day, every morning, every afternoon*

Every morning John <u>buys</u> a newspaper.
Jeden Morgen kauft John eine Zeitung.

- bei **allgemeingültigen** Aussagen

London <u>is</u> a big city.
London ist eine große Stadt.

- bei **Zustandsverben**: Sie drücken Eigenschaften / Zustände von Personen und Dingen aus und stehen normalerweise nur in der *simple form*, z. B. *to hate, to know, to like*.

I like science-fiction films.
Ich mag Science-Fiction-Filme.

Present Progressive / Present Continuous

Bildung
am/is/are + *present participle*

read → <u>am/is/are</u> <u>reading</u>

Bildung von Fragen im *present progressive*
(Fragewort +) *am/is/are* + Subjekt + *present participle*

<u>Is</u> <u>Peter</u> <u>reading</u>? / <u>What</u> is he <u>reading</u>?
Liest Peter gerade? / Was liest er?

Bildung der Verneinung im *present progressive*
am not/isn't/aren't + *present participle*

Peter <u>isn't</u> <u>reading</u>.
Peter liest gerade nicht.

Verwendung
Mit dem *present progressive* drückt man aus, dass etwas **gerade passiert** und **noch nicht abgeschlossen** ist. Es wird daher auch als **Verlaufsform** der Gegenwart bezeichnet.

Signalwörter: *at the moment, now*

At the moment, Peter <u>is drinking</u> a cup of tea.
Im Augenblick trinkt Peter eine Tasse Tee.
[Er hat damit angefangen und noch nicht aufgehört.]

G 18

Bildung
Regelmäßige Verben: Infinitiv + *-ed*

walk → walk<u>ed</u>

Beachte:
* stummes *-e* entfällt

hop<u>e</u> → hop<u>ed</u>

* Bei Verben, die auf Konsonant +
  -y enden, wird *-y* zu *-i-*.

car<u>ry</u> → carr<u>ied</u>

* Nach kurzem betontem Vokal
  wird der Schlusskonsonant verdoppelt.

sto<u>p</u> → sto<u>pped</u>

Unregelmäßige Verben: siehe Liste
S. G 31 f.

be → was
have → had

Bildung von Fragen im *simple past*
(Fragewort +) *did* + Subjekt +
Infinitiv

(Why) <u>Did</u> he <u>look</u> out of the window?
(Warum) Sah er aus dem Fenster?

Beachte:
Die Umschreibung mit *did* wird nicht
verwendet,
* wenn nach dem Subjekt gefragt
  wird (mit *who, what, which*),

<u>Who</u> <u>paid</u> the bill?
Wer zahlte die Rechnung?

<u>What</u> <u>happened</u> to your friend?
Was ist mit deinem Freund passiert?

* wenn die Frage mit *was/were*
  gebildet wird.

<u>Were</u> you happy?
Warst du glücklich?

Bildung der Verneinung im *simple*
past
didn't + Infinitiv

He <u>didn't</u> <u>call</u> me.
Er rief mich nicht an.

Verwendung
Das *simple past* beschreibt Handlungen und Ereignisse, die **in der**
Vergangenheit passierten und
bereits abgeschlossen sind.

Signalwörter: z. B. *yesterday, last*
week/year, two years ago, in 2008

Last week, he <u>helped</u> me with my home-
work.
Letzte Woche half er mir bei meinen Haus-
aufgaben. [Die Handlung fand in der letzten
Woche statt, ist also abgeschlossen.]

Past Progressive / Past Continuous

Bildung
was/were + present participle

watch → <u>was/were</u> <u>watching</u>

Verwendung
Die **Verlaufsform** *past progressive* verwendet man, wenn **zu einem bestimmten Zeitpunkt** in der Vergangenheit eine **Handlung ablief**, bzw. wenn eine **Handlung** von einer anderen **unterbrochen** wurde.

Yesterday at 9 o'clock I <u>was</u> still <u>sleeping</u>.
Gestern um 9 Uhr schlief ich noch.

I <u>was reading</u> a book when Peter came into the room.
Ich las (gerade) ein Buch, als Peter ins Zimmer kam.

Present Perfect (Simple)

Bildung
have/has + past participle

write → <u>has/have</u> <u>written</u>

Verwendung
Das *present perfect* verwendet man,
* wenn ein Vorgang **in der Vergangenheit begonnen** hat und **noch andauert**,

He <u>has lived</u> in London since 2008.
Er lebt seit 2008 in London.
[Er lebt jetzt immer noch in London.]

* wenn das Ergebnis einer vergangenen Handlung **Auswirkungen auf die Gegenwart** hat.

I <u>have</u> just <u>cleaned</u> my car.
Ich habe gerade mein Auto geputzt.
[Man sieht evtl. das saubere Auto.]

Signalwörter: z. B. *already, ever, just, how long, not ... yet, since, for*

Have you <u>ever</u> been to Dublin?
Warst du schon jemals in Dublin?

Beachte:
* *have/has* können zu *'ve/'s* verkürzt werden.

He<u>'s</u> given me his umbrella.
Er hat mir seinen Regenschirm gegeben.

* Das *present perfect* wird oft mit *since* und *for* verwendet („seit").
  – *since* gibt einen **Zeitpunkt** an:

Ron has lived in Sydney <u>since 2007</u>.
Ron lebt seit 2007 in Sydney.

  – *for* gibt einen **Zeitraum** an:

Sally has lived in Berlin <u>for five years</u>.
Sally lebt seit fünf Jahren in Berlin.

Present Perfect Progressive / Present Perfect Continuous

Bildung
have / has + been + present participle

write → <u>has / have</u> <u>been</u> <u>writing</u>

Verwendung
Die **Verlaufsform** *present perfect progressive* verwendet man, um die **Dauer einer Handlung** zu **betonen**, die in der Vergangenheit begonnen hat und noch andauert.

She <u>has been sleeping</u> for ten hours.
Sie schläft seit zehn Stunden.

Past Perfect (Simple)

Bildung
had + past participle

write → <u>had</u> <u>written</u>

Verwendung
Die Vorvergangenheit *past perfect* verwendet man, wenn ein Vorgang in der Vergangenheit **vor einem anderen Vorgang in der Vergangenheit abgeschlossen** wurde.

He <u>had bought</u> a ticket before he took the train to Manchester.
Er hatte eine Fahrkarte gekauft, bevor er den Zug nach Manchester nahm. [Beim Einsteigen war der Kauf abgeschlossen.]

Past Perfect Progressive / Past Perfect Continuous

Bildung
had + been + present participle

write → <u>had</u> <u>been</u> <u>writing</u>

Verwendung
Die **Verlaufsform** *past perfect progressive* verwendet man für **Handlungen**, die in der Vergangenheit **bis zu dem Zeitpunkt andauerten**, zu dem eine neue Handlung einsetzte.

She <u>had been sleeping</u> for ten hours when the doorbell rang.
Sie hatte seit zehn Stunden geschlafen, als es an der Tür klingelte. [Das Schlafen dauerte bis zu dem Zeitpunkt an, als es an der Tür klingelte.]

Will-future

Bildung
will + Infinitiv

buy → <u>will</u> <u>buy</u>

Bildung von Fragen im
will-future
(Fragewort +) *will* + Subjekt +
Infinitiv

<u>What</u> <u>will</u> <u>you</u> <u>buy</u>?
Was wirst du kaufen?

Bildung der Verneinung im
will-future
won't + Infinitiv

Why <u>won't</u> you <u>come</u> to our party?
Warum kommst du nicht zu unserer Party?

Verwendung
Das *will-future* verwendet man, wenn
ein Vorgang **in der Zukunft
stattfinden** wird:
- bei Vorhersagen oder Vermutun-
  gen,

The weather <u>will</u> <u>be</u> fine tomorrow.
Das Wetter wird morgen schön (sein).

- bei spontanen Entscheidungen.

[doorbell] "<u>I'll</u> <u>open</u> the door."
"Ich werde die Tür öffnen."

Signalwörter: z. B. *tomorrow,
next week, next Monday, next year,
in three years, soon*

Going-to-future

Bildung
am/is/are + *going to* + Infinitiv

find → <u>am/is/are</u> <u>going to</u> <u>find</u>

Verwendung
Das *going-to-future* verwendet man,
wenn man ausdrücken will:
- was man für die Zukunft **plant**
  oder **zu tun beabsichtigt**.

I <u>am going to work</u> in England this summer.
*Diesen Sommer werde ich in England
arbeiten.*

- dass ein **Ereignis bald eintreten
  wird**, da bestimmte **Anzeichen**
  vorhanden sind.

Look at those clouds. It's <u>going to rain</u> soon.
*Schau dir diese Wolken an. Es wird bald
regnen.*

Simple Present und *Present Progressive* zur Wiedergabe der Zukunft

Verwendung
- Mit dem *present progressive* drückt man **Pläne** für die Zukunft aus, für die bereits **Vorkehrungen** getroffen wurden.

We <u>are flying</u> to New York tomorrow.
Morgen fliegen wir nach New York.
[Wir haben schon Tickets.]

- Mit dem *simple present* wird ein zukünftiges Geschehen wiedergegeben, das **von außen festgelegt** wurde, z. B. Fahrpläne, Programme, Kalender.

The train <u>leaves</u> at 8.15 a.m.
Der Zug fährt um 8.15 Uhr.

The play <u>ends</u> at 10 p.m.
Das Theaterstück endet um 22 Uhr.

Future Progressive / Future Continuous

Bildung
will + be + present participle

work → <u>will</u> <u>be</u> <u>working</u>

Verwendung
Die **Verlaufsform** *future progressive* drückt aus, dass ein **Vorgang** in der Zukunft zu einem bestimmten Zeitpunkt **gerade ablaufen wird**.

Signalwörter: *this time next week / tomorrow, tomorrow* + Zeitangabe

This time tomorrow I <u>will</u> <u>be</u> <u>sitting</u> in a plane to London.
Morgen um diese Zeit werde ich gerade im Flugzeug nach London sitzen.

Future Perfect (Future II)

Bildung
will + have + past participle

go → <u>will</u> <u>have</u> <u>gone</u>

Verwendung
Das *future perfect* drückt aus, dass ein **Vorgang** in der Zukunft **abgeschlossen sein wird** (Vorzeitigkeit in der Zukunft).

Signalwörter: *by then, by* + Zeitangabe

By 5 p.m. tomorrow I <u>will</u> <u>have</u> <u>arrived</u> in London.
Morgen Nachmittag um fünf Uhr werde ich bereits in London angekommen sein.

11 Passiv – *Passive Voice*

Bildung
Form von *(to) be* in der entsprechenden Zeitform + *past participle*

The bridge <u>was finished</u> in 1894.
Die Brücke wurde 1894 fertiggestellt.

Zeitformen:

- *simple present*

  Aktiv: Joe <u>buys</u> the milk.
  Passiv: The milk <u>is bought</u> by Joe.

- *simple past*

  Aktiv: Joe <u>bought</u> the milk.
  Passiv: The milk <u>was bought</u> by Joe.

- *present perfect*

  Aktiv: Joe <u>has bought</u> the milk.
  Passiv: The milk <u>has been bought</u> by Joe.

- *past perfect*

  Aktiv: Joe <u>had bought</u> the milk.
  Passiv: The milk <u>had been bought</u> by Joe.

- *will-future*

  Aktiv: Joe <u>will buy</u> the milk.
  Passiv: The milk <u>will be bought</u> by Joe.

- *future perfect (future II)*

  Aktiv: Joe <u>will have bought</u> the milk.
  Passiv: The milk <u>will have been</u> bought by Joe.

- *conditional I*

  Aktiv: Joe <u>would buy</u> the milk.
  Passiv: The milk <u>would be bought</u> by Joe.

- *conditional II*

  Aktiv: Joe <u>would have bought</u> the milk.
  Passiv: The milk <u>would have been</u> bought by Joe.

Aktiv → Passiv

- Das Subjekt des Aktivsatzes wird zum Objekt des Passivsatzes. Es wird mit *by* angeschlossen.
- Das Objekt des Aktivsatzes wird zum Subjekt des Passivsatzes.

Aktiv: <u>Joe</u>   buys   <u>the milk</u>.
         Subjekt   *Objekt*

Passiv: <u>The milk</u> is bought <u>by Joe</u>.
          Subjekt   *by-agent*

- Stehen im Aktiv **zwei Objekte**, lassen sich zwei verschiedene Passivsätze bilden. Ein Objekt wird zum Subjekt des Passivsatzes, das zweite bleibt Objekt.

Aktiv: They   gave   <u>her</u>   <u>a ball</u>.
         Subjekt   *ind. Obj.*   *dir. Obj.*

Passiv: <u>She</u>   was given   <u>a ball</u>.
          Subjekt   *dir. Obj.*

oder:

  Beachte:
  Das indirekte Objekt muss im Passivsatz mit *to* angeschlossen werden.

Aktiv: They   gave   <u>her</u>   <u>a ball</u>.
         Subjekt   *ind. Obj.*   *dir. Obj.*

Passiv: <u>A ball</u>   was given   <u>to her</u>.
          Subjekt   *ind. Obj.*

Passiv → Aktiv

- Der mit *by* angeschlossene Handelnde *(by-agent)* des Passivsatzes wird zum Subjekt des Aktivsatzes; *by* entfällt.

- Das Subjekt des Passivsatzes wird zum Objekt des Aktivsatzes.

- Fehlt im Passivsatz der *by-agent*, muss im Aktivsatz ein Handelnder als Subjekt ergänzt werden, z. B. *somebody, we, you, they.*

Passiv: The milk   is bought   by Joe.
       Subjekt   *by-agent*

Aktiv: Joe ◄   buys   ► the milk.
       Subjekt   *Objekt*

Passiv: The match   was won.
       Subjekt

Aktiv: They   won   the match.
       (ergänztes)   *Objekt*
       Subjekt

Der Satz im Englischen

12 Wortstellung – *Word Order*

Im Aussagesatz gilt die Wortstellung
Subjekt – Prädikat – Objekt
(subject – verb – object):

- Subjekt: Wer oder was tut etwas?

- Prädikat: Was wird getan?

- Objekt: Worauf / Auf wen bezieht sich die Tätigkeit?

Für die Position von Orts- und Zeitangaben vgl. S. G 4 f.

Cats catch mice.
Katzen fangen Mäuse.

13 Konditionalsätze – *Conditional Sentences*

Ein Konditionalsatz (Bedingungssatz) besteht aus zwei Teilen: einem Nebensatz *(if-clause)* und einem Hauptsatz *(main clause)*. Im *if*-Satz steht die **Bedingung** *(condition)*, unter der die im **Hauptsatz** genannte **Folge** eintritt. Man unterscheidet drei Arten von Konditionalsätzen:

Konditionalsatz Typ I

Bildung

- *if*-Satz (Bedingung):
  simple present

If you <u>read</u> this book,
Wenn du dieses Buch liest,

- Hauptsatz (Folge):
  will-future

you <u>will learn</u> a lot about music.
erfährst du eine Menge über Musik.

Der *if*-Satz kann auch nach dem
Hauptsatz stehen. In diesem Fall
entfällt das Komma:

- Hauptsatz: *will-future*

You <u>will learn</u> a lot about music
Du erfährst eine Menge über Musik,

- *if*-Satz: *simple present*

<u>if</u> you <u>read</u> this book.
wenn du dieses Buch liest.

Im Hauptsatz kann auch

- *can* + Infinitiv,

If you go to London, you <u>can</u> <u>see</u> Bob.
*Wenn du nach London fährst, kannst du Bob
treffen.*

- *must* + Infinitiv,

If you go to London, you <u>must</u> <u>visit</u> me.
*Wenn du nach London fährst, musst du mich
besuchen.*

- der Imperativ

If it rains, <u>take</u> an umbrella.
Wenn es regnet, nimm einen Schirm mit.

stehen.

Verwendung
Bedingungssätze vom Typ I verwendet man, wenn die **Bedingung
erfüllbar** ist. Man gibt an, was unter
bestimmten Bedingungen **geschieht**
oder **geschehen kann**.

Konditionalsatz Typ II

Bildung

- *if*-Satz (Bedingung):
  simple past

If I <u>went</u> to London,
Wenn ich nach London fahren würde,

- Hauptsatz (Folge):
  conditional I = would + Infinitiv

I <u>would</u> <u>visit</u> the Tower.
würde ich mir den Tower ansehen.

Verwendung
Bedingungssätze vom Typ II verwendet man, wenn die **Bedingung
nur theoretisch erfüllt** werden kann
oder **nicht erfüllbar** ist.

Konditionalsatz Typ III

Bildung
- *if*-Satz (Bedingung):
  past perfect

If I <u>had gone</u> to London,
*Wenn ich nach London gefahren
wäre,*

- Hauptsatz (Folge):
  *conditional II = would + have +
  past participle*

I <u>would have visited</u> the Tower of London.
*hätte ich mir den Tower of London
angesehen.*

Verwendung
Bedingungssätze vom Typ III verwendet man, wenn sich die **Bedingung auf die Vergangenheit bezieht**
und deshalb **nicht mehr erfüllbar**
ist.

14 Relativsätze – *Relative Clauses*

Ein Relativsatz ist ein Nebensatz, der
sich **auf eine Person oder Sache** des
Hauptsatzes **bezieht** und diese **näher
beschreibt**:

The boy <u>who looks like Jane</u> is her brother.
*Der Junge, der Jane ähnlich sieht, ist ihr
Bruder.*

- Hauptsatz:
- Relativsatz:

The boy ... is her brother.
... who looks like Jane ...

Bildung
Haupt- und Nebensatz werden durch
das Relativpronomen verbunden.
- *who* (Nominativ oder Akkusativ),

Peter, <u>who</u> lives in London, likes travelling.
Peter, der in London lebt, reist gerne.

whose (Genitiv) und	Sam, <u>whose</u> mother is an architect, is in my class. *Sam, dessen Mutter Architektin ist, geht in meine Klasse.*
whom (Akkusativ) beziehen sich auf **Personen**,	Anne, <u>whom</u>/<u>who</u> I like very much, is French. *Anne, die ich sehr mag, ist Französin.*
• *which* bezieht sich auf **Sachen**,	The film "Dark Moon", <u>which</u> we saw yesterday, was far too long. *Der Film „Dark Moon", den wir gestern sahen, war viel zu lang.*
• *that* kann sich auf **Sachen** und auf **Personen** beziehen und wird nur verwendet, wenn die **Information** im Relativsatz **notwendig** ist, um den ganzen Satz zu verstehen.	The film <u>that</u> we saw last week was much better. *Der Film, den wir letzte Woche sahen, war viel besser.*

Verwendung
Mithilfe von Relativpronomen kann man **zwei Sätze miteinander verbinden**.

<u>London</u> is England's biggest city. <u>London</u> has about 7.2 million inhabitants.
London ist Englands größte Stadt.
London hat etwa 7,2 Millionen Einwohner.

<u>London</u>, which is England's biggest city, has about 7.2 million inhabitants.
London, die größte Stadt Englands, hat etwa 7,2 Millionen Einwohner.

Beachte:
Man unterscheidet zwei Arten von Relativsätzen:
• **Notwendige Relativsätze**
(defining relative clauses) enthalten Informationen, die **für das Verständnis** des Satzes **erforderlich** sind.

The man <u>who is wearing a red shirt</u> is Mike.
Der Mann, der ein rotes Hemd trägt, ist Mike.

Hier kann das Relativpronomen entfallen, wenn es Objekt ist; man spricht dann auch von *contact clauses*.

The book (<u>that</u>) I bought yesterday is thrilling.
Das Buch, das ich gestern gekauft habe, ist spannend.

- **Nicht notwendige Relativsätze** *(non-defining relative clauses)* enthalten **zusätzliche Informationen** zum Bezugswort, die für das Verständnis des Satzes nicht unbedingt notwendig sind. Dieser Typ von Relativsatz wird **mit Komma** abgetrennt.

Sally, who went to a party yesterday, is very tired.
Sally, die gestern auf einer Party war, ist sehr müde.

15 Indirekte Rede – *Reported Speech*

Die indirekte Rede verwendet man, um **wiederzugeben, was ein anderer gesagt** oder **gefragt hat.**

Bildung
Um die indirekte Rede zu bilden, benötigt man ein **Einleitungsverb.**
Häufig verwendete Einleitungsverben sind:

to say, to tell, to add, to mention, to think, to ask, to want to know, to answer

In der indirekten Rede verändern sich die **Pronomen**, in bestimmten Fällen auch die **Zeiten** und die **Orts- und Zeitangaben.**

- Wie die Pronomen sich verändern, hängt vom jeweiligen **Kontext** ab.

direkte Rede	**indirekte Rede**
Bob says to Jenny: "I like you."	Jenny tells Liz: "Bob says that he likes me."
Bob sagt zu Jenny: „Ich mag dich. "	*Jenny erzählt Liz: „Bob sagt, dass er mich mag. "*
Aber:	Jenny tells Liz that Bob likes her.
	Jenny erzählt Liz, dass Bob sie mag.

- **Zeiten:** Keine Veränderung, wenn das Einleitungsverb im *simple present* oder im *present perfect* steht:

direkte Rede	**indirekte Rede**
Bob says, "I love dancing."	Bob says (that) he loves dancing.
Bob sagt: „Ich tanze sehr gerne. "	*Bob sagt, er tanze sehr gerne.*

In folgenden Fällen wird die Zeit der direkten Rede in der indirekten Rede **um eine Zeitstufe zurückversetzt**, wenn das **Einleitungsverb** im *simple past* steht:

simple present	→ *simple past*
simple past	→ *past perfect*
present perfect	→ *past perfect*
will-future	→ *conditional I*

Bob said, "I <u>love</u> dancing."
Bob sagte: „Ich tanze sehr gerne."

Bob <u>said</u> (that) he <u>loved</u> dancing.
Bob sagte, er tanze sehr gerne.

Joe: "I <u>like</u> it."
Joe said he <u>liked</u> it.

Joe: "I <u>liked</u> it."
Joe said he <u>had liked</u> it.

Joe: "I<u>'ve liked</u> it."
Joe said he <u>had liked</u> it.

Joe: "I <u>will like</u> it."
Joe said he <u>would like</u> it.

- **Zeitangaben** verändern sich, wenn der Bericht zu einem späteren Zeitpunkt erfolgt, z. B.:
- Welche **Ortsangabe** verwendet wird, hängt davon ab, wo sich der Sprecher im Moment befindet.

now	→	then, at that time
today	→	that day, yesterday
yesterday	→	the day before
the day before yesterday	→	two days before
tomorrow	→	the following day
next week	→	the following week
here	→	there

Bildung der indirekten Frage
Häufige Einleitungsverben für die indirekte Frage sind:

to ask, to want to know, to wonder

- **Fragewörter** bleiben in der indirekten Rede **erhalten**. Die **Umschreibung** mit *do/does/did* **entfällt** in der indirekten Frage.

Tom: "<u>When</u> <u>did</u> they arrive?"
Tom: „Wann sind sie angekommen?"

Tom asked <u>when</u> they had arrived.
Tom fragte, wann sie angekommen seien.

- Enthält die direkte Frage **kein Fragewort**, wird die indirekte Frage mit *whether* oder *if* eingeleitet:

Tom: "Are they staying at the hotel?"
Tom: „Übernachten sie im Hotel?"

Tom asked <u>if/</u> <u>whether</u> they were staying at the hotel.
Tom fragte, ob sie im Hotel übernachten.

Befehle/Aufforderungen in der indirekten Rede
Häufige Einleitungsverben sind:

to tell, to order, to ask

In der indirekten Rede steht hier **Einleitungsverb + Objekt + *(not) to* + Infinitiv.**

Tom: "Leave the room."
Tom: „Verlass den Raum."

Tom <u>told</u> <u>me</u> <u>to</u> <u>leave</u> the room.
Tom forderte mich auf, den Raum zu verlassen.

Anhang

16 Liste wichtiger unregelmäßiger Verben – *List of Irregular Verbs*

Infinitive	Simple Past	Past Participle	*Deutsch*
be	was/were	been	*sein*
begin	began	begun	*beginnen*
blow	blew	blown	*wehen, blasen*
break	broke	broken	*brechen*
bring	brought	brought	*bringen*
build	built	built	*bauen*
buy	bought	bought	*kaufen*
catch	caught	caught	*fangen*
choose	chose	chosen	*wählen*
come	came	come	*kommen*
cut	cut	cut	*schneiden*
do	did	done	*tun*
draw	drew	drawn	*zeichnen*
drink	drank	drunk	*trinken*
drive	drove	driven	*fahren*
eat	ate	eaten	*essen*
fall	fell	fallen	*fallen*
feed	fed	fed	*füttern*
feel	felt	felt	*fühlen*
find	found	found	*finden*
fly	flew	flown	*fliegen*
get	got	got	*bekommen*
give	gave	given	*geben*
go	went	gone	*gehen*
grow	grew	grown	*wachsen*
hang	hung	hung	*hängen*
have	had	had	*haben*
hear	heard	heard	*hören*
hit	hit	hit	*schlagen*
hold	held	held	*halten*
keep	kept	kept	*halten*
know	knew	known	*wissen*

Infinitive	Simple Past	Past Participle	*Deutsch*
lay	laid	laid	*legen*
leave	left	left	*verlassen*
let	let	let	*lassen*
lie	lay	lain	*liegen*
lose	lost	lost	*verlieren*
make	made	made	*machen*
meet	met	met	*treffen*
pay	paid	paid	*bezahlen*
put	put	put	*stellen/setzen*
read	read	read	*lesen*
ring	rang	rung	*läuten/anrufen*
run	ran	run	*rennen*
say	said	said	*sagen*
see	saw	seen	*sehen*
send	sent	sent	*schicken*
show	showed	shown	*zeigen*
sing	sang	sung	*singen*
sit	sat	sat	*sitzen*
sleep	slept	slept	*schlafen*
smell	smelt	smelt	*riechen*
speak	spoke	spoken	*sprechen*
spend	spent	spent	*ausgeben/ verbringen*
stand	stood	stood	*stehen*
steal	stole	stolen	*stehlen*
swim	swam	swum	*schwimmen*
take	took	taken	*nehmen*
teach	taught	taught	*lehren*
tell	told	told	*erzählen*
think	thought	thought	*denken*
throw	threw	thrown	*werfen*
wake	woke	woken	*aufwachen*
wear	wore	worn	*tragen*
win	won	won	*gewinnen*
write	wrote	written	*schreiben*

Teil A: Text

The History Boys by Alan Bennett
*In 1983 a group of sixth-formers at an all-boys grammar school in Sheffield have performed
unusually well in their A-level history exams. Thus they have qualified to sit the Oxbridge entrance exams – something that has never been achieved at their school before. As the headmaster wants to ensure success they are placed in a special group of their own. The teachers
expected to prepare them are Hector and Irwin, the latter having been hired exclusively for
this purpose.*

Text 1:
ACT ONE
[…]
    Irwin and Hector
    IRWIN: It's just that the boys seem to know more than they're telling.
    HECTOR: Don't most boys?
        Diffidence is surely to be encouraged.
    IRWIN: In an examination?
5   They seem to have got hold of the notion that the stuff they do with you is off-limits
    so far as the examination is concerned.
    HECTOR: That's hardly surprising. I count examinations, even for Oxford and Cambridge,
    as the enemy of education. Which is not to say that I don't regard education as the en-
    emy of education, too.
10   However, if you think it will help, I will speak to them.
    IRWIN: I'd appreciate it.
    For what it's worth, I sympathise with your feelings about examinations, but they are
    a fact of life. I'm sure you want them to do well and the gobbets you have taught them
    might just tip the balance.
15 HECTOR: What did you call them?
    Gobbets? Is that what you think they are, gobbets?
    Handy little quotes that can be trotted out to make a point?
    Gobbets?
    Codes, spells, runes – call them what you like, but do not call them *gobbets*.
20 IRWIN: I just thought it would be useful …
    HECTOR: Oh, it would be useful … every answer a Christmas tree hung with the appro-
    priate gobbets.
    Except that they're learned *by heart*. And that is where they belong and like the other
    components of the heart not to be defiled by being trotted out to order.
25 IRWIN: So what are they meant to be storing them up for, these boys?
    Education isn't something for when they're old and grey and sitting by the fire. It's
    for now. The exam is next month.
    HECTOR: And what happens after the exam? Life goes on.
    Gobbets!
30   […]
    Headmaster and Irwin
    HEADMASTER: How are our young men doing?
    Are they 'on stream'?
    IRWIN: I think so.

HEADMASTER: You think so? Are they or aren't they?

35 IRWIN: It must always be something of a lottery.

HEADMASTER: A lottery? I don't like the sound of that, Irwin. I don't want you to fuck up. We have been down that road too many times before.

IRWIN: I'm not sure the boys are bringing as much from Mr Hector's classes as they might.

40 HEADMASTER: You're lucky if they bring anything at all, but I don't know that it matters. Mr Hector has an old-fashioned faith in the redemptive power of words. In my experience, Oxbridge examiners are on the lookout for something altogether snappier.

After all, it's not how much literature that they know.

What matters is how much they know *about* literature.

45 Chant the stuff till they're blue in the face, what good does it do?

[…]

Text 2:
ACT TWO
[…]

classroom

AKTHAR: We know, sir.

50 HECTOR: Oh.

DAKIN: About sharing lessons with Mr Irwin, sir?

HECTOR: Ah.

LOCKWOOD: Why is that, sir?

HECTOR: That?

55 Oh. It's just a question of timetable, apparently.

No. What I was going to tell you …

LOCKWOOD: What's the point, sir?

Your lessons are so different from his.

The whole ethos is different, sir.

60 TIMMS: And we relish the contrast, sir.

CROWTHER: Revel in it, sir.

LOCKWOOD: Yin and yang, sir.

AKTHAR: The rapier cut and thrust, sir.

TIMMS: It's all about variety, sir.

65 HECTOR: Hush, boys. Hush. Sometimes … sometimes you defeat me.

DAKIN: Oh no, sir. If we wanted to defeat you we would be like Cordelia and say nothing.

HECTOR: Can't you see I'm not in the mood?

DAKIN: What mood is that, sir? The subjunctive? The mood of possibility? The mood of
70 might-have-been?

HECTOR: Get on with some work. Read.

LOCKWOOD: Read, sir? Oh come on, sir. That's no fun.

AKTHAR; Boring.

HECTOR: Am I fun? Is that what I am?

75 TIMMS: Not today, sir. No fun at all.

HECTOR: Is that what you think these lessons are? Fun?

LOCKWOOD: But fun is good, sir.

You always say …

POSNER: Not just fun, sir.

80 AKTHAR: *(pointing at Posner)* Would you like him to sing to you, sir? Would that help?

HECTOR: Shut up! Just shut up. All of you.

SHUT UP, you mindless fools.

What made me piss my life away in this god-forsaken place?

There's nothing of me left. Go away. Class dismissed. Go.

85 *He puts his head down on the desk.*
There are some giggles and face-pullings before they realise it's serious.
Now they're nonplussed and embarrassed.
Scripps indicates to Darkin that Hector is crying.
Scripps is nearest to him and ought to touch him, but doesn't, nor does Darkin.

90 *Posner is the one who comes and after some hesitation pats Hector rather awkwardly*
on the back, saying 'Sir'.
The he starts, still very awkwardly, to rub his back.
[…] *(773 words)*

Bennett, Alan. (2004). The History Boys. London: Faber & Faber, London pp. 48–49
& 64–65

A Text production

A1 Working with the text
Answer in complete English sentences.

1.1 Compare Hector's and Irwin's attitudes towards education. (4 BE)

1.2 Analyse Hector's character and the way Alan Bennet creates it. (6 BE)

Inhalt: (10 BE)

A2 Composition
Choose <u>one</u> of the following topics.

2.1 "We think that good exam results are very important but they don't constitute
a full rounded education." (Barnaby Lenon, Headmaster of Harrow School,
London)
Write an article for an international student magazine referring to the quotation.
Include a discussion of the role testing has played in your life so far.

2.2 Do the following composition tasks separately:
a) Based on the excerpt from the drama write down Hector's thoughts in the form of
an interior monologue directly following the events in Text 2.
b) Explain your choice of content and style.

2.3 We are all bound by the circumstances we have been born into.
Comment on this notion referring to both the individual and society.

Inhalt: 10 BE

Erreichbare BE-Anzahl Teil A (Summe A1 und A2):
Inhaltliche Leistung: 20 BE
Sprachrichtigkeit: 20 BE
Ausdrucksvermögen: 10 BE
Gesamt: 50 BE

Teil B: Translation / Mediation
Choose <u>one</u> of the following tasks (B1 <u>or</u> B2)

B1 Translation

Fair Chances?

It's been revealed, not for the first time in recent months, that there remains a persistent class-related gap in young people's aspirations relating to higher education. Some 78 % of schoolchildren from the highest earning social groups want to go to university, compared to 55 % from the lowest.

5 The way in which the odds are stacked against the poorest and least-skilled [...] has been summed up with admirable clarity by the geographer Danny Dorling, who produced an alternative map of Britain that sweeps from a "fertile crescent of advantage, where to succeed is to do nothing out of the ordinary, to the peaks of despair, where to just get by is extraordinary".

10 Getting to university, if you're not a member of the anointed classes, is like an assault course: not in the sense that your ascent to the top must be guarded by your parents' sharp elbows, but in that the obstacles to be surmounted seem to spring up everywhere. [...]

(162 words)

Hanley, Lynsey: "University challenged". Guardian.co.uk, 8. April 2008
http://www.guardian.co.uk/commentisfree/2008/apr/08universitychallenge
[download/27. August 2008]   20 BE

Annotation:
lines 7:   crescent – here: area

B2 Mediation
In your English class you have been asked to design a brochure titled *Further Education in Europe*.
Write a summary of the following text focusing on what makes Oxford and Cambridge exceptional.

Die Auserwählten von Oxbridge

Das Studium an den britischen Eliteuniversitäten Oxford und Cambridge gilt als garantiertes Sprungbrett für eine erfolgreiche berufliche Laufbahn im In- und Ausland. Die Kaderschmieden des ehemaligen Empires bilden die geistige Elite einer ganzen Nation aus. [...]
Vergabe von Studienplätzen: Neben dem soliden finanziellen Fundament genießen die Mini-Unis zahlreiche Privilegien: Sie bestimmen das jeweilige Lehrangebot selbst, legen den Inhalt und Verlauf eines Studium sowie der Prüfung fest und verleihen akademische Titel. Außerdem wählt jedes College – wie übrigens die übrigen Universitäten in Großbritannien auch – seine Studenten selbst aus. Neben den Ergebnissen einer schriftlichen Eignungsprüfung haben dabei die Eindrücke aus Interviews und Gesprächen über Lebens- und Berufspläne, Interessen und Fähigkeiten entscheidenden Einfluss auf die Vergabe von Studienplätzen. Obschon – vor allem bei Spitzensportlern – auch ab und an ein Auge zugedrückt wird. Fast 50 Prozent der Studenten in Oxbridge kommen aus Privatschulen; weitere 10 Prozent aus dem Ausland, der Rest aus staatlichen Schulen.
Studienverlauf: Das drei- bis vierjährige Studium in Oxbridge gliedert sich nicht wie in Deutschland in Semester, sondern in Trimester. Der achtwöchige Studienabschnitt von Oktober bis Anfang Dezember heißt *Michaelmas*, das Trimester von Januar bis Mitte März wird in Oxford *Hilary* und in Cambridge *Lent* genannt und die zwei Monate von

April bis Mitte Juni in Oxford *Trinity* und in *Cambrigde Easter Term*. Im ersten Studienjahr müssen die Studenten nicht nur Vorlesungen besuchen, sondern auch einmal wöchentlich ein mindestens fünfseitiges Essay erstellen. Im zweiten Jahr sogar zwei pro Woche. Damit sollen die Studenten unter Beweis stellen, dass sie wissenschaftlich arbeiten können. Das Herzstück des Studiums bildet jedoch die persönliche Betreuung in Form von obligatorischen Treffen mit Tutoren, Lektoren und Professoren. Bei dieser Gelegenheit sitzt ein Student diesem allein gegenüber und muss seinen Lernfortschritt dokumentieren, indem er sein Essay verliest. Nach alter Väter Sitte nimmt der Tutor das Elaborat anschließend systematisch Satz für Satz kritisch auseinander.

Prüfungen und Abschlüsse: Am Ende des zweiten oder dritten Trimesters stehen dann mit den *Moderations*, kurz *Mods*, beziehungsweise den *Preliminary Exams* die ersten großen Herausforderungen an. Denn die Ergebnisse dieser (Vor-)Prüfungen entscheiden darüber, ob ein Student am College bleiben darf. Richtig ernst wird es je nach Fach im Sommer des dritten oder vierten Studienjahres, wenn die Abschlussprüfungen, die *Finals*, erfolgen. [...]

Studentenleben und *social activities*: Am jeweiligen College haben Studenten Kost und Logis frei. Damit sich diese voll auf das Studium konzentrieren können, kümmern sich sogar sogenannte *Bedder*, Putzfrauen, um die Sauberkeit in den meist spartanisch eingerichteten Studentenbuden. Anfang Oktober ziehen die Studienanfänger, *Fresher*, genannt, in das College ein und erfahren beim *Fresher's Blind*, einer Art Willkommensparty, bei der ältere Studenten einen Drink spendieren müssen, die wichtigsten Tricks und Kniffe für die Studienzeit. Wie an allen anderen Universitäten des Landes bilden in Oxbridge die *social acitvities* einen festen Bestandteil des Studiums. Dabei spannt sich der Bogen von sportlichen Wettkämpfen über das Mitwirken in Theaterstücken oder im Chor der Universität bis hin zu *Port and Cigars* (Portwein und Zigarren) und *Tea* mit dem Tutor. Und auch die Mitgliedschaft in der *Student's Union*, der Studentenvereinigung, ist quasi ein Muss. Ebenso das regelmäßige Abhalten von freien Reden in den Debattierclubs der *Student's Union*. [...]

Raab, Karsten-Thilo. "Nur das Beste für die Besten: Die Auserwählten von Oxbridge". Frankfurter Allgemeine hochschulanzeiger.de, 16. Mai 2007
http://www.faz.det/s/Rub244D2E60F0294C4D8AAC6CoC7FC9677B//Doc~EA2 82C0EF1CC8405DB6CCAF21964F8A3F~Atpl~Ecommon~Scontent.html
[download/22 June 2008]   20 BE

Lösungsvorschlag

A Text production

A1 Working with the text

1.1 *The key points are:*
   - *Hector: idealist notion of education and learning*
   - *literature/education to suit the individual, not to please an examiner*
   - *examinations are the enemy of education*
   - *Irwin: pragmatic point of view*
   - *importance of exam results for students' career*

Generally, Hector does not teach his students solely for the purpose of testing and has no problems if his students reflect on their knowledge or the curriculum critically ("diffidence" l. 3). He believes that the knowledge the boys gain in his classes should not be "trotted out to make a point" which means that to Hector learning is for life (l. 28) and not primarily for passing an exam. In fact he calls examinations "the enemy of education" (ll. 8/9). Furthermore, he states that to him learning <u>by</u> heart means learning <u>with</u> the heart; a metaphor expressing a rather personal approach towards education. To Hector, education must apply to the emotions of the students, to suit their individual needs rather than only train them to sit an examination.

Although Irwin seems to agree with Hector in principle, it is obvious that to him it is essential to gear the boys up to their exams. He takes a rather pragmatic view when he says that exams are "a fact of life" (l. 13) and that the boys need to do well in their exams in order to have a career: "Education isn't something for when they are old and grey." (l. 26)

(201 words)

1.2 *The key points are:*
   – *development from self-confidence to frustration and despair*
   – *character depicted through conversations and stage directions*
   – *frustration leads to Hector's misjudgement of the classroom situation*

In the given excerpt, Hector undergoes a transformation from being depicted as a fairly self-confident defender of his teaching methods to ending up in utter despair and helplessness.

In the beginning, the author establishes Hector's character through his conversation with his colleague, Irwin. When Irwin criticises him for not preparing his boys well enough, Hector responds in a rather straightforward and confident way: "Don't most boys? Diffidence is surely to be encouraged". (ll. 2/3) However, he seems to be ready to compromise up to a certain extent with Irwin's ideas of a proper preparation for the exams, "However, if you think it will help, I will speak to them." (l. 10) All the same, the phrase "if you think it will help" strongly suggests that he does not really agree with Irwin.

The balance is tipped when Irwin reduces Hector's teaching to "gobbets" and suggests that Hector make use of them to prepare the boys for the examination. Now Hector is losing his coolness, he becomes passionate, angry and agitated, firing off a sequence of angry questions, raising his voice as indicated by the expressions "gobbets" and "by heart" printed in italics. He rages against the assumption that what he taught the boys should be used in the exams. His whole language turns derisive, bitter and even cynical when he connects the word "useful" with "every answer a Christmas tree" (l. 21).

His last word to Irwin is "Gobbets" which is used almost as a swearword with which he tries to fight off Irwin's accusations.

The second way in which Hector's character is depicted is through the conversation between the headmaster and Irwin. Apart from Irwin's assessment (or accusation) that Hector's students are not well enough prepared, the headmaster describes Hector as an old-school idealist displaying a "faith in the redemptive power of words" (l. 41), somebody who seems to teach literature from a purely aesthetic point of view instead of enabling the students to analyse it ("What matters is how much they know *about* literature", l. 44) It is obvious that the headmaster regards Hector as a failure as his final, rather derogatory, remark "Chant the stuff till they're blue in the face, what good does it do?" (l. 45) shows.

Finally, Hector's character is established in the classroom scene. Here his monosyllabic answers ("Oh.", "Ah.") suggest that he is in a rather depressive state of mind. He also refuses to talk to his students, who are full of affection for him, about the problems with Irwin, which could signify that he has already given in.

When the students tell him that his lessons are "fun", he, probably owing to his general downheartedness, obviously misunderstands his students as being disrespectful and ridiculing his teaching methods. Which means that now even his "disciples" have betrayed him. What follows is an emotional outbreak during which he more or less completely loses his self-restraint. This is shown by his use of language. When he resorts to rude expressions such as "Shut up" or even to four-letter words such as "piss" (ll. 81–83), he shows that he is in utmost despair, close to a nervous breakdown, which is expressed in the sentence "There is nothing of me left." (l. 84)

At the end of the scene Hector's actions and body language, as given by Allen Bennett's stage directions, such as putting his head down on the desk and crying, highlight the impression of a man who has finally given himself up to an embarrassing public display of helplessness. *(588 words)*

A2 Composition

2.1 *The key points are:*
 – *characteristics of an article: heading, introduction, middle part, ending, also use catchy phrases,*
 – *reference to target group (international students): language can/should be slightly casual/not too formal,*
 – *discussion of the role testing has played in your life*

Teaching to the test – a necessary evil?

Let's face it, good test results are important if you want to have a career. But don't we all hate exams? At least I do. After having been exposed to all kinds of exams (written and oral ones) for the past 10 years, I must say that I have had quite enough. To me they constitute the major stress factor at school. Cramming for tests has always turned me off, and quite honestly I don't see the point in doing all the revision when almost everything I have learnt goes out of my head immediately after the exams.

"Exams might not be fun, but they are the only way to ensure that you lazy buggers learn one or two things at school." I hear Mr K. (my most detested teacher whose real name will mercifully remain undisclosed in order to protect the innocent) say. And, take it or leave it, I suppose he is right – at least up to a certain extent. Sure, we all know about the old arguments justifying teachers thinking up tricky and nasty tasks, making us sweat and toil, according to the motto "No pain, no gain".

Another famous quote by the infamous Mr K. reads: "Life is not a pleasure cruise." So what is this all about? It says that life is hard, and that, once we are out there, in the wilderness of a competitive society, we will face numerous situations where we must function and perform, no matter whether we feel like it or not. So, exams are supposed to prepare us for real life situations, including all the stress we suffer when revising instead of having a good time. Oh yes, succeeding in exams requires discipline and time-management (meeting deadlines and observing punctuality, the latter maybe being a typically German obsession). And these are valuable assets for making a career in the afterlife (you know what I mean). So, to cut a long story short, exams don't taste good but (like Guinness Beer) they are good for you, say Mr K. and many others. Now what about all the other stuff school is supposed to accomplish for us. As Mr Lenon states, it should provide a "full rounded education", so there is more to it than just exam success. And I wholeheartedly agree. To me project work, public performances, e. g. drama or music, student exchanges, exhibitions and outings to museums or other interesting sights are very important to develop a student's potential. Personally, I never ever learned as much as when my class and I did an English drama workshop for a week and then performed in front of the school, our parents and our friends. I still know all my lines (and many of the others') by heart. And it was fun working together as a team, with the common aim of putting on a good performance and entertaining our friends.

Another really good project I remember well was a week when our year engaged in some community work called "a good deed for our neighbourhood". There we worked for organisations helping the poor and the disadvantaged. To gain insight into the world of those who are not as well off as we are was a very rewarding experience and a good example of what Mr Lenon refers to as a "round education" – which is definitely more than just exam-geared lessons and cramming for tests. *(572 words)*

2.2 *The key points are:*
  – *Hector's thoughts after the events depicted in Text 2*
  – *interior monologue (free form)*
  – *content of interior monologue must be based on given extract*

a) To leave or not to leave this educational bog hole. That is the question. Or is it nobler in the mind to stay and fight it out? But how can you fight against a system which transforms everything into something practical, something "useful" as Irwin would say. How I hate this pragmatism! What you learn must be useful, and useful means being able to do well in exams. Every fool knows that what the kids learn for exams is for exams only. Hardly anything remains stored up in their brains, and definitely not in their hearts. But then, what's the use of dealing with literature if it doesn't involve the students on an emotional level? Why read Shakespeare and Dickens if you don't have the time to enjoy the beauty of their writings, the wittiness and humour of their language? So what's wrong with my asking students to learn important pieces by heart? I mean Irwin, that narrow-minded idiot, didn't get it at all. Oh yes, I hear our Head say, our students are going to sit an Oxbridge exam, so they need to know about literature, and knowing means taking it apart and then analysing the bits and pieces. It's revolting, just a scholastic exercise, showing off your analytic skills – aren't we all darn clever?
Come on now, old boy. Be reasonable, somehow there must be a compromise. Just to make life a bit easier. Why not give your Head a morsel of some "snappy" target-oriented teaching, just before the exams? Doesn't really hurt, does it?
The students got it wrong anyway, or did they? Did they really mean to reduce me to a funnyman, an entertainer dishing out little tasty chunks of fun, something, or somebody, to laugh at? Me, a laughing stock?
Well, I suppose I got it wrong, I wronged them. Now thinking back on it, they were probably just trying to be friendly, cheer me up as I must have shown that I was in a miserable state.
Well, man, pull yourself together! Your behaviour was completely out of order. Come on, put your act together. First of all apologise, tell them I suffered a nervous breakdown, talk about the problem, my dilemma, when it comes to teaching literature. And work out a fair compromise with the students. Preparation for the exams including the genuine appreciation of literature. Have the cake and eat it. Can this be done? It must be done. It can be done! Can it?

b) When writing this interior monologue I tried to include the two important themes of the given extract, which are Hector's frustration with his colleague's demand for teaching to the test and his nervous breakdown in class in front of his students.
To me the first theme must pose a real dilemma for him as, on the one hand, the teaching of literature should trigger off a certain motivation in students to appreciate the beauty of writing. On the other hand, in a culture where exams play an important role with regard to people's future careers, he must feel under enormous pressure when apparently failing to prepare his students appropriately.
Hector's second problem must be his behaviour in front of his class, where he lost control of himself in a way that must, looking back on it, appear to be absolutely unacceptable. I suppose he would try hard to save the situation by apologising and by telling the students about his problem, his frustration with the system, and then settle for a compromise.

Stylistically, I tried to convey the inner conflict tormenting Hector. That's why the monologue opens up with a rather drastic statement, reflecting Hamlet's famous soliloquy, as the protagonist is in dire straits, with the question taking on an almost existential dimension.

Hector then ponders on the problem, showing his insecurity by asking several questions, which are all of a rhetorical nature as he seemingly knows the answers. I put them in to show how he is desperately trying to reassure himself.

In the following, Hector is taking on an alter ego, an imagined fatherly friend or colleague ("Come on now , old boy.") who tells him to pull himself together and be reasonable. So there is a change from questioning to assuming a more impera-tive stance showing Hector's determination to solve the conflict. This tendency is also highlighted by the change of the pronoun "you" to "I" which is to symbolise that he is now even more determined and has restored his self-confidence.

However, in the end I chose to contrast Hector's determination to succeed ("It can be done.") with a grain of doubt ("Can it?"). I believe that ending the monologue like that helps to create suspense as it opens up the situation to the audience to speculate whether Hector can really change the situation, and his life, for the bet-ter.   *(808 words)*

2.3 *The key points are:*
   – circumstances/determination versus free will
   – examples: historical, political, biographical
   – conclusion: your opinion

Let me begin by saying that I can't agree with that notion. Of course there is no doubt that the circumstances we are born into have a profound influence on us, but they do not wholly determine our actions. Man is equipped with moral and mental faculties that allow him to choose between right and wrong, good and evil, just and unjust.

There are many examples from human history which show that some people managed to have a great career even though they did not come from a wealthy background. Regarding the rags to riches myth of the American Dream, you can see that many suc-cessful Americans (and people elsewhere) have made it from the bottom to the top. Politically speaking you can say that modern western society actually stands for the independence of the individual, for the freedom to fulfil your potential no matter what your social background. It was the French Revolution as a starting point for a devel-opment which did away with the old privileges of the ruling classes, a time when your birth into a certain class would have decided about your life opportunities.

Of course it is still true that if you are born with the proverbial silver spoon in your mouth you will find it easier to succeed in life. At least you do have a lot of opportu-nities which are often denied to people from the lower classes. So I would agree that people's social background still influences their careers. Being wealthy definitely makes your advances in life easier. This applies for example to the availability of tui-tion fees for one's studies.

On the other hand, wealth does not automatically qualify you to make headway. More often than not you are being promoted on your own merits, which means that even if the odds are stacked against you, you can still make it to the top, or at least earn a good living. The same is true for talent. If the aforementioned assumption was right, every concert pianist would produce other concert pianists, but there is no evidence whatsoever that they do. Take the son of Miles Davis, the famous jazz trumpeter. His son did not have a musical career, although he must have grown up in a very musical environment. Also with regard to our moral categories it must be said that if the cir-cumstances determined our lives, all children of criminals would follow their parents' career and become criminals as well. We all know that this is not the case, although you might argue that it is more likely for a child to embark on a criminal career when he or she has grown up in criminal surroundings.

In conclusion, I would say that man is born with a free will and determination, and therefore he can overcome the circumstances he has been born into, even if that can prove to be difficult at times. But in fact, this is what life is about: overcoming difficulties. *(495 words)*

B1 Translation

Faire/gerechte Chancen?

Nicht zum ersten Mal ist in den vergangen Monaten aufgedeckt worden, dass es immer noch eine sich hartnäckig haltende, sozialbedingte/klassenabhängige/milieuabhängige Kluft hinsichtlich der Ambitionen junger Leute im Bezug auf höhere Bildung gibt.

Etwa 78 % der aus der sozialen Gruppe der Spitzenverdiener kommenden Schulkinder wollen auf die Universität gehen, verglichen mit 55 % aus der (sozialen) Gruppe der Niedrigverdiener.

Die Art und Weise wie den ärmsten und am wenigsten ausgebildeten Menschen Steine in den Weg gelegt werden [...] wurde vom Geografen Danny Dorling in bewundernswerter Klarheit/bewundernswert deutlich zusammengefasst. Dieser produzierte eine alternative Landkarte von Großbritannien, die von den „fruchtbaren Vorteilsregionen, in denen es nichts Außergewöhnliches ist, erfolgreich zu sein, bis zu den Gipfeln der Verzweiflung, auf denen es schon das bloße mit dem Leben Zurechtkommen/das bloße Klarkommen außergewöhnlich ist/auf denen es schon außergewöhnlich ist, überhaupt über die Runden zu kommen."

An die Universität zu gelangen, ohne ein Mitglied der erwählten/durchlauchten Klassen zu sein, gleicht einem militärischen Übungsparcours: nicht in dem Sinne, dass dein/der Aufstieg zur Spitze/Gipfel von den scharfen Ellenbogen deiner/der Eltern unterstützt werden muss, sondern (in dem Sinne) dass die Hindernisse, die überwunden werden müssen, offenbar überall auftreten.

B2 Mediation

The keypoints are:
- *article/summary for an international magazine (primarily for young people who might not know about the British university system)*
- *focus on what makes Oxbridge exceptional*
- *observe the formal requirements as regards a mediation (e. g. length, style)*

Oxbridge: The Road to Success

Oxford and Cambridge (or "Oxbridge") are <u>the</u> elite universities in Great Britain, each consisting of numerous smaller colleges, all with their own curriculum. That's why 50% of the pupils at these colleges come from renowned public schools. Once they have passed the entrance examination plus interviews, students are required to hand in essays every week in order to demonstrate that their work meets high academic standards. At the end of the first year all students must pass a so-called Preliminary Exam if they want to continue their studies. However, at the heart of each course of study are the tutorials, which means that students regularly meet up individually with their personal tutors and other academic staff to discuss their work in detail. The colleges provide simple style full-board accommodation. Throughout the year there are activities in which students are expected to participate such as welcome events, sports, drama and music as well as the debating societies of the Student Union. Students graduating after three or four years of study will have obtained excellent career opportunities. *(180 words)*

Prüfungsteilnehmer A

Topic: Children are our Future

Concepts of our family have changed over the centuries.
Comment on the following photos.

http.//www.christenundjuden.org/images/
hannas_familie.jgp

http://www.travailsuisse.ch/de/system/files/storypics/
Familie.jpg

Together with your partners discuss the image of a good family.
Furthermore talk about what should be done to create a more family-friendly society.
Try to agree on realistic measures.

Prüfungsteilnehmer B

Topic: Children are our Future

Concepts of family have changed over the centuries.
Comment on the following photos.

© Tomasz Trojanowski – Fotolia.com   http://www.nzz.ch/images/vater_1.547818.jpg

Together with your partners discuss the image of a good family.
Furthermore talk about what should be done to create a more family-friendly society.
Try to agree on realistic measures.

Lösungsvorschläge

Partner A: Robin

The topic Richard and I have been asked to discuss is "Children are our Future". To start us off I will comment on two photos which show how concepts of family have changed over the centuries.

The first photo I would like to talk about was probably made about a hundred years ago. It shows a family of ten, with the father in the middle, his eight children and his wife next to him. I'm not sure, but I think there is also an elderly woman who might as well also be a grandmother or perhaps another relative, an aunt maybe.

To me this picture epitomises what people nowadays refer to as the good old classical extended family, a time when people had ten children or more and when it was also common for several generations to live under the same roof.

As regards the social makeup of the traditional family, the father was considered the major breadwinner and the utmost authority. He was at the centre of his family and ruled over his wife and children like a patriarch. To me, this is also shown in the picture, as everyone seems to look rather serious, almost as if standing to attention. You can see that family life at the turn of the last century was definitely not as liberal and easygoing as it is today.

The other photo depicts a typical modern nuclear family, although the couple shown there have three young children, which is quite a lot for a family in an industrialised country. The family are sitting at the table and the father seems to be serving up food. This leads to the assumption that he might also have prepared the food himself, while his wife (or girlfriend, I mean, who knows, nowadays) is taking care of their baby child. The atmosphere conveyed by the photo is a rather cheerful one, the woman looks lovingly at her spouse, and he seems to like his role as a "house husband", if that's what he is. Personally, I believe that he is is just participating in the housework, something the husband in the first photo would probably not even have thought of.

Those were different times however, when men and women were supposed to follow certain social behaviour patterns, with the man acting as the sole breadwinner and the woman supporting the family as a homemaker.

Now these patterns have changed: there were the Suffragettes, and women taking on men's jobs during the World Wars, there was Women's Lib in the 1960s and 70s and in the so-called socialist countries, e.g. the GDR, women were expected to work in almost every field, in factories, building sites or as engineers. All this finally led to the emancipation of women, and put more pressure on men to take a more active part in what was formerly known as a "woman's job." So today, modern men know how to change a baby's nappies and can also stack a dishwasher; some can even operate the washing machine.

To cut a long story short, as regards family life, men and women cooperate a great deal more than in former times. Nowadays, it is more or less taken for granted that women have a job just like their husbands, and that it is therefore practical, and logical, well, and fair, I suppose, if both share the housework and the upbringing of their children. So, for me, the basis of a good family is cooperation. But let's discuss that later.

Richard, what kind of pictures have you got? *(592 words)*

Partner B: Richard

Well Robin, what I have got here are two pictures showing modern parents and their children. In the first photo you can see a young woman sitting in a chair with her three-year old daughter on her lap. Both seem to have enjoyed playing a computer game, or perhaps the woman has just been doing some work on the computer with her child sitting with her. Anyway, they both look rather happy.

In the other picture you can see a man in his thirties sitting on a chair. While reading a book, he is rocking a pram. To me he epitomizes a modern father who finds nothing wrong with taking care of his baby child, while, perhaps, his wife is away either working or meeting friends. Anyway, I have heard that a lot of modern dads nowadays take on a lot more responsibilities. For instance they join their wives in prenatal classes, or are even present when the child is being born. My dad actually was there when I was born, patting my mother's head and helping her to breathe properly. My granddad thought that was completely out of order, but then, he is still old school.

So, Robin, the photo depicting the father and his child would fit in with your image of a modern family. Not so many kids as before, but daddies being a lot more involved in the upbringing of their children.

At second sight, you could perhaps also conclude that the two photos represent two single-parent families, with either the father or the mother taking care of their offspring. Of course, that is up to interpretation, but as far as I know the number of single-parent families has increased quite dramatically over the last twenty years or so. At least, some people are worried about this development, saying that a single mom, or a single dad, cannot really give their children all they need. Well, I don't know about that, but I suppose it is rather stressful to combine both a strenuous working life and raising your children just on your own. Honestly, I don't know how people cope! But as I said, single-parent families are a regular occurrence these days, and to me, there is nothing wrong with it. *(375 words)*

Discussion

RICHARD: Well, of course, there isn't. Although a survey carried out recently revealed that for most German youngsters the ideal family is still the traditional one, you know, with a mom, dad and children.

And really, from my point of view, I think that children need both, a father and a mother, not only biologically speaking, but also when it comes to raising children. A father can do and convey things women can't, or at least not to the same extent. And vice versa, of course.

ROBIN: Quite right. I believe there are certain male and female qualities which help children to develop their identities.

RICHARD: So we both agree that the best kind of family is the traditional one. Now, what about the others? Take for instance the so-called patchwork families? Would you find those problematic?

ROBIN: Not really. I mean, some people claim that patchwork families are a fairly new development, but as far as I know, they have been around since the beginning of mankind, with mothers and fathers dying and remarrying. Well, in fact our fairy tales are good examples of conflicts that might arise in patchwork families. Take Cinderella: the bad stepmother and her daughters making life miserable for the father's daughter, Cinderella.

RICHARD: So what you are basically saying is that we don't really need to worry too much about patchwork families, as they have always been a part of our culture, and they are more or less widely accepted. But there is one thing that worries me in that respect. The number of divorces, of families breaking apart. And then people establish new families, with both partners bringing their children into the new relationship. There are so many of them nowadays, and the number is rising. I mean the breaking up of one family and then the need to adjust to another one must be a tough job for the kids. Just imagine, from one day to the other, you have got new brothers and sisters. It must be hard, at least in some cases.

ROBIN: Sure. But then, maybe living in a "new" family offers new opportunities, new friends. Like in a normal family, some people get on with their brothers and sisters, and some don't. But what is worrying me as well is the rising number of divorces. I mean in Germany we have this wonderful new word "Lebensabschnittsgefährte", in English, that would be something like "temporal companion", you know what I mean. Everything is temporal, there is no security, not even as regards your belonging to a family.

RICHARD: True. And I tell you what. It all has to do with a general feeling of temporariness. In the old days, you had a job, and mostly, you had it for life. Now it's hire and fire. You can be laid off in no time, and in their lifetime people will probably have to work for many different companies and doing different jobs to make ends meet. Nothing is certain, so even the security a family once provided has vanished.

ROBIN: Good point. But perhaps that is exactly the reason why so many people, especially young people, cherish the traditional family. Because it does offer the most security a child can have.
How can this security be maintained, I mean, that's the question we should discuss. What could be done to create a more family-friendly society?

RICHARD: Well, then we should look at the economic factors first. What puts families under pressure? The first thing that comes to my mind is the fact that, especially in Germany, it seems to be extremely difficult to combine both work and the raising of children. I mean, in the old days, young families could often rely on their grandparents for support. But today, people are more or less constantly on the move and the grandparents live elsewhere. And our society fails to provide sufficient day care facilities – which means that you either get a job or stay at home to take care of the kids. And for many people this simply doesn't work. Especially academically trained women find it impossible to have both children and a career. So more often than not they decide against having children at all.
The other problem with working families is that many children suffer from neglect because mom and dad are away for too long, and they end up being on their own, sitting in front of the box playing computer games. Or they are out and about in the streets. No wonder that more and more children don't know how to behave themselves or have severe concentration problems and other learning difficulties.

ROBIN: Yes, the media are full of these little "monster kids". The message is that parents just can't cope anymore – that's why there are programmes like "The Super Nanny". I mean most of it is just sensationalist stuff to get the viewers' attention, but there probably is a grain of truth in it. So what needs to be done is this: First, we need more and better day care facilities. As far as I know, the German government has by now acknowledged the problem and started to act. But still, we are lagging behind compared to the Scandinavian countries for example.

RICHARD: Yes indeed, we still do not invest enough money and resources in our children, which means into our future. You see, it's not only the very young children that need to be taken care of. I'm also talking about school children. And here the schools must provide opportunities that children can spend the afternoon at school, doing joyful and meaningful things, and not just hang around in front of the TV. But again, the German government has, up to a certain extent, realized that schools must provide extra-curricular activities in addition to the normal lessons.

ROBIN: Yes, and schools must provide a proper meal a day. Honestly, every day the media confront you with the fact that many families fail to provide any decent food for their kids. Can you imagine that most schools in Germany don't even have a proper dining hall? In this respect, Germany is so backward, compared to Britain or the USA, sometimes you just can't believe it!

RICHARD: You are quite right there. It is unbelievable to see how much money is spent elsewhere, and how little is invested into the next generation. On the contrary, it is a widespread assumption that having children means falling into the poverty trap. They cost so much, or they lower your income because you can't work fulltime. And that's why people decide against having children. So what we need is direct financial support for families.

ROBIN: Now wait a minute, we are still living in a welfare state. There is child benefit, free medical treatment, special allowances for needy families.

RICHARD: There is, but not enough. Or not in the right place at the right time. I have heard of countries where families don't pay any taxes. I mean, so many industrial companies are being subsidized or receive generous tax reductions. I am sure that there is room for better financial support of families in a rich country such as Germany.

ROBIN: In principle, I agree. But then, money isn't everything. What we haven't discussed so far is that in order to create a more family-friendly society we also have to change people's general attitudes towards children. I have the feeling that children are often seen as noisy and in general, unpleasant. Just the other day I heard about a man who went to court because they wanted to establish a kindergarten next to his house. I mean, how selfish can you get?

RICHARD: That's quite a good example, and that kind of hostile reaction is typical of some adults, often those who don't have any children themselves, and who regard other things as more important.

ROBIN: Like what?

RICHARD: Like their own personal freedom, or take a word from the 1980s: "self-fulfillment". As if you were just alone on this planet!

ROBIN: Yeah, I know the type. Not willing to compromise, always trying to find their place in the sun. Always looking for new kicks. Travelling places, the newest gadgets, a luxurious lifestyle. And kids are just in the way …

RICHARD: Absolutely. "Oh, they consume my valuable time, they are noisy, they don't do as they are told, they argue with you, you must drive them to all sorts of activities, piano lessons, parties and what have you.

ROBIN: Now come on, that's just the normal routine. I suppose as parents you must be prepared to make some sacrifices.

RICHARD: And endure some stressful situations, I'm sure. But then, you see, I don't like the word sacrifice. What do parents sacrifice? I mean they get so much back in return.

ROBIN: Right, children can be fun. And it must be wonderful to see them grow up and you can share so many experiences. And being a family gives you a true sense of belonging, of togetherness. I suppose that's worth investing your time.

RICHARD: Indeed, and just to come back to our topic, we need to propagate, well, or remind people of the fact that children are not a curse, but a blessing. That they enrich your life rather than make it difficult.

ROBIN: And they make your life meaningful. The children are our future, we live on in them, and if that's speaking too philosophically, or biologically, you can be sure that, at the end of our working life, it's they who will pay our bills, that is finance our retirement.

(1603 words)

Prüfungsteilnehmer A

Topic: The Internet

You organize an Internet club for younger students.
Comment in the table.

What Internet users go online for (in per cent)

	2004 Feb	July
Finding information about goods or services	79	82
Searching for information about travel and accommodation	69	68
Using email	83	85
Telephoning over the Internet/video conferencing	*	7
General browsing	63	62
Finding information relating to education	35	33
Buying or ordering tickets/goods or services	47	49
Selling goods or services	5	8
Personal banking and financial services	34	36
Playing or downloading games	11	12
Using chatrooms	17	20
Playing or downloading music	25	22
Reading or downloading on-line news	24	26
Listening to web radio/watching web television	12	17
Downloading other software	20	20
Downloading images	22	21
Looking for a job/sending job application	20	23

From: http:/www.e-consultancy.com/publications/internet-stats-compendium/[download/16 April 2008]

Together with your partner discuss the advantages and disadvantages of the Internet. Compile a list of guidelines that young people should be taught.

Prüfungsteilnehmer B

Topic: The Internet

You organize an Internet club for younger students.

Comment on the statistics.

Most common computer crime and security breaches (percentage of organisations having experienced this type)

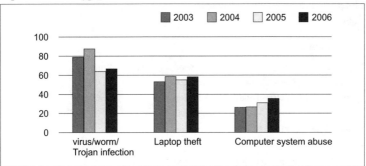

Australian Institute of Criminology 2007. Australian crime: facts and figures 2006. Canberra: AIC.
http://www.aic.gov.au/publications/facts/2006/index.html

Together with your partner discuss the advantages and disadvantages of the Internet. Compile a list of guidelines that young people should be taught.

Partner A: Christian

The topic we are going to deal with is „The Internet". It is our task to organise an Internet club for younger students and compile a list of guidelines for young people who want to use the Net.

But first we need to discuss the advantages and disadvantages of the Internet as such.

Now I have been given a table which was compiled in 2004. It gives you information as to what percentage people used the Internet for what purpose. The table then compares numbers from February and July 2004. It is striking that most users use the Net for rather practical purposes such as emailing (more than 80 percent) or finding information about goods, services, travel and accommodation. It is interesting to see that, at least back in 2004, with 11 respectively 12 percent, chatrooms and playing or downloading games did not play such an important role as some people might think. At least my parents are always on about young people spending most of their time in virtual chatrooms. I suppose that by now this number though might have risen quite considerably. I mean loads of people I know do spend a lot of time on platforms like the *schuelerVZ* or *Facebook* or what have you. But then this is 2009, so it's 5 years on, a long time considering the development of modern communication technologies. Another aspect which might be important, especially with regard to the guidelines we are supposed to develop, is the downloading of images, software and, most of all, music. Now again, the data given in the statistics is probably outdated but downloading music is widespread, and some of the platforms providing music are now regarded as illegal. So people need to be careful, otherwise they might face confrontation with the law. But we should come back to this later.

The first thing we should do when we try to set up an Internet Club, is ask our students as to what purposes they use the Net. Then we can advise them better on how to use it.   *(344 words)*

Partner B: Katharina

I agree. We need up-to-date information, and we need it about the group we're dealing with. Anyway, I have been given statistics about the most common computer crimes and security breaches in Australia. In form of a bar chart, it shows the percentage of organisations that have been experiencing such offences between 2003 and 2006.

All in all it can be deduced that there has been a decrease with regard to viruses, worms and Trojan infections, which was highest in 2004, with about 85 percent of all companies affected, which is now down to roughly 65 percent in 2006 – although there seems to be a slight increase of about one or two percent as compared to 2005. So perhaps the number is rising again.

As regards laptop theft, numbers have remained fairly steady, ranging from circa 55 percent in 2003 to 59 percent in 2006.

The number of computer system abuses has been rising from 30 percent in 2003 to about 35 percent in 2006.

So what do these numbers tell us? I don't really know. I suppose they show that, perhaps because of improved security software, such as firewalls, it is less likely that your computer gets infested by viruses and the like. On the other hand you need to watch out that no one steals your notebook, especially if it contains valuable or sensitive information. As more and more people nowadays are actually in possession of notebooks the problem might perhaps even increase.

The same might be true for computer system abuse. We all know that when students are supposed to be working on an assignment in the computer lab, some of them start mucking about, surfing the Internet, wandering off to undesirable sites, sometimes even downloading the stuff, and all the rest of it. But again, we as private individuals are not really in the line of fire

as regards hacker attacks, like for instance the Pentagon or the White House – or larger organisations.

But then, if we set up an Internet Club we should show people how to make sure that their computer is protected by a firewall and that you have to observe certain rules and regulations if you want to be safe.   *(368 words)*

Discussion

CHRISTIAN: Yes, safety is a problem. We must make sure that the users in our club know the basics about security and the Net. But before we start discussing that issue, we should talk about the advantages and disadvantages of the Internet. I mean, we, and the students we are supposed to teach, need to know what we can do with the Net, and where there might be problems.

KATHARINA: Sure, so I suggest we consider some of the most important advantages the Net offers especially for young people. Well, first of all, at least that is what most of the teachers say, the internet provides a huge source of information. It enables students to quickly read up on any subject – not only in German but also in English, which is why our English teacher is so enthusiastic about it.

CHRISTIAN: Oh yes, he is! And I can understand why. There is so much out there. Quality newspaper articles, high quality history sites, e. g. from the BBC, there is Wikipedia, which gives you up-to-date knowledge of the word …, really, it's all at your fingertips. It is fantastic.

KATHARINA: Now don't get carried away Christian. There is also a lot of rubbish on the Net. I have even heard of people or whole organisations that deliberately spread misinformation on it. So you need to be careful of whom you trust.

CHRISTIAN: Good point that, and this is something we must tell our students. To be critical of the information they receive from the Net. Well, it's media awareness, isn't it.

KATHARINA: True, that's what it is. That's what we should teach them to read carefully and to be critical of all sources of information.

CHRISTIAN: Yep, so we should definitely deal with this problem. Perhaps we could browse the Net together with the students and show them how to differentiate between "good" and "bad" sites.

KATHARINA: Absolutely! It's computer literacy: knowing how to handle the Internet, knowing your way around.

CHRISTIAN: So what other advantages does the Net provide? Apart from providing informa-
tion, it has become an important means of communication between young people. Take my younger sister for example. She is already in the *schuelerVZ*, although she is only ten.

KATHARINA: And you are supposed to be twelve, aren't you.

CHRISTIAN: You are, but you see, she told us that all her classmates and her friends had al-
ready joined, so at the end of the day, my parents gave in, and I could put her in. I mean, we checked the site, and really, it is fairly harmless.

KATHARINA: I agree, and anyway, it has become a mass medium of communication, like it or not. And we should tell our students about it, as there are sites out there, you know, certain chatrooms which should be considered undesirable, to say the least.

CHRISTIAN: I can't agree more. Chatting with the wrong person, perhaps even making contact in the real world, can lead to deadly consequences. So we must definitely warn our students to keep off such sites and identify pedophiles and other perverts.

KATHARINA: Yes indeed. Actually, when we were on exchange in Sweden last year, we noticed that teachers and the government were very eager to teach children tricks of how to avoid such people, and inform their parents and the police.

CHRISTIAN: Talking about parents. I think it would a very good idea to involve the parents at some time, because they often don't have a clue about what their kids can be exposed to.

KATHARINA: Good idea. I know that some parents are extremely naive in this respect. And here we could tackle another problem especially parents are concerned about. It's the fact that quite a few students seem to be spending far too much time chatting on the Internet. Or playing computer games. They become engrossed in the virtual world, and forget about the real world outside, and the real people.

CHRISTIAN: Yeah, becoming a part of an online community. I know a girl who, once she's come home from school, locks herself in and spends almost her entire freetime in front of the computer. I think she has become addicted, a computer junkie. You can guess that her parents are really worried as she seems to have broken off all contact to the real world. She says that she hasn't got any real friends at school. But in the chatroom she is really popular, and has got friends all over the world. I think it's frightening. The real world has been replaced by some sort of computer reality.

KATHARINA: I suppose that is a danger, at least to some. Giving yourself a new identity. What do you call it? An avatar. It's a sort of an alter ego. You give yourself a new name, in fact a new identity, and then you go out there as a completely new person.

CHRISTIAN: Well, yes, changing identities and all that. Now, don't panic. I think most of the time it is fairly harmless, like a role play, well, like an extended role play perhaps. But it's fun, and provides endless opportunities for creative activities. In principle, I think there is nothing wrong with it.

KATHARINA: I agree with you. We should not get hysterical about it, but sometimes it takes on rather frightening dimensions. It's when people get addicted to it, if they sacrifice all their time and their real friendships, you know, if they stop living and communicating in the real world, then I do get worried.

CHRISTIAN: OK, I see your point. Take "World of Warcraft", for example. Personally, I quite like the game. It's full of fantasy and you can really prove yourself. Showing you can master the strategies, the techniques, the planning and all the rest that goes with it. It's great entertainment, and not just mindless killing, like for instance all these ego-shooter games.
But sure, some people do get carried away, so we need to discuss the problem of Internet addiction with our students.

KATHARINA: Agreed. But let's just consider the practical benefits you can derive from the Net. Apart from finding all sorts of information, the Internet is the main medium of communicating your ideas to others. Nowadays, companies are operating worldwide. Construction plans and ideas are sent around the world with people in different countries working on them, which makes exchanging ideas a lot faster and more efficient. So what I want to say is that we should also focus on the Internet as a valuable tool, not only for the big companies, but also for people like you and me.

CHRISTIAN: Super idea, perhaps we could even found a sort of Internet student firm, or just establish contact with other schools, or other Internet clubs. That could be fun.

KATHARINA: And rewarding as well. I mean we live in a globalised world, and as I said before, computer literacy is part of how to communicate in this new world.

CHRISTIAN: OK. So far, we have discussed some of the advantages and disadvantages of the Net. So, Katharina, what kind guidelines would you suggest for our students?

KATHARINA: Well, number one could be: Don't trust everybody. Make sure that you can trust the source of information, or the chatroom member you are dealing with. If in doubt, drop it and log out immediately.

CHRISTIAN: Number two could be: Do not download anything illegal or any offensive materials. You might be found out, and then you or your parents might have to pay for it.

KATHARINA: Number three: As regards chatrooms, *Facebook*, *YouTube* or *schuelerVZ* and the like, make sure not to put any embarrassing photos or information of yourself on the Net. Never, ever! It can always be retraced, and this is what we need to drive home to our students: Your future employers will be looking for stuff like that, and if you have presented yourself in any offensive way, you might not get the job you want.

CHRISTIAN: That's indeed a very, very important point. Especially when they are young, students don't know what they are doing, and they do not think ahead. They can't imagine that their photos, or texts, can be retrieved from the Net for the next million years.

KATHARINA: As long as the Net exists, you mean.

CHRISTIAN: Sure. Well, I was just going to say that perhaps for rule number four we should tell our students to refrain from any cyber bullying, as it has more disastrous consequences on the victims than most people imagine. And it can seriously backfire on themselves if they are found out.

KATHARINA: Very good point. Now, what else is important? Coming back to security, as rule number five we should tell them never to give away any private information such as their full names and addresses or phone numbers in a chatroom, or their (or their parents') banking details, or agree to any dubious contract.

CHRISTIAN: Well, they shouldn't agree to <u>any</u> contract at all! If in doubt, leave it out.

KATHARINA: Perhaps that should be the golden rule. "If in doubt, leave it out." If you feel uneasy with anything, go and tell your friends, or your parents, or us.

CHRISTIAN: Absolutely. And don't give in to peer group pressure. Just because some people do strange things on the Net, it doesn't mean that you have to follow suit.

KATHARINA: Very good point. Another one could be: Use the Net, but leave it alone at times, as there are other things in life you can enjoy, like sports or music.

CHRISTIAN: Oh, the parents and teachers will thank us for that! So rule number six could be: Make sure that you have a life outside the Net.   *(1625 words)*

Teil A: Text 1

Against Going To War With Iraq.
Speech given by Barack Obama on October 2, 2002 in Chicago

Good afternoon. Let me begin by saying that although this has been billed as an anti-war rally, I stand before you as someone who is not opposed to war in all circumstances. The Civil War was one of the bloodiest in history, and yet it was only through the crucible of the sword, the sacrifice of multitudes, that we could begin to perfect this union, and drive
5 the scourge of slavery from our soil. I don't oppose all wars.

My grandfather signed up for a war the day after Pearl Harbor was bombed, fought in Patton's army. He saw the dead and dying across the fields of Europe; he heard the stories of fellow troops who first entered Auschwitz and Treblinka. He fought in the name of a larger freedom, part of that arsenal of democracy that triumphed over evil, and he
10 did not fight in vain. I don't oppose all wars.

After September 11th, after witnessing the carnage and destruction, the dust and the tears, I supported this administration's pledge to hunt down and root out those who would slaughter innocents in the name of intolerance, and I would willingly take up arms myself to prevent such a tragedy from happening again. I don't oppose all wars. And I
15 know that in this crowd today, there is no shortage of patriots, or of patriotism.

What I am opposed to is a dumb war. What I am opposed to is a rash war. [...]

I know that even a successful war against Iraq will require a US occupation of undetermined length, at undetermined cost, with undetermined consequences. I know that an invasion of Iraq without a clear rationale and without strong international support will
20 only fan the flames of the Middle East, and encourage the worst, rather than best, impulses of the Arab world, and strengthen the recruitment arm of Al Qaeda. I am not opposed to all wars. I'm opposed to dumb wars.

So for those of us who seek a more just and secure world for our children, let us send a clear message to the President today. You want a fight, President Bush? Let's finish the
25 fight with Bin Laden and Al Qaeda, through effective, coordinated intelligence, and a shutting down of the financial networks that support terrorism, and a homeland security program that involves more than color-coded warnings. [...]

You want a fight, President Bush? Let's fight to make sure our so-called allies in the Middle East, the Saudis and the Egyptians, stop oppressing their own people, and sup-
30 pressing dissent, and tolerating corruption and inequality, and mismanaging their economies so that their youth grow up without education, without prospects, without hope, the ready recruits of terrorist cells. You want a fight, President Bush? Let's fight to wean ourselves off Middle East oil, through an energy policy that doesn't simply serve the interests of Exxon and Mobil. Those are the battles that we need to fight. Those are the bat-
35 tles that we willingly join. The battles against ignorance and intolerance. Corruption and greed. Poverty and despair. [...]   *(520 words)*

Abridged from: Barack Obama: Against Going To War With Iraq.
http://www.barackobama.com/2002/10/02/remarks_of_illinois_state_sen.php [down-
load/17 November 2009]

Text 2

Sounds good by Philip Collins

The least understood aspect of great rhetoric is that much more is said than words. Every speaker brings a tone to their material that they could no sooner throw off than defy gravity. Tony Blair found lightness without trying. Gordon Brown cannot fail to convey
40 solemnity, even when smiling. And Barack Obama has, to use one of his own terms, a righteous wind at his back.

It's banal, because it's too obvious, to conclude that Obama's words belong in a tradition of classical rhetoric. So does anyone speaking in complete sentences. [...]

The precepts of classical rhetoric help us see how the trick works. But technical compe-
45 tence is the only thing genius has in common with mediocrity. This will not explain why Obama has, even before his inauguration on 20th January, begun to draw level with the last century's greatest political speakers: Winston Churchill, JFK, Martin Luther King and Vaclav Havel.

Obama's rhetoric is rarely flowery. On the page it is not even especially colourful. The
50 least successful passages, in fact, are those in which the prose turns purple. In his November victory speech, for example, Obama suggested that everyone should "put their hands on the arc of history and bend it once more toward the hope of a better day." The best to be said for that is that you know what he means.

But, at his strongest, Obama combines a poetic form of expression with a poetic com-
55 pression of meaning, while rarely straying from ordinary language. His speeches do take wing, but the flight comes from the rhythm of the sentences, as much as the elevation of the language.

An Obama speech is, in fact, like a pop song. The lyrics yield no great mystery. But, set to the right music, a meaning is disclosed that hardly seemed to be hidden in the prose.
60 No writer could give this musical sense to Hillary Clinton. But it is always there in the way Obama hits the important word in each sentence. [...]   *(334 words)*

Abridged from: Philip Collins, "Sounds good" in Prospect, January 2009 issue,
pp. 14/15.

A Text production

A1 Working with the text   25 BE

Analyse Obama's speech and assess to what extent the skills described by Philip Collins in "Sounds good" apply.

Write a coherent text.

A2 Composition   25 BE
Choose <u>one</u> of the following tasks.

2.1 "I am not opposed to all wars. I'm opposed to dumb wars." (ll. 21/22)
Comment.

2.2   Discuss the message of the cartoon.

CALVIN AND HOBBES © *Watterson. Dist. By UNIVERSAL UCLICK. Reprinted with permission. All rights reserved.*

2.3   "DON'T FORGET THE PAST! – The relevance of historical events" is the topic of an international youth conference.
Write a speech for this conference reflecting on the relevance of historical events.

Erreichbare BE-Anzahl Teil A (Summe A1 und A2):
Inhaltliche Reichhaltigkeit und Textstruktur: 20 BE
Sprachliche Korrektheit: 20 BE
Ausdrucksvermögen und Textfluss: 10 BE
Gesamt: 50 BE

Teil B: Translation / Mediation
Choose <u>one</u> of the following tasks (B1 <u>or</u> B2)

B1 Translation

"Wannabe" Washington walks tall

It took more than two centuries, says Joel Kotkin, but Washington DC is finally poised to emerge as America's "undisputed centre of national power and influence." The city has always been something of a "wannabe" among world capitals, lacking the commercial and cultural clout of cities such as London or Paris. Its lowly status reflected the ideals of
5 America's founders, who resented the confluence of power and wealth that defined 19th century European capitals. But this model of decentralised power is now unravelling as a result of the economic meltdown and the "unprecedented collapse of rival centres of power" within the US. From California to the Carolinas, once proudly independent states and cities are now looking to Washington to rescue them from insolvency. [...] In time,
10 people may come to resent the capital's dominance, seeing it as "oppressive and contrary to the national ethos". But Washingtonians won't notice. "They'll be too busy running the country."   *(158 words)*

Best of the American columnists: Koel Kotkin – "Wannabe Washington walks tall"
THE WEEK, *7 Feb 2009, p. 15.*   20 BE

B2 Mediation
While doing research on the topic "Education and work" for your English course you have found the following texts.
Summarize the contents for your fellow students.

Text 1: Rhetorik-Expertin Gloria Beck im Interview mit Spiegel Online
[...]

SPIEGEL ONLINE: Sie waren mehrere Jahre Dozentin für Rhetorik an der Universität Koblenz. Woran hapert es bei Studenten in Sachen Kommunikation?

GLORIA BECK: Studenten übernehmen oft Muster, die sie aus der Schule kennen. Sie for-
5 mulieren Sätze häufig zu umgangssprachlich und deswegen nicht so exakt, wie es das Niveau des Seminars erfordert. Spätestens an der Uni sind alle Studenten Erwachsene, die ihrem Dozenten gegenüber gleichberechtigt und selbstbewusst auftreten sollten. Die Rhetorik liefert ihnen dafür das notwendige Werkzeug. Ich meine damit nicht eine bestimmte Art zu sprechen. Es kommt auf die Strategie an, kompetent aufzutreten.

10 SPIEGEL ONLINE: Und die lautet, die Aufmerksamkeit selbstbewusst auf die eigene Person zu lenken?

BECK: Nicht auf die Person, sondern auf die eigene Kompetenz. Denn das interessiert an der Uni. Niemand gibt Ihnen eine gute Note, weil er findet, dass Sie ein netter Mensch sind. Nur leistungsstarke Studenten erhalten gute Noten. Um aber als solcher erst ein-
15 mal in Erscheinung zu treten, sollten die Fragen und Beiträge im Seminar einer bestimmten Struktur folgen.

SPIEGEL ONLINE: Sie nennen diesen Aufbau „Dreierbeitragsstruktur". Um welche drei Schritte geht es?

BECK: Zunächst muss deutlich gemacht werden, zu welchem Punkt in den Ausführungen
20 des Dozenten man etwas sagen will. Dann formuliert man die eigene Idee, anschließend die Frage. Das dauert etwas länger, wirkt dafür aber kompetenter. [...]

Wichtig ist, dass Inhalt und Aufbau des Redebeitrages stimmen. Und das lernt man am besten, indem man weiß, wie das geht und kontinuierlich übt. Ein erster Schritt könnte

darin bestehen, dass sich die Studenten vornehmen, sich pro Kurs einmal zu melden
25 und eine Frage zu stellen. Dann sticht man aus der Masse hervor und bleibt dem Dozenten positiv im Gedächtnis. [...] *(283 Wörter)*

Rhetorik an der Uni: Alles nur Show: Interview mit Gloria Beck. 20. 02. 2007.
http://www.spiegel.de/unispiegel/studium/0,1518,458398,00.html [down-
load/5. August 2009] 20 BE

Text 2: Rhetorik – Mit den richtigen Worten Karriere machen

[...] „Der Inhalt eines Satzes macht lediglich zehn Prozent der beim Gesprächspartner
erzielten Wirkung aus", erklärt Eduard Klein, Geschäftsführer der Münchner Frontline
Consulting Group. „Die eigentliche Wirkung der Worte wird über den Tonfall und die
30 Körpersprache transportiert." Bei der Körpersprache werden unter anderem Stimme,
Gestik, Mimik, aber auch Kleidung, die Art des Sitzens und der Abstand zu seinem Gegenüber unterschieden.

„Das Gesicht ist der Spiegel der Seele", sagt Roman Braun. Wichtig sei, dass sich die
Mimik entsprechend den sich verändernden Gefühlslagen ändere. Ebenfalls von Bedeu-
35 tung sei der Augenkontakt mit den Gesprächspartnern. „Sind es mehrere, sollten die Au-
genkontakte gleichmäßig verteilt werden", so Braun.

„Eine positive Körpersprache kann von Beginn an eine gute Gesprächsatmosphäre för-
dern. Dazu zählen unter anderem öffnende Handbewegungen; darüber hinaus sollten die
Arme nicht vor der Brust verschränkt sein", sagt Arnold Kitzmann, Leiter des Manage-
40 ment-Instituts Kitzmann in Münster. „Wer in einer Diskussion punkten will, sollte zudem
dafür sorgen, dass die Anderen ihn auch verstehen. Dafür ist eine klare und deutliche
Aussprache unerlässlich." [...]

„Äußerst wichtig in einer Diskussion ist die eigene Überzeugung", stellt Eduard Klein
heraus. „Man muss von dem überzeugt sein, was man sagt. Nur dann können die eigenen
45 Worte auch eine Wirkung entfalten." „Man wirkt in einer Diskussion nur dann überzeu-
gend, wenn man authentisch ist", sagt Arnold Kitzmann. „Das Wertvollste bei einer
Kommunikation ist die Natürlichkeit. Es ist schön, rhetorische Mittel zu kennen. Wenn
ich sie aber nur einstudiert wiederhole, kann ich keine persönliche Ebene aufbauen und
darunter leidet dann auch die Glaubwürdigkeit."

50 In einer leidenschaftlichen Diskussion kann es durchaus auch mal zu verbalen Angriffen
der Gesprächspartner kommen. Es ist gut, auf solche Momente vorbereitet zu sein. Bei
einer aufbrausenden Replik sollte man in jedem Fall einen ruhigen Kopf bewahren und
sich nie eine emotionale Ebene begeben, rät Rhetorik-Trainer Braun.

Stattdessen sollte man in ruhigem Ton seine Aussage wiederholen und gegebenenfalls
55 ausführlicher erläutern.

Auch kann es vorkommen, dass man von einer angesprochenen Thematik wenig versteht.
In diesen Fällen sollte man in jedem Fall ehrlich bleiben und seine Unwissenheit in diesem bestimmten Punkt einräumen . [...] *(332 Wörter)*

Falk Osterloh: Rhetorik – Mit den richtigen Worten Karriere machen.
02. 04. 2009. http://www.welt.de/finanzen/karriere/article3488742/Mit-
den-richtigen-Worten-Karriere-machen.html [download/5. August 2009] 20 BE

Lösungsvorschlag

A Text production

A1 Working with the text

The key points are:
- *contradiction: anti-war rally but not opposed to war in general*
- *difference between "dumb wars" and just wars*
- *examples from (American) history*
- *Obama's personal involvement*
- *appeal to patriotism*
- *stylistic devices: metaphor, parallelism, anaphora, personal pronouns (I, we), personification ...*
- *language: poetic form of expression, ordinary language, rhythm of the sentences*
- *resemblance of the speech to a pop song*

Obama starts his speech "Against Going To War With Iraq", given in Chicago on October 2, 2002, with a contradiction, which must come across like a provocation: although he is officially taking part in an anti-war rally, he makes sure that he is well-prepared to fight a war if necessary: "I stand before you as someone who is not opposed to war in all circumstances" (l. 2). Musically speaking, if you compare the speech to a pop song, as Philip Collins does in line 58, this opening serves like an intro to a song. Thus, Obama draws attention to his speech, as his listeners will be eager to hear how he can resolve this apparent contradiction.

To do so, Obama continues by pointing out several examples of justified wars. First he mentions the American Civil War, which, for Obama, not only kept America together as a nation ("perfect this union" l. 4), but also put an end to slavery. To justify this war, Obama uses positively connoted metaphorical expressions such as "the crucible of the sword" and "the sacrifice of multitudes" (ll. 3/4), which, for me, aim to evoke an image of a glorious victory and consequently trigger a feeling of togetherness and patriotism among his audience. In this respect I would contradict Collins when he says: "Obama's rhetoric is [...] not even [...] colourful" (l. 49). Here, and elsewhere, Obama's rhetoric is indeed colourful, as the expression "drive the scourge of slavery from our soil" (ll. 4/5), a metaphor combined with powerful alliteration ("s"), shows.

The next war Obama mentions is the Second World War. Here, Obama appeals to the audience's sympathy by demonstrating his own family's involvement, as he explains how his grandfather fought in Europe and how he witnessed the horrors of the Nazi death camps. Obama appeals to America's sense of being the world's leading nation, as his audience knows that America's involvement in the Second World War, together with the reconstruction of Europe and the rise of America as a superpower, is generally conceived as a great success story.

The same is true for the third war he mentions, the fight against terrorism. Obama knows how important it is to make a stance against the terrorists of 9/11, especially in 2002 when this speech was given. Accordingly, his language indeed becomes very belligerent. Terms such as "hunt down and root out" (l. 12) are intended to show absolute determination to protect the "innocents" (l. 13). This is highlighted by Obama's own personal pledge that he "would willingly take up arms" himself (l. 13). With the sentence "And I know that in this crowd today, there is no shortage of patriots, or of patriotism" (ll. 14/15), Obama connects directly with his listeners, as no patriotic American could deny the arguments put forward so far. This strategy could reflect what Collins describes as the "righteous wind at his back" (l. 41): you simply cannot disagree with Obama when he advocates that issues like freedom, democracy, tolerance and security are worth fighting for.

All three parts about just wars end with the sentence "I don't oppose all wars" (ll. 5, 10, 14). This classical element of repeating the most important message of one's speech (evoking recollections of Martin Luther King's famous "I have a dream" speech) does indeed resemble a chorus in a pop song. Like a refrain, it will remain firmly rooted in people's memories. It also adds to the sense of rhythm that Collins detects (l. 56).

So far, Obama has prepared the ground for the very message he wants to convey, which is his opposition to George Bush's war policies. Comparing the speech to a pop song, the anaphora "What I am opposed to is a dumb war. What I am opposed to is a rash war" (l. 16) serves like a new chord, perhaps a rather dissonant one. A new tone has been added, and the audience knows that Obama will now come to the core of his speech.

To do this he makes use of rather factual, objective terminology, ("length", "cost", "consequences", "rationale", "support" ll. 18/19). These terms are then contrasted with the disastrous consequences for America if President Bush were to engage in a "dumb war". Phrases like "only fan the flames of the Middle East" (l. 20), or "strengthen the recruitment arm of Al Qaeda" (l. 21), a personification of the enemy, are intended to create an atmosphere of fear.

To undermine his opponent even more, the rather colloquial, rhetorical question "You want a fight, President Bush?", which is repeated throughout the rest of the speech (ll. 24, 28, 32), evokes images of a street fight, portraying Bush as a rather mindless bully. In contrast, Obama offers "coordinated intelligence" (l. 25) and invites everyone to get active ("Let's").

The short phrase "Poverty and despair" (l. 36) at the very end of the given excerpt shows that Obama "combines a poetic form of expression with a poetic compression of meaning" (ll. 54/55), as this expression is preceded by enumerations and therefore serves as the culmination point of his speech; the condensed message, formulated in telegram style.

All in all, Obama comes across straight; there is no "great mystery" (l. 58), and the vital messages are constantly repeated. Together with the dramatic outline of the speech and the way Obama works with contrastive ideas and rhetorical elements, his speech does indeed have the quality of a pop song. No wonder that his speeches have inspired other people to turn them into songs, e. g. his slogan "Yes we can", which, as a song, served as an original addition to his election campaign.   *(945 words)*

A2 Composition

2.1 *The key points are:*
   – quotation put into the context of Obama's speech
   – examples of dumb wars and/or justified wars
   – reasons for/against going to war
   – your own conclusion

When Obama talks about a "dumb war", he refers to the war against Iraq, which, in his mind, would be fought "without a clear rationale" (l. 19). To me, this means that there must be wars which are fought on a rational basis, or which are at least morally justified. Obama himself mentions two such wars, the fight against Nazi Germany (and Japan) and the American Civil War. The latter is even seen as a means "to perfect" the union (l. 4). The word "perfect" can also be seen as the opposite of "dumb", and in the 1860s a war seemed the "perfect" solution to keep America together as a nation and economic unit – and do away with slavery.

If we agree with Obama, a justified war would then have to follow a clear rationale and be part of a superior moral aim. However, there is a catch. We all know that moral superiority has often served as the justification for aggressive action against other people, the reason for conquests or the colonization of continents, frequently resulting in the extermination of whole peoples and nations.

When Nazi Germany invaded Poland and the Soviet Union, many Germans conceived themselves as belonging to the master race and therefore as justified in subduing and murdering millions of people they regarded as "worthless". Of course it was right to fight Nazi Germany, as it represented perhaps the most loathsome political system ever established on this planet. Of course it was right – and far from dumb – to stop the Nazi hordes from murdering even more people. And the fact that the USA finally gave up their isolationist policies and joined the Allies probably saved the lives of millions of people, because it helped to bring down Germany and Japan faster. Furthermore, if you look at the Marshall Plan and the way America helped in the reconstruction of Germany (and Japan) after the war, you could easily argue that America, along with the other Allied forces, was driven by both a moral obligation and a calculating rationale, as an economically strong and politically stable (West) Germany served as an efficient barrier and ally against the Soviet Union during the Cold War.

So, all in all, the war against Hitler was anything but a "dumb war", as the victors – at least the western allies – not only won the war, but also managed to lead the defeated parties back into the world community, profiting from trade with the now prosperous former enemies.

However, looking back in history, I suppose there are hardly any other examples of "rational" wars, as most wars were fought either for political power or for sheer conquest. If you look at the second Iraq war, which Obama criticizes as a "dumb war", I can almost wholeheartedly agree. Iraq, unlike Nazi Germany, did not pose a threat to the rest of the world. Neither did it serve as a safe haven for international terrorists, nor was it in possession of weapons of mass destruction. Additionally, and this is where the Iraq war lacks true "rationale", there have never been any serious or feasible plans (and financial means) for the political and economic reconstruction of the country.

Looking back at human history, perhaps all wars have been "dumb wars", as the "sacrifice of multitudes" (l. 4) is too high a price to pay, even if you have the best intentions. Mahatma Gandhi has shown that you can defeat even the greatest empire by non-violent means, and Martin Luther King and the Civil Rights Movement (taking Gandhi as an example) also achieved their aims without using force. In this respect, the liberation of India and the emancipation of the African Americans are examples of truly "smart wars"; of fights that deserve a prominent place in our history books, as they demonstrate that great political goals can also be realized without killing one another. In this context, I would like to leave the last words to Mahatma Gandhi who, commenting on the vicious circle of violence and counter-violence, once said that "An eye for an eye makes the whole world go blind." *(684 words)*

2.2 *The key points are:*
- *refusal to take on responsibility*
- *influence of the media*
- *participation in the decision making process, e. g. voting*
- *blame "the system"/"things" rather than fix them*

In the cartoon we see a little boy with his friend, a talking tiger, racing down a slope in a cart. The boy tells the tiger that, as a grown-up, he will not read up on any complex issue, nor will he be prepared to take on any political responsibility. Although he will not vote for any political party, he intends to complain that the government does not represent him, which would in turn justify his ongoing unwillingness to participate

in the political life of his country. This self-fulfilling prophesy is ironically side-stepped by the tiger, who calls it an "ingeniously self-fulfilling plan".
I cannot agree more with that. The little boy is a typical example of people who have either lost faith in our political system, or who simply do not want to make the effort to participate in the complex life of a democracy. The latter is shown by the refusal of the boy to read the newspaper. Considering this, if you live in a democratic society, you have the opportunity to inform yourself independently. That means that, thanks to freedom of speech, people have access to a great variety of information and opinions. I admit that, partly due to the internet, we are currently immersed in such a vortex of information that it is difficult, and sometimes exhausting, to know your way around. However, newspapers especially help you to keep up with what is happening, often exposing political wrongdoings and misconceptions. Which means that if you throw away this right to be informed, you also forsake one of the most important political principles of a democracy: freedom of speech, which serves as a prerequisite of acting as a responsible and mature citizen.
We all know that people who do not bother to inform themselves can easily be mani-pulated. Today, many people prefer the sensationalist reports of the so-called tabloid press to quality newspapers. The result is that these people are often vulnerable as re-gards simplistic, often radical, political messages. In this case, the aforementioned vi-cious circle of non-participation and the result, the situation "when everything goes down the tubes", comes full circle, as a democratic society cannot exist without peo-ple taking an active part.
On the other hand, I can understand that people, especially the younger generation, get frustrated with politics. More often than not you get the impression that govern-ments, even on a local level, either do what they like, or are at the mercy of various lobbies. You could also add that national governments are in many ways at the end of their tether, as globalization has unleashed mechanisms which can no longer be con-trolled by the people we vote for.
But does that mean that active participation in a democratic society is futile? Far from it – it is our only chance, and we should not forfeit it easily. It took centuries to estab-lish democracies in Europe and elsewhere, and even if our modern democracies are still far from perfect, we should make sure that we support and strengthen them from within. This means we should at least take the trouble to make our way to the ballot box, as it is a well-known fact that radical minorities tend to profit from a general "vot-ing fatigue". If we do not take care, we might end up with people in power that we do not want at all; people who would take away our freedom. Because by not showing any interest and commitment, we are showing that we do not really care.   *(586 words)*

2.3 *The key points are:*
    – a text containing some typical characteristics/rhetorical devices of speeches
    – should attract the reader's as well as the listener's attention
    – historical examples/events and their relevance

Good morning everybody.

"Don't forget the past!" There you go. For generations, history teachers have justified their bombarding us with dates, facts and figures by reminding us of the relevance of our past to our education. I don't know about you, but I often experienced history les-sons as being somewhat out of context, failing to show the relevance of past events for our lives. But if you take the trouble of looking at history more closely, or happen to have a good history teacher (such a species does exist, so I have heard), then the rel-evance of the past soon becomes clear.
Just one little example: people in Germany, like me, and I suppose most fellow Euro-peans, often fail to understand the gun control controversy in the USA. You see, we

tend to regard everyone who is in the possession of guns and speaks out against any gun regulations as "trigger-happy nutters", or even fascists who want to take the law into their own hands. Don't get me wrong, I do not advocate the private possession or proliferation of firearms, but when I learned that the right to bear arms is part of the American constitution, (you remember, the Second Amendment and all that), then the whole controversy appeared to me in a new light. I learned that in the past, Americans fought for this right, the right to defend yourself either against common criminals or against a state that has turned on its citizens, e. g. by trying to establish a dictatorship. This shows that we need to know about the past if we want to understand the present.

Back home in Europe we are faced with the challenge of multi-cultural societies. Take, for instance, Great Britain. Only when we understand that due to the legacy of the British Empire, thousands of people from the ex-colonies were asked to come and live in Britain to help the economy back on its feet after the Second World War, can we understand why today, some parts of Britain, especially inner city areas, have a very high percentage of Asian or Caribbean population.

As you can see, our current societies are the result of events and developments in the past. Knowing these facts helps to counteract racist ideas about the "invasion of foreigners" who only come to live in our midst because they want to take advantage of our social security systems. Once you have seen behind the scenes, you know that things are more complex, and you won't fall for political groups using certain minorities as scapegoats or targets for their aggression. Nobody in his right mind would nowadays fall for neo-fascist or Nazi ideology if he knew about the atrocities committed during the so-called Third Reich, and the carnage of the Second World War. Nobody would justify imperial wars as they happened in the past if they knew, for instance, that Spain and Portugal ravaged a whole continent, South America, to strip it of its gold and land. Nobody would justify the extermination of the Native Americans during the colonization of the West. All these crimes against humanity would nowadays be considered as what they were: crimes which ought to be punished by a world community which, in form of the United Nations, has established international laws and regulations to prevent such aggressive acts from happening again.

I hear you say, though, that so far the United Nations hasn't been very efficient, and that there are still wars tormenting the world, like the ones in Afghanistan and Africa, with armies of child soldiers killing and pillaging, and being raped and exploited by ruthless warlords who treat the civilian population like dirt.

I admit that we still have a long way to go, but let us not deny the fact that in many respects people have learned their lesson. The Third World War, the biggest threat to mankind ever, has not happened. Some people might say that this was only due to coincidence, that it was pure luck, but looking back, I firmly believe that our parents' and our lives were spared partly because the political leaders saw a bit of sense, as people on both sides knew that a war between the superpowers would have been the last war on earth.

In fact, the Cold War came to an end when the Berlin Wall came down, and this year we will celebrate the 20th anniversary of Germany's reunification, achieved by peaceful means, with not a single shot being fired. A truly remarkable achievement if you look back into German history.

And there are more examples of such historical achievements. Take Gandhi's successful fight for Indian Independence, which was achieved by means of non-cooperation and other forms of civil disobedience. Take Martin Luther King and the Civil Rights Movement. Doesn't the fact that, today, the USA is led by an African American president show that progress and justice can be achieved, that human society does in fact move forward, that things also change for the better?

As I said before, there is still a long and winding road ahead, and the world is far from perfect. But our past has shown us that things can be changed. And although it has become a bit of a cliché, I would like to quote Barack Obama once again: "Yes, we can." And I say, yes, we can change the present and make provisions for our future if we don't forget the past. Yes, we can make the world a better place if we learn our lessons from history and draw the right conclusions. And yes, history lessons might be boring at times, but we are all part of history, our own history and the history of others, so we might as well take a more active stance towards it.

Thanks for your attention   *(969 words)*

B Translation/Mediation

B1 Translation

„Möchtegern"-Washington geht aufrecht[1]

Joel Kotkin sagt, dass es mehr als zwei Jahrhunderte dauerte, aber Washington DC sei nun endlich bereit, Amerikas „unangefochtenes Zentrum[2] nationaler Macht[3] und Einflussnahme" zu werden. Die Stadt war immer schon so etwas wie ein „Gernegroß"[4] unter den Hauptstädten dieser Welt, (allerdings) ohne die wirtschaftliche und kulturelle Schlagkraft von Städten wie London oder Paris. Ihr bescheidener Status spiegelte die Ideale der amerikanischen Gründungsväter wider, die der Verquickung von Macht und Wohlstand, die kennzeichnend für die Hauptstädte Europas des 19. Jahrhunderts war, ablehnend gegenüber standen[5]. Aber im Zuge des wirtschaftlichen Niedergangs[6] und des „noch nie da gewesenen Zusammenbruchs[7]" konkurrierender Machtzentren" innerhalb der USA ist dieses Modell dezentraler Macht dabei sich aufzulösen. Von Kalifornien bis Nord- und Süd-Carolina blicken nun Staaten und Städte, die einst stolz auf ihre Unabhängigkeit waren, auf Washington, in der Hoffnung, dass sie so vor der Insolvenz gerettet werden. Irgendwann werden die Menschen sich möglicherweise über die Dominanz der Hauptstadt ärgern und sie als „unterdrückerisch und dem Nationalethos widersprechend" begreifen. Aber die Menschen in Washington werden davon keine Notiz nehmen[8]. „Sie werden zu sehr damit beschäftigt sein, das Land zu regieren."

Anmerkungen
1 Auch: *erhobenen Hauptes*
2 Auch: *unbestrittener Mittelpunkt*
3 Auch: *Größe*
4 Auch: *„Möchtegern"*
5 Auch: *die die Verquickung von Macht und Wohlstand [...] störte*
6 Auch: *Zusammenbruchs*
7 Auch: *Einsturzes*
8 Auch: *das nicht merken*

B2 Mediation

The key points are:
- *importance of successful communication for people's careers*
- *strategies of speaking*
- *extra-lingual aspects of communication (e. g. body language)*
- *creating an appropriate atmosphere, (e. g. by being honest, in control)*

Rhetoric and beyond

The two given texts, articles from German quality papers, deal with the importance of successful communication for people's university education and future careers. They both highlight the fact that communication is far more than the application of purely rhetorical skills. Gloria Beck, an ex-university lecturer from Germany, focuses on speaking strategies. To her, a clear structure and overall coherence in your argumentation will make you a successful speaker. To achieve this she suggests a three-step structure for arguments, consisting of what exactly you are referring to, your own idea, and your question. To improve the quality of your contributions, you should refrain from using colloquial language. Furthermore, she advises students to participate actively in classroom discussions by asking the right question at the right time in order to attract their professors' attention. All these skills need to be acquired by constant practice.

The second text points out that rather than rehearsed rhetorical phrases, features such as body language, intonation, facial expression, eye contact, and even the clothes people wear, make up about 90 per cent of all communication. In addition, you need to be convinced of your own ideas and know your facts if you want to make a good impression. When, during a discussion, you are confronted with a harsh verbal attack, try to keep your cool. Finally, in order to stay honest and trustworthy, you should be open enough to admit the fact that in certain areas you might not have sufficient factual knowledge. *(249 words)*

Prüfungsteilnehmer A

Topic: Volunteer Work

Your school has a partner school in the US. You know that the students there are required to do a certain amount of volunteer work each month.

Comment on the cartoon.

Francartoons

Together with your partner discuss the benefits and limitations of volunteer work as an obligatory part of school life in Germany.
Try to agree on how such a project could be organised.

Prüfungsteilnehmer B

Topic: Volunteer Work

Your school has a partner school in the US. You know that the students there are required to do a certain amount of volunteer work each month.

Comment on the cartoon.

I'm sorry, this is the line for people who volunteered to help their community. You're looking for the eternal damnation department.

© Ralph Hagen, www.cartoonstock.com

Together with your partner discuss the benefits and limitations of volunteer work as an obligatory part of school life in Germany.
Try to agree on how such a project could be organised.

Lösungsvorschläge

Partner A: Anna

The topic Beatrice and I have been asked to discuss is voluntary work. We all know that for many years, voluntary work has been an integral part of school life in America, where students are supposed to do a certain amount of voluntary work each week. Now the question is whether voluntary work should become an obligatory part of school life in Germany, and if so, how it could be organized.

Now, to me, making voluntary work an obligation for all students seems to be a contradiction in terms, as "voluntary" means "willingly". So generally, I should think that imposing voluntary work on all students would not really work out well, and would probably be difficult to implement. On the other hand, I think that voluntary work would indeed be beneficial for both those who engage in voluntary work, and those being helped, e. g. disadvantaged children or elderly people. But of course, all this needs to be carefully organized, otherwise volunteers might end up like the woman in the cartoon I've been asked to comment on. This woman has apparently applied for work as a volunteer, but the answer she gets from her superior is rather off-putting, even insolent, as he describes her future job as comprising, quote, "a range of experiences including exhaustion, emotional overload, lack of support and stark terror", unquote. So to me, the message of the cartoon refers to the exploitation of volunteers as a cheap workforce, as people you can take advantage of, as people you can treat badly or just neglect because they obviously haven't got any rights. So at the end of the day, volunteers might end up in a rather unpleasant situation, being denied proper support by their employers. As regards our project, we definitely must take care that the situation depicted in the cartoon cannot happen. *(306 words)*

Partner B: Beatrice

I couldn't agree more. Our volunteers must not be left in the lurch under any circumstances. But before we come to the organization of our volunteer scheme, let me describe my cartoon. It depicts a scene at the gates of heaven, with two men trying to get past St. Peter. However they are rejected because, apparently, they have never volunteered to help their community, and therefore are sent to hell, which in the cartoon is called "the eternal damnation department", symbolized by a devilish figure sitting behind a desk. So, there seems to be a divine reward for those involved in voluntary work. And I think that that is something we ought to discuss first. To what extent does voluntary work offer a reward? *(124 words)*

Discussion

ANNA: Well, Beatrice, think of the term "rewarding experience". I think this means that the deed, the activity people engage in, is a reward in itself, as it might broaden your horizons and make you a more rounded person.

BEATRICE: What do you mean by that?

ANNA: What I mean is that voluntary work gives you the opportunity to experience situations you might never face otherwise. Take elderly people for instance. We are young, we don't really know how it feels to be old, when you aren't able to cook for yourself anymore, or wash yourself properly. Only when you volunteer, when you get involved with such a situation, do you get to know what it's like. Before you are old, that is.

BEATRICE: I see what you mean. And I agree. Coming back to my cartoon, I am sure that having been involved in some meaningful voluntary work will give you a lot of satisfaction, you know, the reassurance that you have done something really positive, that you have helped somebody in need. In fact, the example you have just mentioned is quite convincing. You hear it on the news every day: "The ageing society." Soon there will be a great deal more elderly people, with fewer and fewer younger people to attend to their needs.

I'm sure that taking care of elderly people will be a big challenge for us and the next generations, and perhaps this is where the schools might come in. If there aren't enough nurses for the elderly, students and other people might have to jump in and help.

ANNA: You're right, but then this is not America. We still live in a welfare state, where the community takes over when an individual encounters severe difficulties. In America, charity plays a much more important role than here. Therefore I suppose it is more widely expected that high school students get involved in voluntary work. Because otherwise, that work would not get done.

BEATRICE: I agree, there are cultural and political differences, but at the end of the day, there are still a lot of things that could be done.

ANNA: Absolutely. Going back to the growing number of elderly people, I think that someone must help, or at least lend a hand now and again. But are high school students really qualified to do this? I mean, you need some skills and certain knowledge when dealing with elderly people.

BEATRICE: I suppose that depends to what extent the people you take care of, are … I think "challenged" is the politically correct word here.

ANNA: Sure. There are certain limitations, and of course, students cannot really take on any more extensive responsibilities, but they could assist a nurse in her or his job, or read out the papers to those who are visually impaired. They could play games with them, card games, or Ludo.

BEATRICE: Or just talk to them. You know, I've been to a home for elderly people to visit my grandma, and one of the most horrible things I encountered was the fact that many of the residents complained of being bored to tears.

ANNA: Yeah, the same routine day in, day out. No wonder people feel alone and abandoned in such places. I suppose contact with younger people could make a big difference.

BEATRICE: I'm sure it does. I've seen people reacting ever so positively when children started talking to them, or when there was a little concert, you know, a choir or a band playing some music.

ANNA: Well, there we are then. People of all ages could participate when it comes to making elderly people's lives a little more enjoyable. So why shouldn't we make it an obligatory part of our school life? How about at least one good deed per term? That would be two afternoons or evenings in the whole year. That's not really asking too much, is it?

BEATRICE: Not at all, and really, I should think that a great majority of students would participate on a voluntary basis, without teachers telling them to do so. But does that really make sense? People need constant contact with other people. So, really, individual visits once or twice a year wouldn't really help much, would they?

ANNA: Better than nothing I would say. But you're right, if we want students to do voluntary work for only one or two days a year, we need to think of specific activities. How about performing a little play, or music, or organizing a party for the elderly? That would still make sense, and it could be easily organized. Such projects could be done by a whole class, as a joint effort to do something good for the rest of society.

BEATRICE: Not a bad idea. It would help to foster a feeling of togetherness in the class and you could even involve the parents.

ANNA: Well, this does work. We once did a little Christmas show in a hospice. It was great to have an audience, and it felt even greater to have brought so much joy to everyone.

BEATRICE: Ok, so far we can agree on the occasional visit, once or twice a year. But what about something more regular? Could that be done?

ANNA: Well, perhaps the class could act like a godfather, and be responsible for just one or two people. Then the students could take turns in visiting their "godchild", you know what I mean?

BEATRICE: Yes, I do. I think that's a very good idea, you know, you could have a picture of the person you take care of in the classroom, perhaps even build up a file, with photos and reports and things, making it all more personal. Establish a real personal relationship.

ANNA: Sounds good to me. I suppose it could work, theoretically. It all depends on the people, students and teachers, whether they really want to make it happen.

BEATRICE: Yeah, now you're talking about the limitations of such projects. And here we come back to what we said in the beginning. I can't imagine people working as good volunteers if they don't want to do so. They should either do it wholeheartedly, or not do it at all.

ANNA: I don't quite agree with you there. Those people who don't really want to do anything, like the blokes in your cartoon, could be involved in some other projects, like cleaning up the environment, you know, stuff you don't need to do wholeheartedly since you're not dealing with real people, but things which need to be done all the same.

BEATRICE: Sounds a bit like forced labour to me. I'm not sure if that could be implemented. And perhaps such measures would put regular jobs in jeopardy.

ANNA: That needs to be avoided, of course, but that's up to the politicians. If voluntary work was introduced at a national level, the appropriate legal measures would have to be taken. But I was wondering about what could be done to get more people involved on a truly voluntary basis.

BEATRICE: You mean how to motivate people? Well, how about setting each student a couple of days for voluntary work, then leave it up to him or her what to do and when to do it. Maybe some students would prefer doing voluntary work in their holidays, or perhaps they could do something abroad. That might be very motivating.

ANNA: Good idea, you would have your cake and eat it, so to speak: do something rewarding and get to know another culture. Well, as far as I know there are lots of organizations around that help people find a placement as a volunteer.

BEATRICE: Sure, but the problem might be that some organizations charge horrendous fees. So that might put people off.

ANNA: Well, it might, but then schools need the resources to offer various possibilities to their students, for instance by being connected to a larger network of organizations and institutions, especially on a local level.

BEATRICE: Yes, that's important. That way the school would liase with the local community, a matter of give and take. But how could that be organized?

ANNA: Well, I suggest we look at American high schools and find out how they do it.

BEATRICE: Good idea. The internet should provide enough information and ideas. Of course we need to involve students, like the school captains, and teachers, and put these ideas to the school community – which would involve parents as well. Actually, some parents might even work in areas where voluntary work might be needed. So here we could perhaps establish direct contact to children's homes, kindergartens and so forth.

ANNA: And we should address the community at large: the local government, social institutions and so forth.

BEATRICE: Alright, and then we need a proper concept: we need to establish which age group can do what and when. I suppose that depends on current legislation, as there are certain limitations on what kids are allowed to do at a certain age.

ANNA: Well, yes, these are the technicalities. But how do we motivate people to do voluntary work in the first place? I mean if having "a rewarding experience" is not enough?

BEATRICE: How about some of the reward culture we find at schools in English speaking countries? Like awarding prizes for the most charitable class, or individual.

ANNA: You mean medals and certificates and the like? Your picture on the school homepage, or in the local paper?

BEATRICE: Maybe more than that. Maybe you could even find sponsors who would donate a real prize, e.g. finance a trip abroad or something like that.

ANNA: That would definitely motivate me. Perhaps such a sponsor could also assist you in spending a gap year abroad and finding an attractive location. Or just pay for your flight.

BEATRICE: Now don't get carried away, Anna. We're still talking about voluntary work, not a competition to win an attractive gap year.

ANNA: Well, why not? People get scholarships for academic achievements, why not give money to somebody who works hard to help his or her fellowmen?

BEATRICE: OK, it definitely wouldn't hurt to make voluntary work more attractive. Give it a positive image, and people will come and join.

BEATRICE: Right, but we really do have a moral obligation to help those in need. And that doesn't mean travelling to exotic countries, it means helping right here, in our community. *(1739 words)*

Prüfungsteilnehmer A

Topic: Freedom

In autumn this year Germany will celebrate the 20th anniversary of its reunification.
Comment on the following quotation.

"Liberty means responsibility. That is why most men dread it."
(George Bernard Shaw, Irish dramatist & socialist, 1856–1950)

Together with your partners discuss how people have achieved their freedom throughout history.
Try to agree on what must be done to maintain it.

Prüfungsteilnehmer B

Topic: Freedom

In autumn this year Germany will celebrate the 20th anniversary of its reunification.
Comment on the following quotation.

"Only the educated are free."
(Epictetus, Roman, Greek-born slave & Stoic philosopher, 55 AD–135 AD)

Together with your partners discuss how people have achieved their freedom throughout history.
Try to agree on what must be done to maintain it.

Prüfungsteilnehmer C

Topic: Freedom

In autumn this year Germany will celebrate the 20th anniversary of its reunification.
Comment on the following quotation.

"In the truest sense, freedom cannot be bestowed; it must be achieved."
(Franklin D. Roosevelt, 32nd president of US, 1882–1945)

Together with your partners discuss how people have achieved their freedom throughout history.
Try to agree on what must be done to maintain it.

Lösungsvorschläge

Partner A: Katrin

As you know, the topic we are supposed to discuss is freedom. An appropriate topic, I think, as Germany will celebrate the 20th anniversary of its reunification this year.

It's our task to talk about how people have achieved their freedom throughout history and then agree on what must be done to maintain it.

I have been given a quotation by George Bernhard Shaw, an Irish dramatist and socialist, who once said that, quote, "Liberty means responsibility. That is why most men dread it", unquote. What Shaw means here, I think, is that every one of us (not only men) must do something, and take action in order to retain our freedom. And that's what many people find difficult. They would rather sit back and relax, you know, like the typical couch potato who wants to live a carefree life and move as little as possible. Then there are people who would like to change things but don't know how. They feel helpless, powerless and inadequate. That's why they dread the responsibility for their own life, their own freedom.   *(179 words)*

Partner B: Bernhard

Another factor for achieving and maintaining your freedom is education. According to Epictetus, a philosopher from ancient Rome, quote, "only the educated are free", unquote. I'm not too sure if I can agree with this statement, as some rich and powerful people might well be rather uneducated, but still free. But in general, education is the key for having a career, for making headway in society, and for shaping your future. Furthermore, education has often been at the core of the development of new theories, either political or theological. Martin Luther, for instance. He was a scholar who translated the bible into the vernacular, making the text accessible to a far greater number of people than before, liberating them, or at least those who could read, from the doctrine of the Catholic Church. And that triggered the Reformation, an event that changed the history and culture of Europe. Or take Karl Marx and Friedrich Engels, who wrote books which laid the foundation of communism and the socialist revolution in Russia.   *(170 words)*

Partner C: Valerie

I'm not too sure if the Russian Revolution brought freedom to the people, at least not in the long run, but it certainly changed the history of the world. I have been given a quote by Franklin D. Roosevelt, the famous American president. He once said that, quote, "in the truest sense, freedom cannot be bestowed, it must be achieved", unquote. You can see, Katrin, that Roosevelt and Shaw have something in common. They both claim that freedom is a result of human effort. You must do something to achieve it and do something to keep it.   *(97 words)*

Discussion

BERNHARD: And one of those efforts is to educate yourself, to get a good schooling in order to understand what is going on – and what needs to be done to gain or defend your freedom. You need to stay in touch with current developments, realize when things are going wrong and act accordingly. Only then can you take on true responsibility.

But we all know that getting an education isn't only fun: sometimes it is boring, or hard work.

KATRIN: But according to Epictetus, being educated is the only way to be free. Free of ignorance and prejudices.

VALERIE: Perhaps we should now look at how people have gained their freedom throughout history and some examples of what people did in the past to achieve this.

BERNHARD: Right. Now, why don't we talk about the American Revolution, or The War of Independence, as it is called? I mean, Independence Day is one of the most popular and spectacular holidays, and not only in America.

VALERIE: That's true. Just think of the movie "Independence Day", where you had the world unite against a hostile alien race that wanted to wipe humanity off the planet.

KATRIN: Oh yes, and guess who led the fight against the extraterrestrials? It was the American President himself. And it was American scientists who found out how to defeat the aliens. A world fighting for its freedom, united under American leadership on Independence Day.

BERNHARD: Ok, it was somewhat patriotic, and perhaps a bit over the top. Directed by a German, funnily enough. But millions of people all over the world liked the film, and so did I. It showed that with intelligence, coordination and the will to succeed you can even overcome a far superior enemy. So there we are: These are the core qualities of having a successful revolution, of how to change things for the better.

KATRIN: I agree. If we look back to the American Revolution, the "baddies" were the British who imposed unjustified taxation on the colonists, without allowing them to participate in the decision making process: "No taxation without representation." No wonder that after some time people started to think about running their colonies on their own.

VALERIE: Sure, who wants to be exploited? Everybody wants to reap the benefits of their labour, so the Americans gradually organized themselves and started to fight against British suppression. First there were protests and petitions. Then, when that didn't have any effect, there were spectacular events such as the Boston Tea Party, but finally, as the British still wouldn't see sense but sent in their army, the whole thing resulted in military action. We all know how it ended. With the birth of the United States of America.

BERNHARD: And the birth of the American Constitution, a document many people see as the first proper blueprint of a democratic society. Where everybody has the same rights, the right to fulfil his potential. The "pursuit of happiness". So, in a way, the American constitution laid the political foundation for the American Dream. And if you look back to Europe at that time, that really is a great achievement.

KATRIN: Absolutely. People in Europe were ruled by absolutist monarchs and societies were structured hierarchically. With a privileged ruling class, and people at the bottom who were little more than slaves.

VALERIE: But there was a big shake up, just about 10 years after the Americans had gained their independence: The French Revolution. The king himself and many other members of the ruling classes were executed. Well, it was a rather bloody business, with a lot of political chaos in its aftermath, but the French Revolution is still celebrated as one of the most decisive moments in European history.

KATRIN: So what have we learned so far? That successful revolutions, actions that set people free, are always part of a violent struggle, with people either being shot or hacked to pieces. I suppose we should also consider more peaceful examples. For instance Mahatma Gandhi or Martin Luther King.

BERNHARD: Or the German Revolution; I mean our reunification twenty years ago. Perhaps those three have something in common.

VALERIE: They do. First, there were people who could think independently. Take Martin Luther King. He, among others, did not accept the widespread belief that black people were inferior by nature, that segregation was right and that therefore "black people should know their place". So again, the process of achieving liberation starts in your mind. It starts with making use of your education, with generating good ideas, which, at the end of the day, are so convincing that many people join your cause.

KATRIN: Spot on, Valerie. The same was true for Mahatma Gandhi. He was a lawyer, so he also fought the British Empire on legal grounds. He said that according to their own legislation, the British were not supposed to exploit and discriminate against the people of India. And he used the press. Whenever the British arrested him or beat up his followers, he made sure that the press was there. And so people all around the world knew what was going on and sympathized with him. This put the British under enormous pressure. The same was true for Martin Luther King. His media presence, like his famous speech "I have a dream", made him world famous. Suddenly millions of people, also white people, were on his side and supported the Civil Rights Movement. In the end, the American government had to give in to many of his demands. To conclude we can say that media presence is vitally important if you want to achieve, or defend, your freedom.

BERNHARD: And how do you get the media's attention? By spectacular actions. Take Gandhi's "Salt March", on which he and thousands of his followers went to the sea and made salt, which Indians were forbidden to do because the British had the monopoly on making salt. So he publically broke the law, in front of the police, and in front of the cameras of the world's press. This made him world famous, and as he didn't use any violence, people sympathized with his cause.

VALERIE: Yes, these symbolic actions combined with media presence are a very efficient instrument. The "Boston Tea Party" I mentioned earlier is another example. But you also need to make sure that you have enough followers in the first place. The bigger a demonstration, the more attention you get from the media, and the more difficult it is for the government to control or subdue it. You can hardly arrest 100,000 people who have taken to the streets.

KATRIN: True, if you have sufficient numbers, people can neither ignore nor put you down so easily. When my dad told me about the big demonstrations in Leipzig, you know, the "Montagsdemonstrationen" (the Monday Demonstrations) in 1989, he said that first, many people were scared of the police, but then so many demonstrators came together that the police didn't dare to intervene. So that was a great victory for freedom, and at the end, the whole movement against the SED regime had gained so much momentum that the ruling class had to give up the fight and step down.

VALERIE: Without a single shot being fired. But remember, it all started on a rather small scale. With people congregating in churches, small groups which created a network of resistance over the years, and which came up with ideas and slogans. And then these ideas caught on and attracted more and more people.

BERNHARD: Yes, people realized that it was up to them if they wanted things to change. They informed themselves, for instance they watched West German TV, which would give them a different side of the story, as opposed to the one told by the state controlled media in the GDR. So again, education has always played an important role.

KATRIN: And it still does. I think we should now discuss how we, as citizens, can take on our responsibility and maintain our freedom. As we said before, education is vitally important. If you keep yourself informed, if the school system allows for a good education, then you realize what is going wrong.

BERNHARD: So what is going wrong?

KATRIN: Take the internet. It gives companies, as well as the state or organized crime the possibility to control every one of us. Take Google, for instance, do we really know what they are up to? They are collecting data about people worldwide; it looks as if they can find out almost everything. Like Orwell's "Big Brother is watching you". It sends shivers down my spine. And I feel that all of this is going completely unchecked, so it's high time we do something about it. Like petitioning our parliament, or making other people aware of this problem, joining an action group, or voting for a party that acknowledges the problem ...

VALERIE: Act responsibly, that's what you mean, I suppose. And you are right, but it's not quite as easy as it seems. There are so many problems, and so many things you could do, theoretically. But then there is so little time. There's school, or a job, friends and lots of other things going on.

BERNHARD: True, but all the same. If you don't act, you silently accept things as they are, and one day you might find yourself in deep trouble. I mean you don't need to be a revolutionary like Gandhi, or a great campaigner like Martin Luther King. But you should be able and willing to tell right from wrong and then show enough commitment to defend your rights.

VALERIE: Bernhard, I think you have just touched on a very important point. You should know your rights, and you should appreciate how good it is to be free, to live in a free democratic society like we do here in Germany. If you see these Neo-Nazis, then you are reminded of what it was like in the Third Reich, of how people were treated, of what the Germans did to the Jews and to millions of other innocent people.

KATRIN: And how they lost the war, how they were smashed by the Allies, representing the free world, who would not accept the rule of fascism. And who were willing to pay a high price for the defence of freedom.

VALERIE: So history must play an important role in people's education and upbringing, because it shows how valuable our democratic society is. And that you don't get away with murder.

BERNHARD: And people must learn that there are many forms of resistance that can bring results. You don't need to take up arms to make yourself heard. Legal action, demonstrations, petitions, industrial action and so on are ways of voicing your opinion in a democratic society which have been quite effective. People should know about these possibilities, and be prepared to act accordingly.

KATRIN: Then it will help to get information on where you can turn, which groups you could join. For instance, a political party, or an environmental group, like Greenpeace, a trade union or a human rights organization such as Amnesty International.

VALERIE: Yes, then you are part of a network, and I think it helps enormously if you know that you aren't standing alone, that there are many people out there who share your ideas; and once you are part of a larger group, you can achieve a lot.

KATRIN: And don't forget that it's not only politics that count. Maintaining your freedom starts with your family and friends. You should stand up for your rights in your family also; for example, parents should listen to their children, and people should resist peer group pressure when it comes to doing silly things, well, at least things you don't want to do.

BERNHARD: Right, and at school, students should intervene when people are being harassed, either by teachers or other students. Don't sit and watch. Do something. *(1996 words)*

Teil A: Text 1

Change drink habits? You're joking

Sisyphus (and this is true) was sentenced by the gods to roll a huge rock up a steep hill for eternity. Each time he would bring the boulder just about to the summit, and then something would cause the blasted stone to roll right down to the bottom again. The ancient Sisyphus was punished for his cleverness, but we modern Sisypheans are condemned by
5 our stupidity to have the same debate about how to alter the behaviour of our fellows, over and over and over again.

The issue might be a health scare, an environmental scare, a crime scare or a combination of all of these. Whatever – the inevitable rubric is as follows.

One: dreadful case or cases, headlines, news stories, moral panic, bishops (optional), MPs,
10 voluntary organisations, something must be done.

Two: government consultation, strong words, determination, much already done – much remaining to be done.

Three: proposals involving tougher sentencing, banning of something in public, strengthening police powers.

15 Four: proposals involving education, a publicity campaign, special lessons in schools.

Five: vested interests (brewers, head teachers, lawyers) on why measures are impractical or reek of the nanny state; opposition on why measures are impractical and don't go far enough.

Six: Institute of Ideas or similar contrarians on why murder or smoking […] were never a
20 problem in the first place.

Seven: fail to evaluate last set of measures, begin again with something else.

Yesterday it was, once more, drink. Or, rather, kids and drink, which is a quadrupled panic. This concern arises partly out of the endless recent publicity about binge drinking and antisocial behaviour, and partly because of worries about the health of individuals. Kids
25 being involved meant that the main minister in the frame was Ed Balls, the Children's Secretary. So we got ideas for extending ASBOs to persistent public drinkers, greater police powers to disperse youthful drinkers, a two-strikes policy for retailers flogging booze to the unbearded and – on the soft side – an education campaign for parents on what drink advice to give to their progeny (other than "drunk for a penny, dead drunk for twopence").
30 And we had the Shadow Secretary, Michael Gove, on how this was no good, though no one quite got round to asking him why. Expect the Institute of Ideas (actually alcohol liberates young minds) later in the week.

But in the midst of this hyperactivity Mr Balls said this: "We need a culture change about drinking, with everyone from parents, the alcohol industry and young people all taking
35 more responsibility." In other words the measures were of little use without the culture change. People who currently think that getting blasted, wasted, rat-arsed, hammered, legless, mellow, jolly or wrecked is a good thing need to begin to believe that it is a very bad thing. Radio presenters need to stop joking with victorious sportsmen that there'll be "sore heads" in the morning. Sometimes, in social situations, I am astonished at just how much

40 glug otherwise sensible folk can get down their necks in an evening. So cultural change is
right. Without it, everything is just more laws.

[…] But what can governments do about the anti-learning culture in our schools and on
our screens, where "swots" are to be pitied and the playing of football is the sole reliable
virtue? It's in the culture. Like racism or smoking, it takes decades to shift. It isn't Balls;
45 it's us.   *(571 words)*

Aaronovitch, David: Change drink habits? You're joking. The Times, 3 June 2008.
http://www.timesonline.co.uk/tol/comment/columnists/david_aaronovitch/article
4053603.ece [downloaded /1 December 2008]

Text 2

Report condemns government response to alcoholism and binge drinking

Government responses to Britain's "shocking" rise in binge drinking and alcoholism have
ranged from "the non-existent to the ineffectual", the health select committee warns today.

Supermarkets and the drinks industry have more influence on government alcohol policies
than health experts, the scornful report by MPs says.

50 Minimum prices, combined with restrictions on advertising and sponsorship, could save
thousands of lives and billions of pounds a year.

The publication of the long-awaited report has triggered a fresh broadside of condemnation from health professionals frustrated by the failure of the government's strategy to
tackle the escalating problems of drink-related violence and deaths.

55 The call for minimum pricing – already endorsed by England's chief medical officer, Sir
Liam Donaldson, and backed by the Scottish government – does not receive the support of
the three Conservative MPs on the health committee.

But the whole committee calls for a sharp rise in taxes on spirits and "industrial white ci-
der", improved treatment services for alcoholics, a mandatory labelling scheme for drinks,
60 and tougher regulation of alcohol promotion and advertising.

On minimum pricing, it says that a lower limit of 40 p per unit of alcohol would cost a
moderate drinker only 11 p more a week and could save 1,100 lives a year. If the level
were set at 50 p a unit, it would save 3,000 people from liver disease and other fatal conditions.

65 Price controls would curb self-harm among young binge-drinkers and poorer, high-volume
consumers, the report suggests, and they would encourage a switch-over to weaker wines
and beers. […]

English drinking habits have been transformed over the past 60 years, it warns. Average
consumption has risen from an annual 3.5 litres of pure alcohol per head in 1947 to 9.5
70 now. "The alcohol problem in this country reflects a failure of will and competence on the
part of government department and quangos," says the report. […]   *(315 words)*

Bowcott, Owen: Report condemns government response to alcoholism and binge drinking.
The Guardian, Friday 8 January 2010.
http://www.guardian.co.uk/society/2010/jan/08/binge-drinking-alcoholism-report/print
[downloaded /11 February 2010]

(total number of words: 886)

Annotations:

l. 19   Institute of Ideas: non-governmental organisation dedicated to expanding the boundaries of public debate

l. 26   ASBO: Anti-Social Behaviour Order (a civil order made against a person who has been shown to have engaged in anti-social behaviour)

A Text production

A1 Working with the text 25 BE

Analyse and compare how both texts serve their purposes.

Write a coherent text.

A2 Composition 25 BE

Choose <u>one</u> of the following tasks.

2.1 In his article, David Aaronovitch talks of an "anti-learning culture in our schools and on our screens, where 'swots' are to be pitied and the playing of football is the sole reliable virtue" (ll. 42–44).

Write a letter to the editor of *The Times* commenting on this assertion.

2.2 Discuss this modern Sisyphus image focusing on at least one of the issues shown on the boulder.

"Someday, son, this will all be yours."

global warming, debts, conflicts, waste disposal, overpopulation, unemployment

2.3 Choose a work of literature from an English-speaking country. Comment on the way its character or characters have responded to challenges.

Erreichbare BE-Anzahl Teil A (Summe A1 und A2):
Inhaltliche Reichhaltigkeit und Textstruktur: 20 BE
Sprachliche Korrektheit: 20 BE
Ausdrucksvermögen und Textfluss: 10 BE
Gesamt: 50 BE

Teil B: Translation/Mediation

Choose <u>one</u> of the following tasks (B1 <u>or</u> B2),

B1 Translation

Penalising Teenage Boozing

Parents who give their children alcohol risk being hit with court orders under a new government clampdown on teenagers drinking in public.

The move follows research showing more than half of underage drinkers get their supplies from home, while 11- to 14-year-olds, who are unlikely to be served in pubs or shops, are
5 now drinking double the number of units they did in 1990.

Parents of persistent offenders will face interventions from courts and social workers to improve their parenting skills, while police powers to disperse groups of teenagers in public parks and on street corners will be extended to children as young as 10.

Although fewer children drink than in the 1980s, those that do appear to be starting
10 younger and drinking harder. [...]

Children falling foul of a new offence of persistently possessing alcohol in public will have to sign behaviour contracts spelling out alcohol's health effects and the intimidatory impact of their activities on others. *(159 words)*

Hinsliff, Gaby: Parents to face court over young drinkers. The Observer, 1 June 2008.
http://www.guardian.co.uk/society/2008/jun/01/drugsandalcohol.health/print
[downloaded /1 December 2008] 20 BE

B2 Mediation

You have been invited to take part in a youth conference on values in society organized by the European Commission in Brussels.

In preparation for a discussion with other participants write a summary in English of what the following text says about children's values.

Erster Kinder-Werte-Monitor des Kindermagazins GEOlino in Zusammenarbeit mit UNICEF

Im Auftrag von GEOlino und in Zusammenarbeit mit UNICEF hat das Marktforschungs-institut Synovate Kids+Teens im Juni und Juli 2006 insgesamt 908 Kinder im Alter von 6 bis 14 Jahren aus ganz Deutschland in persönlichen Interviews zu ihren Wertvorstellungen befragt.

5 Danach verfügt die Altersgruppe der 6- bis 14-Jährigen über einen ausgeprägten Gerechtigkeitssinn und eine große Hilfsbereitschaft. Diese „idealistische" Orientierung steht aber nicht im Widerspruch zu einer insgesamt pragmatischen Grundeinstellung. So hat für die heutigen Kinder – anders als noch in den 1980er Jahren – Leistungsbereitschaft eine genauso hohe Bedeutung wie Gerechtigkeit oder Hilfsbereitschaft sie haben.

10 Für alle befragten Kinder haben die Kinderrechte einen hohen Stellenwert. Am wichtigsten ist ihnen das Recht, ohne Gewalt aufwachsen zu dürfen. Zum einen wollen sie selbst vor Gewalt geschützt sein, zum anderen ist es ihnen besonders wichtig, dass Kinder in Kriegs- und Krisengebieten Schutz und Hilfe finden.

Die meisten Kinder haben heute offenbar gute und vertrauensvolle Beziehungen zum
15 Elternhaus. So nennen sie als wichtigste Vermittlungsinstanzen und Vorbilder für ihre Werte Eltern und Großeltern. Im Teenageralter gewinnen Freunde und die Zugehörigkeit zu sozialen Gruppen bei der Wahl von Vorbildern an Bedeutung. Berühmte Personen, die Medien und die Kirchen spielen bei den 6- bis 14-Jährigen bei der Wertevermittlung eine untergeordnete Rolle. Am wenigsten bringen die deutschen Kinder Politiker mit der Ver-
20 mittlung von Werten in Verbindung.

„Kinder entwickeln schon früh ein Bewusstsein für Gerechtigkeit und die Bereitschaft, sich für andere einzusetzen. Wir wollen ihnen die Erfahrung vermitteln, dass es sich lohnt, danach zu handeln – in der Familie, in der Schule, im Verein und auch in der Politik", sagte Entwicklungsministerin Heidemarie Wieczorek-Zeul bei der Vorstellung der Studie
25 in Berlin.

„Wer Kinder stärken will, muss ihre Familien stärken und ihnen gute Lern- und Bildungsmöglichkeiten verschaffen. Deshalb ist es so schlimm, dass in Deutschland die soziale Herkunft mehr als in den meisten anderen Industrieländern über den Schulerfolg von Kindern entscheidet", sagte Dietrich Garlichs, Geschäftsführer von UNICEF.

30 „Die heutigen Kinder haben Zugang zu mehr Informationen und wissen mehr über ihre Rechte als frühere Generationen. Sie wollen ernst genommen und nicht nur als Konsumenten betrachtet werden", sagte Gerd Brüne, Verlagsleiter der GEO-Gruppe, in deren Auftrag die Umfrage im Sommer 2006 durchgeführt wurde.

Bereitschaft zu sozialem Engagement

35 Entgegen der verbreiteten Einschätzung, dass Heranwachsende heute eher auf sich bezogen sind, zeigt die Umfrage, dass die meisten deutschen Kinder gerne bereit sind, sich für Menschen oder Werte einzusetzen. Am stärksten ist die Einsatzbereitschaft ausgeprägt, wenn es darum geht, Freunden zu helfen. Großes Interesse besteht aber auch am Engagement für Tiere, Vereine sowie ärmere oder hilfebedürftige Menschen – am geringsten ist
40 bei den 6- bis 14-Jährigen das Interesse am Umweltschutz. Der Schwerpunkt des Engagements liegt dabei im Lebensumfeld der Heranwachsenden. Klassische Organisationen wie Parteien, Gewerkschaften oder Bürgerinitiativen spielen nur eine untergeordnete Rolle.

Nach der Umfrage haben die meisten Kinder ein gutes und komplexes Verständnis von Werten:

45 **Mut haben**
Hierunter verstehen die Kinder in erster Linie, „sich etwas zutrauen", „Ängste zu überwinden" – und zwar auch stark zugunsten anderer, um zum Beispiel Schwächeren zu helfen oder Gerechtigkeit herzustellen:
„Wenn jemand geschlagen wird, laut zu sagen: ‚Lass das sein!' " (Junge, 6 Jahre)

50 **Verantwortung**
Diesen Wert bringen die Kinder vorrangig mit „sich um Andere, um Schwächere kümmern" in Verbindung. Dies betrifft vor allem ihr Nahumfeld in der Familie oder andere Kinder – und auch Haustiere. Die Kinder erkennen klar, dass es hilfsbedürftige Menschen gibt, um die man sich kümmern muss:
55 „Dass Eltern sich um Kinder kümmern müssen, dass man andere Leute nicht ausschließt, dass man Menschen, die auf der Straße liegen, hilft." (Mädchen, 9 Jahre)

Toleranz
beziehen die Kinder vor allem auf das Akzeptieren anderer Meinungen:
„Meine Freundin ist peinlich. Sie hört Tokio Hotel. Sie ist aber dennoch meine Freundin.
60 Das ist tolerant." (Junge, 11 Jahre)

Am zweithäufigsten verstehen die Kinder unter Toleranz die Achtung gegenüber anderen Nationen.
„Alle Menschen sind gleich." (Junge, 7 Jahre)   *(638 words)*

UNICEF (Hrsg.): Familie und Freundschaft sind wichtiger als Geld: Erster Kinder-
Werte-Monitor des Kindermagazins GEOlino in Zusammenarbeit mit UNICEF.
UNICEF Presse, 24. 10. 2006. http://www.unicef.de/3990.html
[downloaded /17 September 2008]   20 BE

A Text production

A1 Working with the text

The key points are:
- *both texts are articles published in British quality papers*
- *different ways of dealing with the topic and influencing the reader (informative, critical, provoking, entertaining)*
- *tone (e. g. factual, witty, humorous, ironic), stylistic devices (e. g. accumulation, ellipsis, alliteration, personal pronouns), vocabulary/register (formal/informal)*

Both texts were published in British quality papers and highlight the problems surrounding the consumption of alcohol by young people in Britain today. However, whereas David Aaronovitch offers a pointed and at the same time entertaining and humorous critique of the government's policies, calling for change and a different approach towards the problem, the text by Owen Bowcott appears to be primarily factual, aiming at merely informing the reader.

Already in the headline to his article, Aaronovitch shows his scepticism as regards the government's aim to change young people's drinking habits by putting forward a rhetorical question and then answering it in the negative, using a fairly colloquial and even disrespectful phrase ("You're joking").

The failure of society to act against alcoholism is further illustrated by the author telling the story of Sisyphus in a rather colloquial way, thereby adding colour and a humorous effect to his argument ("the blasted stone", l. 3) Here, Aaronovitch illustrates mankind's dilemma, the fact that throughout modern history ("over and over and over again", ll. 5/6), man has been trying hard to alter his behaviour, but to no avail. The phrase "condemned by our stupidity" (ll. 4/5) confronts the reader directly and is aimed at arousing his curiosity to find out whether the following text can offer a solution.

In the following part, the author presents seven areas of failure when it comes to tackling larger issues such as health and environmental problems. The number "seven" could be an allusion to the biblical "seven deadly sins". The telegram style (ellipsis) used throughout this part, which beforehand is rather mockingly described as "the inevitable rubric" (l. 8), adds to the ironic and even sarcastic tone ("banning of something", l. 13) and highlights the author's criticism of efforts to change human nature, which he describes as mere activism ("hyperactivity", l. 33). This pointlessness connects to the Sisyphus story: Having (once again) failed to solve one problem, society starts to "[…] begin again with something else" (l. 21), using the same strategies that failed before.

The tone becomes almost derisive in the following paragraph. The expression "once more" (l. 22) shows that the problem has been tackled many times before, unsuccessfully, and employing hyperbole ("quadrupled panic", l. 22), Aaronovitch sets the ground for more criticism. At the same time, by referring to different politicians and institutions, as well as to the current debate on the topic, Aaronovitch adds some seriousness to his argument, making his text even more compelling as he combines the factual with spicy criticism.

The extensive use of alliteration and contrast when referring to public policies adds to the entertaining value of the text: The expressions "persistent public drinkers" (l. 26), "greater police powers" (ll. 26/27) and the term "progeny" (l. 29) first create a pompous atmosphere of self-importance on the side of the government, which is then contrasted with either humorous phrases such as "flogging booze to the unbearded" (ll. 27/28) or informal, even slightly disrespectful utterances such as "no one got quite round to asking him why" (ll. 30/31).

However, in the next paragraph, Aaronovitch becomes more serious when he suggests a more realistic solution to the problem by quoting the Children's Secretary (whom he had ridiculed before for his "hyperactivity"). After all, he partly agrees with Mr Balls' suggestion. To connect with his humorous approach in general, and to make the minister's ideas even more explicit, Aaronovitch translates Balls' speech into informal language by using an extended enumeration of colloquial terms for being drunk ("getting blasted" etc., ll. 36/37). Especially the contrastive terms ("good thing" – "bad thing", ll. 37/38) make it clear that that only a culture change at large can bring about a change of people's attitudes and drinking habits.

In the concluding sentence Aaronovitch appeals to the reader to think in new, respectively in the author's terms, almost literarily going out with a bang by speaking to "us" directly and by using a rather saucy, sexually charged pun: "It isn't Balls; it's us." (ll. 44/45).

In contrast to Aaronovitch's text, Owen Bowcott writes in a far more neutral, matter-of-fact style, keeping to the formal language a reader would expect from a report in a quality paper.

This is already reflected in the headline, where Bowcott just summarises the view of the health select committee, whereas Aaronovitch starts with a provocation.

Throughout the article Bowcott tries to convey the seriousness and objectivity of his writing by extensively quoting different sources, showing that he is at pains to give a comprehensive and reliable account of the debate.

However, like Aaronovitch, Bowcott's article is also a harsh critique of the government's apparently fruitless attempts to curb alcoholism and binge drinking. The excerpt of the article ends on very critical note, as the expression "failure of will and competence" (l. 70) suggests.

Furthermore, negatively connoted expressions such as "condemn" (headline) and "scornful" (l. 49) are noticeable. Especially the phrase "has triggered a fresh broadside of condemnation" (ll. 52/53), a drastic, violent metaphor using (or alluding to) military ("broadside") as well as religious and legal terminology ("condemnation"), evokes an image of the health experts acting as a firing squad executing the government.

The deliberate use of such emotionally laden language, together with the fact that throughout the article the government is not given any space to respond to the criticism of the health select committee, clearly shows which side Bowcott is on.

In conclusion, when comparing the two articles, it can be stated that both authors heavily criticise the government, albeit with different means. Aaronovitch takes sides rather openly by using humour, irony, sarcasm and colourful, even playful language to influence the reader, which makes his text both entertaining and informative. Bowcott, however, resorts to the form of the (seemingly) neutral report, using formal language to give his article a more serious and factual tone in order to convince readers of his opinion.

(997 words)

A2 Composition

Sir,

I am writing to you in response to the article by David Aaronovitch which, by and large, I consider an entertaining, witty and clear-cut analysis of the fruitless endeavours by the British government to tackle the problem of alcoholism.

However, I do not agree with Mr. Aaronovitch's statement on our learning culture, which he describes as being virtually non-existent. In fact, I feel greatly distressed by the way he depicts young people's attitudes as being hostile to any form of formal education, an attitude he describes as "the anti-learning culture at our schools".

According to Mr. Aaronovitch, all youngsters (or at least the boys?) seem to be dreaming of a career as a football-pro, with the "swots" (I would call them "serious, responsible, rationally-minded and hard-working people") being regarded as outsiders, either vicitimised or pitied, as if they were doing the wrong thing.

Does Mr Aaronowitch really assume that the values and virtues of our generation only center around drinking, having fun and dreaming of football stardom without willing to work hard for it? Are we just a bunch of mindless (drinking) football supporters?

As far as I am concerned, the majority of us students are highly motivated. They know that good grades do matter and they feel good about obtaining them. Our self-esteem is not based on how much we can drink, but on how successful and creative we are.

And what about our schools? Are they really just a refuge for the lazy and unmotivated?

Mr Aaronovitch might have in mind some derelict inner city schools, where disadvantaged children find it indeed hard to accomplish their education, with distressed teachers, social workers and parents helplessly standing by. Of course, there are problem schools with problem children. But these are the exceptions, not the rule. In fact, most schools, at least in my country, and I am sure that applies to yours as well, are trying hard to fulfill their teaching targets and provide a good education.

And as regards distressed schools, there is an overall willingness in our society to alleviate the situation. Take the notorious Rütli-School in Berlin, which once was portrayed as being the worst school in the whole of Germany. In almost no time it was transformed into a well-run school with a positive learning culture. So people do care about education.

Another favourite commonplace the adult world in general seems to relish, and Mr Aaronovitch fell victim to as well, is the worn-out cliché of young people's addiction to the media, of young people being glued to the box, watching idiotic programmes all around the clock, playing violent and mindless computer games, or chatting on the net for hours on end. As much as this might apply to some youngsters, it is definitely not true for the majority of my generation. Perhaps the obsession with this topic is fostered by the high attention troubled teens receive in the media?

Be that as it may, I should think people ought to be more relaxed about our generation and our values, as I firmly believe that most youngsters know how to handle television, computer games and the Internet without being caught up in the sort of "anti-learning culture" Mr Aaronovitch describes in his otherwise brilliant article.

Yours truly,
Jan (18), Leipzig (Germany)   *(547 words)*

2.2　*The key points are:*
  – *reference to the situation depicted in the picture*
  – *tackling at least one of the topics mentioned (e. g. global warming, overpopulation)*
  – *pros and cons as regards the message of the picture ("discuss")*

Modern Sisyphus

The given picture depicts the dilemma of modern man, symbolized by a man rolling up a giant rock representing the problems of human society, such as global warming, conflicts, overpopulation and others. There is an obvious allusion to the Sisyphus story and consequently, we can assume that the rock will, at one point or the other, roll down again, with the next generation having to roll it up again as indicated by the words "Someday, son, this will all be yours."

In general, the given image illustrates the assumption that however hard we try to solve the most pressing problems we are faced with, we are bound to fail, as the Sisyphus stone will inevitably roll down again and we will have to start all over again. So, like Sisyphus, we can never accomplish our goals.

The question is, though, whether the myth of Sisyphus can really serve as an appropriate depiction of the human condition.

At first sight, there seems to be an overwhelming amount of facts to support this. Just by looking at our history, we are indeed faced with an endless amount of strife. In fact, human history could be described as an endless and perhaps never-ending story of wars and conflicts. In "the good old days" wars were generally approved of as being a rightful means to increase one's own cultural, religious and economic influence. Just take the endless wars for hegemony between the European powers, or the colonization of Africa involving the displacement of millions of Africans in the cause of slavery.

However, amidst all the suffering and wrongdoings, humanity as such did try to improve the situation. The enslavement of the African people finally came to an end, and the fact that America now has an African American president can be seen as proof that conflicts can be brought to a positive ending.

On the other hand, slavery as such has not been wiped off our planet. It still exists (unofficially) in many parts of our world, in form of child labour or, predominantly in Africa, in terms of thousands of child soldiers being brutalized and exploited every day. In this respect, the stone has rolled downhill again, with humanitarian organizations trying – rather helplessly – to alleviate the situation.

Another example of both improvement and relapse into conflict can be noticed when looking at international postwar history. The setting up of the United Nations and the widely held view (quite contrary to the aforementioned periods) that you must not make war with other nations has limited the number of conflicts between states considerably, and that alone can be described as a success story. The fact that the Cold War did not develop into a "hot war" and the formation of the European Union could indeed give hope that man is reasonable enough to resolve conflicts without resorting to violence.

However, those historians who were quick to usher in a period of worldwide peace after the iron curtain had come down have been proven wrong. There are still numerous conflicts worldwide, such as civil wars and ethnic cleansing; there still is the looming threat of international terrorism; and in general, people still seem to be ready to take up arms (with the arms industries making more profit than ever before) to solve their problems. In this respect we are just trying to roll up the stone once again.

The same is true for conflicts on a more personal level. At least in the western world, women have achieved a lot during the last decades, such as voting rights, the right to work in almost any job they choose and equal access to education. Nevertheless, there is still discrimination in the work place, e.g. in terms of unequal pay, and a lot of women are still subject to domestic violence. So amidst all the progress, the stone is still not up the hill. Yet, looking back at human history, it has not rolled back either, as the situation has definitely improved.

In conclusion, it can be said that, in spite of many setbacks and new starts, the Sisyphus image does only partly apply to human existence, since there has been considerable progress in many areas, slowly but surely. The question is, will we ever reach the top? Is there a chance for the stone to stay up? I do not dare to answer this complex question, but as an optimist, I see the stone moving upwards. *(741 words)*

2.3 *The key points are:*
  - *One or more characters of a work of literature from an English-speaking country.*
  - *How do the main character (and other characters) respond to challenges?*
  - *What are their aims and ambitions?*
  - *Reasons for the characters' success as well as failure.*
  - *You can use a more neutral or a more personal style.*

One of the first great works of English literature that comes into my mind when talking about challenges is William Shakespeare's *Macbeth*. Although written more than 400 years ago, it still speaks to us through its dramatic intensity and deep insight into human nature and behaviour. To me, Macbeth is, in many ways, a typical representative of modern man. Modern man as he is trying to realize his ambitions and satisfy his needs, setting things in motion and unleashing powers he cannot control, and therefore dismally failing in the end.

In the beginning, Macbeth serves his country well and is rewarded by his king for his craftsmanship and bravery as a war leader. When the three witches foretell that one day he will be king of Scotland, he first reacts in a reasonable, almost rational way. He knows that, albeit being of noble birth, he is not of royal blood, so he cannot possibly become king. At this point Macbeth himself is contented with this situation, and in rational terms he should be, but his wife – a character that is both crafty, ruthless and (over)ambitious – finally talks him into grasping the opportunity of a life time: to kill the king in order to become King of Scotland himself.

Lady Macbeth describes the regicide as a true challenge, something an ambitious man must respond to positively by taking action. First, Macbeth opposes the plan arguing along moral lines. He refers to moral obligations such as hospitality, mutual trust, political and personal loyalty to the king, and the fact that Duncan has indeed been a very competent leader. At first, these obligations count more than his (or his wife's) individual ambitions. But when Lady Macbeth accuses him of not being a real man (also by questioning his sexual prowess), of being a weakling incapable of realizing his dreams, he finally gives in and accomplishes the deed.

His own ambitions have got the better of him and make him act against all reason and turn him into a traitor and murderer. As a consequence, throughout the play, Macbeth will be painfully aware of the fact that, although he has won the challenge of becoming king, he has lost his moral integrity.

Haunted by pangs of remorse, a childless marriage and a wife falling into madness, he finds himself isolated and threatened by real or imagined enemies. In fact, Macbeth is not able to reap the benefits of his crime as he has set off an avalanche of almost uncontrollable carnage: retaining his position as king is another challenge calling for even more blood.

Macbeth also fails to meet the challenge of being a worthy successor of the previous king. Instead of being a trustworthy guardian of his people, he develops into a ruthless tyrant whose country is going to rack and ruin, hit by natural disasters – in Shake-

speare's time believed to be the godly punishment for Macbeth's violation of the natural world order by seizing the throne.
The last challenge Macbeth fails to meet is facing reality and saving his own life by fleeing the country. So great is his hubris, that he now considers himself invincible. Ironically, the belief in his own strength is, once again, based on information from the witches, creatures from the underworld a clear-thinking man should not have trusted in the first place.
In summary, it could be said that Macbeth, as a true tragic hero, fails to meet the challenges of his life due to his tragic misjudgment when it comes to temper his ambitions, by trusting in the wrong people and finally by being unable to control the forces he has conjured up by his deeds. *(610 words)*

B Translation/Mediation

B1 Translation

Saufen von Teenagern unter Strafe gestellt

Infolge neuer, verschärfter Maßnahmen der Regierung gegen Heranwachsende, die in der Öffentlichkeit trinken, riskieren Eltern, die ihren Kindern Alkohol geben, gerichtlich belangt zu werden.

Diese Maßnahmen resultieren aus Forschungsergebnissen, die zeigen, dass mehr als die Hälfte aller minderjährigen Alkoholkonsumenten ihren Nachschub von Zuhause erhalten, und dass 11- bis 14-Jährige, die in Kneipen und Geschäften praktisch nicht bedient werden, mittlerweile die doppelte Anzahl von Einheiten konsumieren wie im Jahre 1990.

Eltern von Wiederholungstätern werden in Zukunft mit Interventionen durch Gerichte und Sozialarbeiter konfrontiert werden, die darauf abzielen, sie bei Erfüllung ihrer Elternpflichten zu stärken. Außerdem werden die Befugnisse der Polizei, Ansammlungen von Teenagern in öffentlichen Parks und an Straßenecken auflösen zu können, auf Kinder ab dem zehnten Lebensjahr[1] ausgedehnt werden.

Obwohl insgesamt[2] weniger Kinder trinken als in den 1980er-Jahren, scheinen die, die es tun, früher anzufangen und deutlich mehr zu trinken.

Kinder, die wiederholt[3] mit dem Gesetz, welches ihnen den Alkoholbesitz in der Öffentlichkeit untersagt, in Konflikt geraten, werden Verhaltensvereinbarungen unterzeichnen müssen, in denen sie deutlich dazu Stellung beziehen müssen, wie sehr Alkohol die Gesundheit beeinträchtigt und wie bedrohlich ihr Verhalten auf andere wirkt.

Anmerkungen
1 Auch: *bis auf Kinder im zarten Alter von zehn Jahren*
2 Stilistische Ergänzung
3 Auch: *erneut*

B2 Mediation

The key points are:
- *importance of the family*
- *values, e. g. social commitment, the will to work hard*
- *focus on children's rights*
- *importance of traditional political institutions*

In a survey, conducted and published by Unicef and the German youth magazine GEOlino in 2006, children and youngsters throughout Germany were asked about their personal and political values.

It showed that nowadays 6 to 14 year-olds seem to adhere to a complex value system including a sense of justice, the general readiness to help those in need and – in contrast to the 1980s – the willingness to work hard.

Today's German children seem to be firmly rooted within their families, with their parents and grandparents, rather than celebrities or politicians, acting as role models. Furthermore, they seem to show a great deal of social commitment regarding their immediate environment. However, they also show empathy towards disadvantaged people in general.

On a political level, they are committed to animal rights and are ready to play an active part in various associations, clubs and societies. However, they show less interest in joining classical political institutions or in environmental protection. All the same, they keep themselves better informed than previous generations and, knowing their rights as children, they want to be taken seriously, especially concerning the right to grow up in a non-violent environment.

Personal courage, especially when it comes to helping the weak and helpless, tolerance and respect for other individuals and nationalities are also considered vital values.

(216 words)

Prüfungsteilnehmer A

Topic: Speed of Life

You are working on a project about the pressure of fast-paced modern life and are preparing a presentation on ways of coping with stress.

Comment on the following photos.

© QI

© 2011, Sheri Christianson, AtlantaPhotos.com

Together with your partner decide on what causes stress.
Compile a list of strategies to cope with stress effectively.

Prüfungsteilnehmer B

Topic: Speed of Life

You are working on a project about the pressure of fast-paced modern life and are preparing a presentation on ways of coping with stress.

Comment on the following photos.

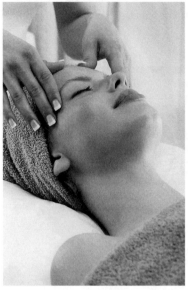

© Ljupco Smokovski | Dreamstime.com

© Jacob Wackerhausen / iStockphoto.com

Together with your partner decide on what causes stress.
Compile a list of strategies to cope with stress effectively.

<h1 style="text-align:center">Lösungsvorschläge</h1>

Partner A: Pauline

Jonas and I are asked to discuss a project about the pressure of fast-paced modern life and prepare a presentation on ways of coping with stress effectively.

In order to do this, we would have to find out about the various factors causing stress.

Now, I have been given two pictures, one of them is a photo showing a big motorway crossing with several lanes and exits, and full of cars. This photo could stand for modern man's dependency on cars, epitomising the speed of modern life. As many people have to commute to their workplaces, they spend a lot of time in their cars, and of course, they try and travel as fast as possible because commuting takes away so much of their valuable time. They have to live fast, "living in the fast lane", metaphorically speaking, with all the stress that goes with it.

The second picture is collage showing a big clock and a man, probably an office worker, carrying two piles of folders in his arms and, like a pirate just about to board an enemy ship, he has a pen stuck in his mouth. The clock tells him that he is late (twelve o'clock as the proverbial deadline is just past) and consequently, he looks stressed.

To me, he symbolises modern man who is under a lot of pressure because he cannot keep up with the pace of work. All in all, the picture could allude to the fact that in many ways people have become alienated from their work and have become part of a giant machine they can neither control nor slow down.

Talking about speed, the photos are connected in that they both show how people are being exposed to the speed of life, that is, to the fast-paced rhythm of work and travel we have to succumb to. This puts a lot of stress on all of us – a process that is life-threatening. So people need to find a strategy to slow down and reduce the speed of life. Although the man looks fairly young, I guess he might end up with some heart disease or burn-out syndrome sooner or later.

(360 words)

Partner B: Jonas

I have also been given two pictures, and in fact, they do stand in contrast to yours. The first one shows a woman who has her temples massaged, nice and gently as it seems. It looks as if she is enjoying it a great deal, as her eyes are closed and her overall facial expression shows that she is very relaxed. Since her head and body are wrapped up in towels, you could conclude that she has been to the sauna before or enjoyed some other kind of spa treatment. Keeping body and soul together, just let go, or just treat yourself are mottos represented in the picture.

The second photo shows a woman walking her dog in a park. You can guess that she has to do this regularly, I suppose at least twice a day. So this picture represents an active way of life, but a life that connects you to an animal, and nature in general. This woman does not walk her dog in the noisy streets but in the quietness of a park. I think animals, especially dogs or cats, can have a very soothing and relaxing effect on people, helping them to calm down and unwind after a stressful day at work.

So my pictures somehow present antidotes to the stress experienced in your pictures, Pauline. They suggest relaxation, being close to nature, taking care of an animal as well as physical exercise as strategies to cope with stress.

(244 words)

Discussion

PAULINE: I see. Well, I think that animals, or pets, do in fact play a very important role when it comes to handling stress. You see, a dog for instance is always in a good mood, or have you ever seen a depressed dog? So in the morning, before you set off to work, you experience a great deal of friendliness, the dog wagging its tail joyfully, looking forward to be taken out for a stroll.

JONAS: Yeah, I get your point, Pauline. But doesn't that obligation cause stress as well? You know, having to walk the dog every day, first thing in the morning, last thing in the evening, even when it rains, or hails, or snows, or when it's dead cold outside. Whatever the weather, however tired you are, you have to do it.

PAULINE: Sure, you should think twice before buying a dog. You need to be prepared to make some sacrifices. And you need to live in the right surroundings. But believe me, taking care of living creature is ever so rewarding, it does alleviate stress. It will also automatically give you discipline and thereby help you to structure your life more effectively, which in many ways can help to reduce stress as well. In fact, my granddad always says that if it hadn't been for the dog, he would never have taken so many walks outside, and consequently he would never be as fit as he is now. He says that walking the dog and playing with it is so relaxing, and it helps you to get focussed, to reflect on your problems in peace and quiet.

JONAS: I see, it can help to unwind after a stressful day at work. So what else is causing stress, and what could be done about it? What about the millions of commuters, who spend so much of their valuable time on the road? They must be absolutely shattered when they come home. And then they have to take care of their kids, or do the odd household chores. No wonder they can't relax properly. Perhaps they should be thinking of moving closer to their workplace. But I suppose many people have realised that, and instead of settling down in the suburbs, as it used to be the fashion for many decades, many people nowadays find it more attractive to move back and live in inner city areas.

PAULINE: That does make sense. Just think of the time you can save; especially when you have children. Then you need a good infrastructure, including schools, kindergarten, sport facilities etc. Otherwise you end up as your kids' chauffeur, which will make your life really hectic and frustrating because you won't have enough time for yourself.

JONAS: Absolutely, and it's stressful for the kids as well. So finding a place to live not too far away from your workplace is very important. Well, it's the basis of a good life without too much stress, isn't it?

PAULINE: Quite so. And you should also try and live in a reasonably safe and quiet neighbourhood, preferably with friendly people as neighbours, and with enough space in the house so that everyone has the possibility to retire if he or she wants a quiet time.

JONAS: I can't agree more. Permanent conflicts with your neighbours, domestic strife in general, or a constant flow of traffic going past your house are the major sources of stress. As the British say: "My home is my castle". It's your final retreat and the place where you should feel at ease. But what about work? How much time do you really have to relax? Even if you have a wonderful home – if you want a job, you have to be flexible. Which means you have to be available all around the clock, work never stops. That leaves little time to switch off.

PAULINE: Sure, it's not that easy. But I sincerely hope that it can be done somehow. Like switching off your mobile, refraining from checking emails over the weekend – by just trying to protect your privacy and not being available all the time. I mean, by and large, this is also a political issue, for the trade unions for example.

JONAS: And for the government and the employers as well, because so many members of the workforce are on sick leave, showing burn-out syndromes or other symptoms of overstress, like physical or emotional fatigue. At the end of the day it's costing them money, so they should do something about it.

PAULINE: True. Actually, lots of companies have already come round to the opinion that they should do something about the well-being of their workforce, like establishing kindergartens to help women cope with the double burden of waged work and the bulk of household responsibilities.

JONAS: Oh and I know that some firms have set up rest areas or fitness facilities for the employees to relax and recuperate. So there is something being done to reduce stress at the workplace. But then I suppose that accounts for only a few employees, and it is still quite a long way to go.

PAULINE: Sure, and there is still one major problem as regards work. Boredom. People having to do a job they don't like because it offers no inspiration, no challenges, no fun. I think having to do a job I couldn't relate to would actually kill me.

JONAS: So how do you cope with stress caused by boredom? Well, I think you need to find something that appeals to you, something you experience as being rewarding. Then you don't really count the hours and don't experience the whole thing as stressful. For example, at school we spent hours on end practicing with the orchestra, or rehearsing plays or doing projects. That didn't feel like stress. And quite a few lessons were interesting, and you got something out of them, didn't you?

PAULINE: That's right; it was fun, now and again. I suppose you mean that you should try and see the positive aspects as regards your job; find something you really enjoy, something that makes it more bearable, so to speak. For me that has always been the PE lessons, or maths, or meeting my friends.

JONAS: Absolutely. Working together with other people also means sharing your problems. And that makes it a lot easier to cope. To sum up, thinking positive and being sociable can do a lot to reduce stress at work.

PAULINE: Well, not only at work. Having friends and getting along with your workmates is very important for your well-being in general. We all know how stressful it is for people who experience bullying or just don't get along with people, at work or in private.

JONAS: Yes, getting on with others is perhaps the most important factor of all. We are social beings, and it's vital that we feel at ease with the people around us. So that means we also need to be prepared to work on our relationships with others. Like being open-minded, tolerant and friendly, and perhaps even caring.
But apart from that, we also need some distraction, something that is not part of our daily work routine, something we can look forward to when coming home from work, or from school. Take sports for instance. It has been scientifically proven that running, for instance, makes you feel happy and more relaxed as your body produces certain substances that reward you, so to speak, for having worked hard.

PAULINE: The term reward is quite important, I think. I mean, let's face it: you cannot really have a life without stressful situations. So by giving yourself a reward, either by spending time doing sports or some other activity, you can restore your power and your motivation. Take my mom, for example: she's got long working hours, but twice a week, no matter what, she does a thorough workout in the gym and relaxes in the sauna afterwards.

JONAS: Yes, she is doing the right thing, I suppose. But you see, there are so many people claiming that they haven't got the time for hobbies or for sports. Maybe you need a fixed schedule, a schedule that tells you: "Right, it's Saturday, and at such and such a time you go jogging with your friends or go to the gym."

PAULINE: Well, I think you have hit the nail on the head. If you really want to enjoy any kind of sport you should try and work out regularly and you should set yourself reasonable and realistic targets. Not like my uncle, who wanted to run a marathon just after having done some light jogging for about two months.

JONAS: Absolutely, because if you want too much, you end up having just another kind of stress, often referred to as leisure stress. I suppose in general you should reflect your own ambitions and abilities and look at yourself from a realistic point of view. Sometimes it might be difficult to strike the right balance, but you could ask your PE teacher or your coach when starting to work out.

PAULINE: Good idea. In fact, I remember our PE teacher telling us that, when it comes to performing well at sports, you need a sufficient amount of rest, too. So some people, I would describe them as the hyperactive, really need to bear that in mind. I'm talking about people who feel guilty wasting time when they just sit back and relax. They forget that our body and soul need time to unwind; time when you do nothing at all, just chill-out in order to recover from the stress we have been exposed to.

JONAS: So another strategy to keep out the stress is to be aware of the fact that you need some rest periods, and that you should be somewhat realistic about your abilities and aspirations. Frustrated ambitions contribute a lot to you feeling stressed out, I suppose.

PAULINE: Spot on. A negative self-image or a constant feeling of being inadequate is perhaps the most important stress factor in people's life. So, up to a certain extent, being contented with what you are and what you have can definitely help you to cope with stress more effectively. So how should we present our ideas to our audience?

JONAS: Perhaps we could do a wall chart or a PowerPoint presentation, with images such as the ones given to us in this exam, in order to raise people's attention – and then comment on the images. As an introduction to our topic.

PAULINE: Great. And we could illustrate our ideas further by drawing up some role plays, for example in form of and expert talk, or some mini-plays depicting typical situations that cause stress.

JONAS: … and show how the problem could be solved by giving practical examples.

PAULINE: Sounds good, and entertaining. I think people might actually enjoy this.

JONAS: And perhaps we should round off our presentation by having a discussion with our audience at the end. That way the whole thing would be more communicative and it would involve our audience more actively.

PAULINE: That's a good plan!   *(1858 words)*

Prüfungsteilnehmer A

Topic: Health Awareness

You are organising a project day on health awareness at your school.

Comment on the quotation.

"The only way to keep your health is to eat what you don't want, drink what you don't like, and do what you'd rather not."

(Mark Twain, American writer, 1835–1950)

Together with your partners plan this day.
Consider how you could make as many of your fellow students as possible take an active interest in the topic.

Prüfungsteilnehmer B

Topic: Health Awareness

You are organising a project day on health awareness at your school.

Comment on the quotation.

"So many people spend their health gaining wealth, and then have to spend their wealth to regain their health."

(A. J. Reb Materi)

Together with your partners plan this day.
Consider how you could make as many of your fellow students as possible take an active interest in the topic.

Prüfungsteilnehmer C

Topic: Health Awareness

You are organising a project day on health awareness at your school.

Comment on the quotation.

"If you are young and you drink a great deal it will spoil your health, slow your mind, make you fat – in other words, turn you into an adult."

(P. J. O'Rourke, American comedian)

Together with your partners plan this day.
Consider how you could make as many of your fellow students as possible take an active interest in the topic.

Lösungsvorschläge

Partner A: Anton

We have been given the task to plan and organise a project day on health awareness at our school. We should also consider how we could make people interested in taking an active interest in the topic.

Let me read out the quotation on my sheet, first. I think it is quite revealing and amusing. Quote: "The only way to keep your health is to eat what you don't want, drink what you don't like, and do what you'd rather not." unquote. Now, this is from Mark Twain, the author of *Huckleberry Finn*, *Tom Sawyer*, and lots of other humorous writings. And I'm sure this quote is also somewhat tongue in cheek. But he's got a point. A healthy lifestyle does indeed involve certain restrictions, for instance as regards the food you eat. Hamburgers and chips taste great, at least most people think so, including my humble self, but everyone knows that they are not exactly healthy. The same is true for what most people drink, sugary soft drinks or beer and other alcoholic drinks.

Now this leads to the third point Mark Twain refers to: our behaviour. Staying out late at night, boozing, watching too much TV, spending too much time in front of our computer, and not exercising regularly – all this amounts to a rather unhealthy life style. But for too many people, activities like drinking alcohol or playing computer games are vital parts of their life. It's fun, and people won't do away with it quickly, even though it's exactly the kind of thing "you'd rather not" pursue, as Twain correctly remarks, and, subconsciously, people know that. Perhaps this might be the biggest problem: to get people truly interested. We should not preach too much about a super-healthy life style, because just telling people that certain things are not good for them is preaching either to the converted or to those who know but don't care. Finger-wagging won't help. But of course, in our project, we need to deal with food and drink, including alcohol, and I suppose other drugs, so we'll have to find a way.   *(350 words)*

Partner B: Belinda

I agree. We should not be moralizing too much. But of course, we need to discuss food and drink.

There is a saying that goes: "You are what you eat." Maybe that's taking it a little bit too far, but a healthy diet is definitely an important part of our project.

Well, I have also got quite a witty quote, by someone called A. J. Reb Materi. He or she says that, quote: "So many people spend their health gaining wealth, and then have to spend their wealth to regain their health." Although this statement is sort of verging on the sarcastic, I think it is quite true. There are many people working themselves to the bones by doing physically demanding jobs, by working overtime, or by being exposed to too much stress that they have to spend a lot of money to reinvest it into their health. For instance, they spend their money on massages or physiotherapy, or to see a psychologist. I mean, there are so many people around nowadays, young and old, who attend all sorts of therapies and need emotional as well as physiological support. Really, I think everyone knows somebody suffering from "burn-out syndrome" or the like. There are just so many people who can't cope with the stress anymore. No wonder people buy all sorts of tranquillizers or stimulants, more often than not taking both at the same time. Or they go for other performance-enhancing drugs. Apart from the requirements at work or at school, there are other demands put forward, e. g. by the beauty industries: You've got to look gorgeous, so as a girl you must be as slim as those anorexic models you see in the ads or on TV, like in *Germany's Next Top Model*. Boys must be fit, not fat, and look it. So there is a lot of pressure, not only on working adults, but also on young people. And I know quite a few fellow students who spend a lot of money on medicines, performance enhancing drugs or on therapies in order to function better, to fit into the system and obtain good grades. So, as regards our project, we should perhaps be looking at strategies, especially for people at our age, of how to combat stress in a more healthy fashion.   *(383 words)*

Partner C: Claudia

Sure. But we should also look at how the adult world influences young people's behaviour. The quotation I've got actually points out that people start following an unhealthy life-style when they are young because they seem to imitate the life-style of adults. Like the quotes before, I like this one because it is witty and poignant at the same time: P. J. Rourke, an American comedian, says that, quote, "If you are young and you drink a great deal it will spoil your health, slow your mind, make you fat – in other words, turn you into an adult." unquote. So it's not the kids in the first place, it's the adults who seem to be getting it quite wrong. It's them who are overweight due to an unhealthy life-style; it's them who sit in front of the box, watching mindless soaps and drinking away all of their reason. Therefore, it is necessary that we question the role adults play when it comes to health education. Knowing that young people imitate their parents or other adults, we should perhaps think about in how far the latter set a negative example and what can be done about this.

Furthermore, O'Rourke points out that people adopt an unhealthy lifestyle at an early age. That means that we should definitely look at our present youth culture and discuss to what extent unhealthy lifestyles are being promoted by parents, peer groups and the media, like the tradition of drinking alcohol as the initiation into the adult world.   *(251 words)*

Discussion

ANTON: Absolutely. I suppose I'm one of the typical examples of how you're being taught to start drinking at an early age. In my football team we started celebrating our victories by drinking beer when we were about fifteen. In fact, our coach bought us the first drinks. "Come on boys, you are real men now, so it's time to go for the real thing. Cheers."

CLAUDIA: Well, I suppose this is somewhat part of the football culture. But girls go and imitate the behaviour of adults as well. Although it might be the boys who lose control quicker.

BELINDA: That could be. But before we discuss this matter any further, I think we should try and set up a programme or schedule, of what could be done on this project day.

ANTON: Right. So perhaps we should have some workshop on youth culture and how young people literally learn from the adults to live unhealthily. For example, why do people drink although they know it doesn't do them much good?

CLAUDIA: Yes, in this respect we should also deal with the importance of peer group pressure. Why is it prestigious to drink? Why is drinking linked to a certain social recognition? Why is it such an important part of our culture?

BELINDA: Yeah, but we should not just concentrate on drinking. A healthy diet and a healthy lifestyle are equally important. Like eating the right food, getting enough exercise and enough rest.

ANTON: Enough rest? You mean people should chill out more?

BELINDA: Up to a certain extent, yes. Some people are either working too hard, or they are engaged in so many different activities in their free time that they forget to give their minds and bodies enough rest. I have heard that even young people nowadays are suffering from burnout syndrome. Look at some kids' schedules. Sports, violin lessons, extra tuition, drama society and so forth.

ANTON: And attending therapies. You are quite right. Well, Belinda, you really do have a point.

Many people are just doing too many things, they want everything and they want it now. A good example are some guys I know from the gym, you know, fitness fanatics who spend so much time weightlifting that they simply overtrain. They don't give their bodies enough rest, and as a result, instead of being refreshed and feeling fit, they feel stressed out and frustrated. The next step, and believe me more boys get hooked on this than you might think, would be to take performance-enhancing drugs in order to keep up with things.

CLAUDIA: But I don't think that overtraining, as you call it, is such a big issue among us students. Isn't it the other way round, that most people don't do enough sports?

ANTON: Well, what I wanted to say was that young people put demands on themselves they cannot possibly meet. So people's personal goals as regards physical fitness and their self-image should be included in our project. We should be talking about young people's expectations and aspirations.

BELINDA: Alright, I'm beginning to see what you mean.
So how do we get people motivated to join our project and turn up in greater numbers?

ANTON: First of all, we need to make the project sound interesting, you know, without coming across like teachers or social workers. I mean, we did have biology lessons on health, and everyone knows that carrots are healthier than fatty burgers and that drugs and smoking are not really any good for you. So we don't need that kind of stuff.

CLAUDIA: I agree. As Anton rightly said before, we should neither preach nor moralise. I think we should be informative as well as entertaining. Offer a fresh perspective.

BELINDA: Good idea. How about a day that provides action, entertainment and information? I could imagine inviting a psychologist or somebody from the advertising industries talking about beauty ideals, how they are created and to what purpose. Maybe it could be interesting to refer to the history of the human body, to show how beauty ideals have changed; how arbitrary, how relative, they are.
And how people fall victim to beauty ideals and expectations, and what they can do about it. I mean, people should learn to accept who they are and what they look like. I think this workshop could be interesting for girls, who are often quite insecure about their bodies.

CLAUDIA: Good idea, perhaps we could even invite an ex-model or somebody who has suffered from anorexia, somebody who can give our students some first-hand experience of what it is like to succumb to those weird beauty ideals. Or a doctor. Perhaps we could even involve some of our parents to join in as experts.

BELINDA: How about a cooking workshop in which students learn how to prepare some healthy and tasty food? There could in fact be a little competition, like in those TV shows, and in the end a student jury gives some kind of reward to those who produced the tastiest and the healthiest meal. They could actually run a little restaurant for the whole day. "Fit, healthy and yummy!", or something like that.

ANTON: Sounds great, and it would attract people, I'm sure.
Well, I would suggest a rather practical workshop for boys, too. They have their own problems, believe me. Many of them should do more sports because if they did, they would feel a lot better. Perhaps we could do a workshop on sportive activities for the "not so sporty", you know what I mean? New sports, sports that are fun to do and fairly easy to learn; and not quite so competitive. Or fitness training. Why not invite a professional fitness trainer or get some first-hand experience by going for a workout in a proper fitness studio? That would definitely be more appealing than doing press-ups in the gym during PE lessons, I should think. I know a school that does just that, and they are quite successful in attracting the otherwise inactive.

BELINDA: "Attracting" is the word. Maybe we could stage a play or do a workshop which leads up to a play. First you talk about the problems, e. g. bad eating habits, extreme dieting, lack of exercise, computer addiction, fitness madness, abuse of steroids and other performance enhancing drugs in sports as well as in everyday life. And then you write a little play about it.

CLAUDIA: So a group of students would be writing this play themselves and then perform it? I like the idea. The big advantage is that it would more or less automatically include what they are really interested in. Perhaps we could put it on as the final event – because I suppose most of the problems we will be dealing with in the workshops should be incorporated.

ANTON: If it is presented in a humorous, entertaining way as well as being informative, it could attract a big audience. And it would round off the whole day quite nicely.

BELINDA: Perhaps we could do it like a revue, a show with different scenes, and each workshop group contributes a part, with a host connecting the different scenes.

CLAUDIA: Great. That would involve everybody, at least as contributors to the script if not as actors. But it would require quite good coordination and time management.

ANTON: Yes, but I think it could be done. We just need to make sure that people know that they have to contribute a little scene and we should definitely set a time limit, depending on how many groups we have

BELINDA: So, we agree on practical workshops including reflections on a healthy life-style, involving sports, beauty ideals and a healthy diet, with a theatrical performance in the end. Doesn't sound too bad, does it? *(1297 words)*

Teil A: Text

A dark and shrewdly funny look at ambition and betrayal

How do you make a compelling film about the start-up of a website, even one as massively popular as Facebook? *The Social Network* shows us how it's done.

You begin with a highly coloured source like Ben Mezrich's controversial 2009 book *Accidental Billionaires: The Founding of Facebook, A Tale of Sex, Money, Genius and Be-*
5 *trayal.* Then you get Aaron Sorkin *(The West Wing)* to write the screen adaptation, replete with witty, high-speed dialogue that crackles like autumn leaves.

After that, put his script in the hands of flashy director David Fincher *(Fight Club, Se7en),* who can give things like writing computer code and arguing intellectual property the suspense and urgency of a thriller. Finally, place at its centre a splendid dysfunctional-genius
10 performance by Jesse Eisenberg and propel the action with a deliciously insistent score by Trent Reznor and Atticus Ross.

The end result is not only engrossing, but also shrewdly funny. Fincher and Sorkin have great fun exposing the immature undergrad heart beating beneath Facebook's multi- billion-dollar empire. Set among the Ivy League elite, it's a kind of *Gossip Girl* with geeks,
15 and it exploits the irony that the world's biggest online social network was created by people who were socially inept.

Eisenberg stars as Harvard sophomore Mark Zuckerberg, a brilliant, ambitious but spectacularly tactless computer programming wizard who, in the first minutes of the film, is dumped by his understandably exasperated girlfriend (Rooney Mara). In a burst of mi-
20 sogynistic sexual frustration, he creates Facemash, the prototype of what would become Facebook. Hacking into the dormitory records of Harvard's houses, he filches photos of female students and juxtaposes them in pairs on his site, inviting users to decide which one is hotter.

Facemash is a campus sensation that gets Mark into trouble with the authorities but
25 catches the attention of the patrician Winklevoss twins (Armie Hammer and Josh Pence). The duo, along with their dweeb sidekick, Divya Narendra (Max Minghella), have plans to launch an exclusive social network site for Harvard and they woo Mark to help them create it. The Jewish Mark, who is keenly aware of his lower caste status at WASP- infested Harvard, strings them along while independently building his own site with his pal
30 Eduardo Saverin (Andrew Garfield), a Brazilian immigrant and fellow wunderkind/misfit.

Fincher flips back and forth between these heady early days and the subsequent lawsuits served against Mark by the Winklevosses and Saverin. The latter is the more painful of the two, and the film soon becomes a tale of betrayed friendship.

As Mark and his partners begin to expand Facebook's reach beyond Harvard, the busi-
35 ness-savvy Eduardo starts canvassing for ads to support the site. But Mark, who finds the idea distasteful, instead falls under the spell of California golden boy Sean Parker (a perfectly cast Justin Timberlake), co-founder of Napster. Sean lures Mark and his team to sunny Palo Alto to join the Silicon Valley community, leaving Eduardo stuck in New York on an internship and out of the loop. It's the stuff of adolescent drama: a cool new-
40 comer drives a wedge between two BFFs – only with world wide web domination hanging in the balance.

Fincher and Sorkin savour the absurdity, taking computer geekdom to mock-heroic levels, complete with its own bold rallying cry: "Refresh!" But under the comedy there lurks a quiet pathos in the figure of Eisenberg's lonely character. […] His eccentricities –wearing
45   a bathrobe to a business meeting or cargo shorts in the middle of winter – aren't signs of lovable nerdiness, but of a flippant disregard for anything outside his own teeming brain.

[…] Eisenberg expertly conveys Mark's sadness and sense of frustration with himself.

You can see why Zuckerberg is drawn to Garfield's more handsome Eduardo, who has the insouciance of a budding Wall Street hotshot. But that also makes him a more desir-
50   able candidate for one of Harvard's snooty clubs, a fact that secretly provokes Mark's jealousy and leads to unresolved tensions between the two.

Timberlake lends his own charisma to the role of Parker, while Hammer and Pence make for amusing stereotypes as the blond, blueblood Winklevoss boys. A pair of over- privi-leged jocks, they're more than ripe for comeuppance from a vengeful nerd like Mark
55   Zuckerberg. (If you're wondering how Pence and Hammer look identical, it's because Fincher used the same digital manipulation employed in his last film, *The Curious Case of Benjamin Button*, to replace Pence's face with Hammer's.)

You could complain about the lack of strong female characters. Apart from Mara as Mark's razor-sharp ex-girlfriend and a sympathetic but romantically uninterested lawyer
60   played by Rashida Jones, the young women here are all groupies, bimbos or – in the case of Eduardo's girlfriend, Christy (Brenda Song) – psychos. Then again, this is the world of frats and roomies and bromances, the male-fantasy land of beer commercials and MTV spring-break parties.

People have been skeptical about the idea of a full-on feature film about something as
65   new as Facebook (witness the parody trailers for Twitter and YouTube flicks). But the very audacity of this movie is what makes it both funny and dead-on. There are certain pictures that come to define a particular period in time. I'm guessing that, years from now, we'll look back on *The Social Network* as the film that captured the speed, chutzpah and sheer unbelievability of the first big internet sensations.   *(897 words)*

Martin Morrow. "Review: The Social Network". Canadian Broadcasting Centre News.
30 September 2010.
http://www.cbc.ca/news/arts/film/story/2010/09/30/social-network-review.html
[downloaded 8 August 2011].

Annotations:

l. 28	WASP	acronym for White Anglo-Saxon Protestant
l. 40	BFFs	acronym for Best Friends Forever
l. 62	bromances	a close but non-sexual relationship between men; term coined by a skateboard magazine in the 1990s (from brother and romance)

A Text production

A1 Working with the text   25 BE

Explain how Martin Morrow reaches the conclusion that *The Social Network* is a compelling film and assess whether he succeeds in writing an appealing review.

Write a coherent text.

A2 Composition   25 BE

Choose <u>one</u> of the following tasks.

2.1 Once a year your school shows films in English for students of grades 11 and 12.

Write a speech to be delivered as an introduction to the event praising film as a unique form of art.

2.2 Discuss the message of the cartoon.

Annotation:
Google bought Google Earth in 2004,
Google Street View was launched in 2007.

2.3 "The elevation of appearance over substance, of celebrity over character, of short-term gain over lasting achievement […] distracts you from what is truly important." *(Barack Obama, Arizona State Commencement Speech, 2009)*

Comment on this notion.

		Erreichbare BE-Anzahl (Summe A1 und A2):
A1	Working with the text	Inhaltliche Reichhaltigkeit und Textstruktur: 10 BE
		Sprachliche Korrektheit: 10 BE
		Ausdrucksvermögen und Textfluss: 5 BE
A2	Composition	Inhaltliche Reichhaltigkeit und Textstruktur: 10 BE
		Sprachliche Korrektheit: 10 BE
		Ausdrucksvermögen und Textfluss: 5 BE
		Gesamt: 50 BE

Teil B: Translation/Mediation

Choose <u>one</u> of the following tasks (B1 <u>or</u> B2),

B1 Translation

Dicing with data

In the space of a week two of the best-known internet companies have found themselves in a pickle over privacy. Facebook faces criticism for making more information about its users available by default. Meanwhile Google has been castigated by a bevy of privacy regulators for inadvertently collecting data from unsecured Wi-Fi networks in people's
5 homes as part of a project to capture images of streets around the world.

Although the two cases are distinct, they have revived fears that online privacy is being trampled underfoot as internet behemoths race to grab as much data as possible. And they have provoked calls for tougher action by regulators and governments to prevent web firms from abusing the mountains of personal data they now hold. Danah Boyd, a social-
10 networking expert, has even argued that Facebook, with its hordes of members around the world, is now so embedded in people's lives that it should be regulated [...].   *(155 words)*

"Dicing with data". The Economist. 20 May 2010. From the print edition.
http://www.economist.com/node/16163396/print [downloaded 30 August 2011].   20 BE

B2 Mediation

In your English class you are collecting material on the role technology plays in our lives.
Write a summary of the given text for your classmates that serves as a contribution to the topic.

„Bots sind wie Parasiten"

Der US-amerikanische Autor und Programmierer Daniel Suarez, 45, im Interview mit KulturSPIEGEL

KulturSPIEGEL: Herr Suarez, in Ihren Romanen „Daemon" und „Freedom™" erschaffen Sie eine Welt, in der kleine Computerprogramme, sogenannte Bots, uns kontrollieren und unser Schicksal bestimmen. Müssen wir Angst haben?

Daniel Suarez: Nun, was ich schreibe, ist natürlich reine Fiktion, aber diese Fiktion ist
5 nicht so weit weg von der Realität. Die Menschen sollten besorgt sein. Denn schon heute sind wir von einer Armee von Bots umgeben, die unser Leben tiefgreifend beeinflussen.

Können Sie Beispiele nennen?

Nehmen Sie das, was kürzlich an der Wall Street passiert ist ...

... am 6. Mai verlor der Dow Jones plötzlich fast tausend Punkte ...

10 Zum Glück nur für kurze Zeit; aber das waren Bots, die miteinander gehandelt haben – ohne menschliche Kontrolle. Hunderte Milliarden Dollar verdampften in 20 Minuten. Dasselbe bei medizinischen Entscheidungen: Erst kürzlich wurde der Fall mehrerer Frauen bekannt, die hier in den USA ihre Krankenversicherung verloren, nur weil bei ihnen Brustkrebs diagnostiziert worden war. Es war kein Mensch, der diese Entscheidung traf,
15 sondern ein Bot. Diese Programme können grauenhafte Dinge tun. Und niemand stellt das in Frage. Bots prüfen auch Ihre Bonität und entscheiden damit, ob Sie einen Kredit, eine Wohnung oder sogar, ob Sie ein Vorstellungsgespräch bekommen. Und solche Daten verschwinden nie wieder.

Woher kommen die Daten?

Sie werden ständig gesammelt. Denken Sie an Ihr Handy. Ihre Telefongesellschaft weiß zum Beispiel genau, wo Sie sind. Und nicht nur das: Forscher der Northeastern University in Boston haben kürzlich die Daten von 50 000 Handy-Nutzern analysiert. Nach einiger Zeit konnten sie mit 93-prozentiger Sicherheit voraussagen, was jeder Nutzer als Nächstes tun wird. Das lässt sich dann mit Kreditkarten-Käufen korrelieren oder mit den Aufnahmen von Überwachungskameras.

Wird die Datenflut bereits ausgewertet?

Ich wäre erschüttert, wenn es nicht so wäre – einerseits natürlich als Teil des Kampfs gegen den Terror; andererseits jedoch auch, um Sachen zu verkaufen. Bots sind sehr gut darin, riesige Mengen von Daten nach Mustern zu durchforsten. Dabei ist es egal, ob es darum geht, einem Geheimdienst bei der Suche nach Oppositionellen zu helfen oder den Leuten Eis genau in jenem Augenblick anzubieten, in dem sie unbedingt ein Eis wollen. Wer ausgefeilte Bot-Programme entwirft, kann eine Menge Geld verdienen. […]

Aber hinter den Bots stehen doch immer noch Menschen, die sie programmieren und ihnen Aufträge geben.

Sicher, und ich glaube auch nicht an eine riesige Verschwörung. Es ist nicht so, dass da böse Leute in der Ecke sitzen und „ha, ha, ha, ha" machen. Die Programmierer sind alle ehrbare Menschen. Aber das Ganze kann leicht aus dem Ruder laufen. Es gibt Botnets mit zehn Millionen Maschinen. Wer kontrolliert sie? Sagen Sie mir, von wo aus Ihre Daten attackiert werden. Bots lassen sich nicht einfach ausschalten.

Man könnte den Stecker ziehen.

Wie wollen Sie beim Internet den Stecker ziehen? Das ist unmöglich. Rechenzentren haben längst Generatoren und sind nicht mehr auf das Stromnetz angewiesen. Wo sollte man außerdem ansetzen? Wenn Sie 20 Prozent des Internets abschalten, wäre es immer noch da. Wir erschaffen hier gerade etwas sehr Mächtiges, ohne die Folgen zu verstehen. Bots sind wie Parasiten. Sie entwickeln sich die ganze Zeit weiter. Wir könnten die Kontrolle verlieren.

Was sollten wir also tun?

Wir müssen die Kontrolle über unsere Daten zurückgewinnen. Der Schlüssel ist Transparenz. Wenn Sie wissen, woran Sie sind, können Sie entsprechend handeln.

Wie schützt sich ein Software-Spezialist wie Sie?

Ich habe keine Facebook-Seite. Ich twittere nicht. Ich biete nicht viel Angriffsfläche. Manchmal nehme ich sogar die Batterie aus meinem Handy, um nicht lokalisiert werden zu können. Eine sehr kleine Gruppe von Mächtigen entscheidet, was mit unseren Daten geschieht, und diese Leute nutzen Bots, um ihre Ziele umzusetzen. Das hat nichts mehr mit Demokratie zu tun. Es geht nur noch um Effizienz. Das ist das wirklich Beängstigende daran. Wir sollten diesen Weg nicht gehen. Andernfalls steuern wir in eine teuflische Zukunft. *(646 Wörter)*

Philip Bethge. „Bots sind wie Parasiten". Spiegel Online. 28. Juni 2010.
http://www.spiegel.de/spiegel/kulturspiegel/d-71083990.html
[downloaded 8 August 2011].

(Rechtschreibung und Zeichensetzung folgen der Vorlage.)   20 BE

Lösungsvorschlag

A Text production

A1 Working with the text

The key points are:
- *reasons why Morrow considers The Social Network a compelling film:*
- *good adaptation of a controversial book: exciting, entertaining and informative, brilliant cast, important issue (historical document)*
- *assessment whether the text is appealing to you:*
- *well written, colourful language (similes, metaphors, puns, portmanteau words, antithetical expressions ...*
- *aimed primarily at young people (facebook users)*

In his review of "The Social Network" published on the website of a Canadian TV station in 2010, Martin Morrow celebrates the film as being well-made, exciting, highly entertaining and informative.

According to Morrow, the film is based on a fascinating ("highly coloured" l. 3) and controversial book which has been adapted very compellingly into a fast running and witty screenplay, with the director succeeding in giving the otherwise fairly dry issue of "writing computer code and arguing intellectual property the suspense and urgency of a thriller." (ll. 8/9), supported by excellent actors and a great soundtrack.

As regards the plot and the theme of "The Social Network", Morrow describes the film as multifaceted as well as entertaining and informative ("both funny and dead-on", l. 66) as it is highly successful in conveying the paradox that the greatest communication network the world has seen so far, has in fact been created by socially rather incompetent people.

He concludes his review by saying that "The Social Network" constitutes a contemporary document, shedding light on an important cultural and historical phenomenon.

To my mind, Morrow has (more or less) succeeded in writing an appealing review by structuring his text clearly and by using language in a creative and sophisticated way to attract the reader's attention and motivate him to watch "The Social Network."

To begin with, Morrow employs a heading aimed at arousing the reader's curiosity with the help of an antithesis ("dark and shrewdly funny") and together with the words "ambition and betrayal", which sound almost Shakespearian in tone, alluding to Macbeth, makes the heading sound truly "dramatic" in a literal sense.

Morrow then addresses the reader directly ("you") and answers the rhetorical question of how to make a compelling film by presenting his appraisal of "The Social Network" in form of a recipe, in which the source, the screen-play, the acting and the music are presented as ingredients of a most tasty dish ("deliciously insistent", l. 10).

Another striking feature of Morrow's review is the constant use of colourful language which adds spice and vividness to the text.

First, there is the mix of sophisticated, elevated language ("insouciance", "audacity", "misogynistic") and colloquial, even slangy expressions like "sidekick", "stuff", "bimbos" which make the text appear sophisticated and accessible, formal and personal at the same time.

Secondly, Morrow employs a number of stylistic devices such as the elaborate use of adjectives throughout the text ("flashy director", l. 7). In addition, there are compound adjectives of an antithetical nature which the author has created himself, like in "splendid dysfunctional-genius performance" (ll. 9/10) or "wunderkind/misfit" (l. 30). These telegram-style messages make the reader stop and think.

Another creative use of language are similes like "high-speed dialogue that crackles like autumn leaves" (l. 6), which is again of an antithetical nature as the reader (at least I do) associates the term "high speed" with the noise of a highway but thinks of a romantic, colourful Indian summer at the words "autumn leaves", an interesting combination (perhaps not too meaningful though, but sounding good) which puts the reader's mind in motion.

Altogether Morrow displays a wide variety of literary devices ranging from portmanteau words such as "bromances", acronyms ("BFF"), alliterations ("filches photos of female students" ll. 21/22), metaphors ("falls under the spell of California golden boy Sean Parker" l. 36), and puns like "WASP infested Harvard" (ll. 28/29) all adding to the literary quality of the text.

Morrow is also at pains to target his intended audience, the Facebook generation, by using student jargon like "frats and roomies" (l. 62) and the allusion to the TV series "Gossip Girl".

Strategically, and rhetorically, Morrow makes a clever move, when anticipating criticism of the film as regards the lack of strong female characters. By putting this problem into perspective in a rather self-mocking, ironic way when he describes the film as depicting "the male-fantasy land of beer commercials and MTV spring-break parties." (ll. 62/63), Morrow manages to defuse the argument to pave the way for the final paragraph praising the film as a "dead-on" movie.

In conclusion, I should think that the given text is a well-written and well-conceived review, although a bit lengthy, and in parts over the top when Morrow seems to use language more for the jokes or for displaying his linguistic virtuosity as a writer. Besides, the constant name-dropping made it hard for me to concentrate on the content, but then, this review was written for a specific readership and in this respect will have served its purpose.

(758 words)

A2 Composition

2.1 *The key points are:*
  – *write a speech: include rhetorical and stylistic devices typical of speeches*
  – *target group: fellow students (aged 16–18), so your speech does need to be too formal*
  – *affirmative text : "praise"*
  – *context: presentation of English films at school*

Dear fellow students, dear film lovers and lovers of the English language,

Once again, we have come together to celebrate the most astonishing and mesmerizing art form on this planet: film. And to kill two birds with one stone, we will enjoy all the contributions in the original, which means in English. Oh my God, I hear you say, he's now talking about the benefits of watching films in the English original and how it improves your language competence and all the rest of it.

Well, folks, I won't. Instead, I will talk about film as a unique form of art, as something that easily constitutes the most fascinating medium you can enjoy.

But why should film be the greatest of all art forms? What distinguishes film from other genres? What makes film so successful, so impressive?

Well, here we go. First, there is the moving image. When the first films were shown more than a hundred years ago, people screamed in panic, ducking for cover when a train approached. They took the moving image for real, and – folks don't laugh at this – we still do today. Even if we know that all the action is made up, carefully planned and directed, as well as professionally executed by perfectly trained actors, stunt men and special effects artists, this world of make-believe and illusion still leaves extremely strong impressions on everyone of us. Even to this day, film displays a magic we can hardly elude, as film is able to create imaginary worlds so close to reality, even if it shows things like giant starships or alien creatures which do not exist anywhere in the universe but in the film maker's mind.

Add the music, (have you ever come across a film without music? Very unlikely, although there might be some …), which in itself is a very powerful art form to trigger off our feelings, evoking passion, fear or aggression, tenderness or romance. Whatever emotion you can think of, music can generate it, play with it, and put you into an ecstatic frame of mind. Now combine this with the powerful images created by painters, sculptors and designers, shown on a huge, larger-than-life screen, aided by elaborated special effects and you have the one and only art form that can reach parts of your brain and heart other art forms cannot reach.

And let's not forget the power of the camera person – guiding our eyesight, and your hearing by choosing between angles, close-ups or wide-angle shots, thereby creating an almost perfect illusion. Then, as the result of the editing process, the cutter finally creates an assembly of powerful images, actions, sounds, speech and music fired at us in a well-composed rhythm, occupying our senses to a degree and intensity unrivalled by any other forms of art. This is what makes film so unique, the coming together of all arts in one, the total work of art.

Honestly, what could rival film? Opera perhaps, which I would call the fore-runner of film, a splendid century-old combination of drama, art, music and dancing, but then – opera is still limited to the stage. We see that all the props, the whole stage design, as impressive and aesthetically pleasing as it might be, just constitutes a cardboard reality – never ever capable of unleashing the power of the moving image, never succeeding in unfolding the magic of film.

Now follks, sit back, relax and make yourself comfortable to enjoy this unique form of art in form of our first film being shown tonight. *(589 words)*

2.2 *The key points are:*
   – *refer to cartoon and its message*
   – *discuss: pros and cons*
   – *examples: Google Earth, Google Streetview and other internet applications*
   – *conclusion*

The cartoon shows a humorous depiction of the growing intrusion of our privacy by internet search engines, namely Google. Even in our sleep, perhaps the most private moment, we are not safe, as cameras, linked to internet data bases all around the world record every step we take, even if it is only something as profane as the state of our tonsils.

Of course, the sheer content of the cartoon is exaggerated, verging on the absurd. Its message however is not. We all know how much our lives are influenced by modern information technology, with all its advantages and its dangers.

Going back to the cartoon, it is obvious that Google provides us with some useful and practical information. Finding out about places, as remote or far away as they may be, via Google Earth enhances our knowledge as we can obtain valuable impressions of the geographic make-up of our planet at the touch of a button. Furthermore, we can see for ourselves how cities grow, how the infrastructure of certain regions develops, how the rainforests disappear and much more. So Google Earth can be seen as a useful tool to enable more of us (i.e. everyone who has access to the Net) to inform themselves. In this respect Google Earth can be conceived as democratizing the flow of information in general.

Google Street View might be a different matter, though. Conceived as a tool for orientation (What is the area I might want to move to like?) people fear that it reveals too much of their privacy as their homes can easily be identified by billions of people all around the globe. Furthermore, people fear security risks, as potential burglars (or even terrorists) might use Google Street View for their own dark purposes. That's why especially in Germany people have grown critical of Google Street View with some of them taking legal action to ensure that they have the right to have their homes made undistinguishable. Critics have also demanded that faces be blurred out if they accidentally appear on one of the panoramic photos taken by Google.

But then the data collected by Google Street View are only the tip of an iceberg of information gathered by internet companies and institutions worldwide. Be it data from unsecured WLAN systems inadvertently collected by Google when setting up Google Street View, or the deliberate drive for information on consumer habits which make private companies spy on us, we find it increasingly difficult to distinguish who we allow access to our private lives. The complex world of bits, bytes and bots have made it almost impossible to know what is being revealed about us, and to whom. As a result the risk of data abuse has been increasing ever since the proliferation of the Internet. It might be as real as identity theft in order to empty your bank account, or as threatening as a surveillance state gaining full control over you because it knows everything about you. In fact, we have come a lot closer to Orwell's dystopia of *1984,* as the combination of surveillance cameras and the electronic footprints we leave behind when using mobiles or the Internet could indeed create a "Big Brother" watching over you all the time, even while you're sleeping, as the cartoon shows.

On the other hand it would be wrong and misleading to demonize the Net. It is not a Leviathan, a giant political monster which it just out there to infringe our freedom and exert complete control on us. Apart from the useful services it has created (such as online shopping or banking) and together with an unprecedented wealth of information it provides, mostly free of charge, the Net can also be seen as having liberated mankind from ignorance. Knowledge is now available to almost anybody on the planet, no matter where they live. It has transformed our planet into what we now refer to as the global village, making communication faster and easier. The Net, together with modern technologies like smartphones, can bring people together, forming new communities . In this respect, internet platforms such as Facebook are actually said to have furthered the democratization process worldwide and helped fighting totalitarian regimes, e.g. in Egypt or Tunesia.

To conclude, I should think that the Internet, provides both freedom enhancing and freedom endangering elements. It is up to us to make choices, either by taking political action regulating and restricting companies as regards their practices of data collection, or by choosing carefully which personal data we want to make available on the Net for example on Facebook or when using our mobiles. As the Net could not (and should not) be switched off, nor be controlled completely, we have to learn how to live with it.

(796 words)

2.3 *The key points are:*
  – *Topics: appearance over substance, celebrity over character, short-term gain over lasting achievement*
  – *Comment: can be critical or affirmative, neutral or personal*

When Obama says that people pay too much attention to superficiality like their outward appearance, celebrities or short-term gains, he only states the obvious. There is no alternative but to agree.

Of course we should regard substance more important than appearance. At least in theory I would put inner values, moral guide lines and character qualities such as tolerance, forgiveness, helpfulness and integrity over appearance as represented by a beautiful outfit, fashionable clothes or a trendy hairstyle. But sometimes it is not so easy to distinguish between "substance" and "appearance."

Fashion for instance has two faces. First, there is the desire in people to become themselves an object of desire, which means to look beautiful and attract people's attention for all sorts of reasons. To me, there is nothing wrong with that, and although fashion is a rather short-lived business, it represents respect for our bodies and our appearance in society and therefore stands for the substantial value of self-respect. However, when people start being obsessed with looking "cool" or trendy, when they can hardly think of anything else but their looks, then they have put appearance over substance and as a consequence fail to understand what is truly important. To my mind this applies when people undergo plastic surgery or give in to elaborated body ornaments such as large tattoos or piercings. There are body cults which are harmful, like young men taking steroids to pump up their muscles, or young girls going on crash diets, becoming anorexic just to obtain the perfect figure.

And this is when certain celebrities come into play. Assisted by hordes of personal trainers, photographed at the right moment and photoshopped thereafter, the media often present them as perfect role models. And people fall prey to this. Instead of looking behind the scenes and realizing that character, as defined by compassion, intelligence and achievement, can be found in anybody, also, and perhaps foremost, in ordinary people like you and me.

I'm sure that less hero-worship and more concentration on ourselves would be indeed very beneficial for our self-esteem. On the other hand, celebrities are often crucified, especially in the tabloid press. Then their private life is drawn into the public sphere, we become witnesses to the most private moments, preferably embarrassing failures, and we can conclude, with malicious joy, that celebrities are just as human and fragile as we are. But then we just indulge in sensationalism, in stories mostly made up or blown out of proportion by the media, focusing on the banal, on trivia that have nothing to do with our own lives, or any relevant social and political issues. It's even more problematic if people are celebrated who are proud of displaying negative character traits such as greed, sexism, violence or racism.

The third weakness in people Obama points out is the fact that we tend to put short-term gain over lasting achievement, which is just all too human. We spend more money than we can actually afford to just to buy the latest gadget, just to wake up to realty with the dept collector on our doorstep. It is a fact of life that more often than not people do not think of the long-term consequences of their actions.

Unfortunately this also happens on a much larger scale, when politicians ignore the experts' warnings but carry on, just to win the next election. This, by the way, includes Obama himself, who saw himself forced to make concessions in order to re-main popular with the American electorate.

Considering the shortcomings of national politics in general, I hope that international organizations, working on a global scale and acting from a global perspective will eventually set the stage for a policy that really tackles the world's pressing problems by elevating lasting achievement over short-term gain once and for all.   *(643 words)*

B Translation/Mediation

B1 Translation

Das Würfeln mit den Daten

Innerhalb von zwei Wochen fanden sich zwei der bekanntesten Internetfirmen in Bezug auf das Thema Privatsphäre in einer äußerst peinlichen Situation wieder.[1]
Facebook sieht sich der Kritik gegenüber, automatisch[2] mehr Informationen über seine Nutzer verfügbar gemacht zu haben.

Unterdessen ist Google von einer Schar Aufsichtsbehörden, die für die Wahrung der Privatsphäre verantwortlich sind, scharf angegriffen worden.
Der Grund war das versehentliche Sammeln von Daten aus ungesicherten Wi-Fi Netzwerken von Privathäusern als Teil eines Projektes, welches Bilder von Straßen auf der ganzen Welt festhält.
Obwohl beide Fälle verschieden sind, haben sie wieder Ängste aufleben lassen, dass die Privatsphäre im Netz (Online-Privatsphäre) mit Füßen getreten wird, da die Internet-Giganten[3] miteinander wetteifern[4], so viele Daten wie möglich in ihren Besitz zu bringen.
Und sie haben Rufe nach strengeren Maßnahmen seitens der Regulationsinstanzen und der Regierungen provoziert, Internetfirmen daran zu hindern, die Berge persönlicher Daten, die sie mittlerweile angehäuft haben, zu missbrauchen.
Danah Boyd, eine Expertin für soziale Netzwerke, hat sogar argumentiert, dass Facebook, mit seinen Unmengen von Mitgliedern weltweit, bereits so im Leben der Menschen verankert ist, dass es reguliert werden sollte.

Anmerkungen
1 Auch *in Bedrouille/ in der Klemme*
2 by default: hier (beim Computer) automatisch, standardmäßig
3 behemoth: biblisches Ungeheuer, steht nicht in allen gebräuchlichen Wörterbüchern, aber im Duden (als Fremdwort) und in einigen einsprachigen Wörterbüchern
4 Auch: *sich ein Rennen liefern*

B2 Mediation

The key points are:
– *Summary for your (German) English class , neutral tone, not too formal*
– *so-called "bots" as a danger to democracy, the individual and society*
– *how bots work (collect data from the Interne and make decisions affecting our lives)*
– *No world conspiracy, but data can be used to control and manipulate people,*
– *As full control of the Net is impossible, the individuals are advised to be careful about their personal data*

This is a summary of an interview with the American novelist and IT-expert Daniel Suarez which was published by *Spiegel Online*[1] in 2010 in which Suarez expresses his concerns about so-called "bots" – small computer programmes that can interact with each other – on our personal freedom.
Suarez claims that bots collect data from the Internet and can even make decisions affecting people's lives, e. g. whether they qualify for a bank loan or a job interview. Suarez considers this development a serious threat not only to our personal freedom but to our democracy and society at large,
The data these bots collect come from our mobile phones, credit cards or from surveillance cameras and Surarez is sure this data is not only being used by the police but also by private companies or powerful individuals in order to manipulate us.
Although Suarez does not believe in a world conspiracy of people using bots delibe-rately to establish a dictatorship, he is afraid that it might be increasingly difficult to control who is using them and to what purpose.
Asked what we could do in order to curb this harmful development he said that we will not be able to control this technology fully, as we can hardly switch off the Internet, but should be ever more careful about submitting our personal data to the Net.   *(221 words)*

Anmerkung
1 Der Leser ("your English class") müsste den *Spiegel* (als "serious German news magazine") kennen.

Prüfungsteilnehmer A

Topic: Being happy

In some federal states in Germany the subject "Happiness" is being taught at schools. Comment on the quotation.

Happiness is nothing more than health and a poor memory.
(Albert Schweitzer, philosopher and medical missionary, 1875–1965)

Together with your partner discuss what it means to be happy.
Try to agree on the question whether the subject "Happiness" should be compulsory.

Prüfungsteilnehmer B

Topic: Being happy

In some federal states in Germany the subject "Happiness" is being taught at schools. Comment on the quotation.

When I was young, I used to think that wealth and power would bring me happiness. I was right.
(Gahan Wilson, author and cartoonist, born 1930)

Together with your partner discuss what it means to be happy.
Try to agree on the question whether the subject "Happiness" should be compulsory.

Lösungsvorschläge

Partner A: Lisa

We are asked to discuss what it means to be happy, and whether the subject "happiness" should become a compulsory subject at school. Interestingly enough, it has already been incorporated into the curriculum of some German states.

But let me start off our discussion with a statement by Albert Schweitzer, who once said or wrote (quote): "Happiness is nothing more than health and a poor memory." (unquote)

You see, I quite like this. Well, even if it is probably somewhat meant tongue- in- cheek, I think it contains more than just a grain of truth.

To me, health is indeed an important, if not the most important, prerequisite to happiness. Perhaps it is not happiness itself, but being unhealthy or even seriously ill means a serious infringement on your personal freedom because it really limits your range of motion and the scope of what you can do. Or, and I think that's quite a worst case scenario, you constantly suffer from pain and that really makes your life miserable. On the other hand it must be said that there are very ill, or physically and/or mentally impaired people who seem to be a lot happier than their healthy counterparts.

Well, and young people like us just take good health for granted. I suppose you need to get older to really appreciate good health.

Now, the question is: What does Schweitzer mean by "poor memory"? I suppose he does not mean becoming senile or suffering from Alzheimer's disease and forgetting everything. I think that you could translate the term "poor memory" with "the ability to cope with unpleasant experiences". This is indeed the important ability to stop thinking – not necessarily forgetting – about the hurtful moments in our lives. It's self-protection, self-preservation. Especially if people have suffered from severe traumata. I'm sure that, even if you cannot completely forget these terrible events, trying to put them out of your mind helps. Because then you stop being preoccupied with these experiences, they stop clogging up your brain. As simple, or perhaps even simplistic, as it sounds, I suppose there is a lot of truth in it and I'm a hundred percent sure that happiness starts right there, in your mind. If you look at things positively, you feel good. And bad thoughts make you feel bad and unhappy. As we know from depressed people, bad thoughts and memories can make you seriously ill.

But anyway, there is more to happiness than good health and thinking positive. What have you got, Gerion? *(419 words)*

Partner B: Gerion

You are quite right there, Lisa. You see, my quote is also quite humorous. Gahan Wilson, an author and cartoonist born in 1930, once said: (quote) "When I was young, I used to think that wealth and power would bring me happiness." (unquote) Now, you would expect him, or at least I expected him to continue with something like "But of course I was wrong. The key to really happiness is..." Well, but you are mistaken. Wilson actually ends by saying. (quote)"I was right." (unquote)

I really like the way he plays with the listeners' expectations. And I like it, because it is just plain honest. I mean, it's a commonplace to say that true happiness is not really based on material gain, but at the end of the day, we all know that money makes the world go round. Let's put it like this. Wealth is not everything, but it helps. And it helps a lot. Just imagine being really poor, growing up in a slum, being forced to do drugs or prostitute yourself, or work yourself to the bone in a sweatshop. Now, there is nothing romantic or positive about being poor, on the contrary.

So having enough money in your pockets is, like health, a vital prerequisite for happiness, but, here I do agree with you, Lisa, there is more to happiness than just wealth.

Perhaps more important than wealth, although it is often linked to it, is power. Power does definitely make people happy, otherwise there would not be so many people striving for it. It is not for nothing that successful (which means rich and powerful) men enjoy the company of young attractive women. Success makes sexy. And it constitutes a powerful aphrodisiac, not just sexually, I suppose, but it also seems to improve people's overall vitality. Success gives you a lot of positive energy based on self-confidence which in return makes you look at the world and yourself a lot more optimistically. *(329 words)*

Discussion

LISA: I agree, the striving for power is indeed a very powerful drive. No wonder, some people walk over dead bodies to get it, but does it really make them happy? I suppose throughout history there have been numerous people in power suffering from depression, or have just not been very happy at all. Just think of the dictators or gangsters who have to live in permanent fear of being assassinated or brought to justice.

GERION: Ok, it's not that easy. As you said before, there is no simple formula to define happiness. I'm sure it takes a whole lot of elements to make somebody happy. Like good friends for example, the fact that you are part of a well-meaning and supportive community.

LISA: Like your family. Really, I mean, what comes first? The first thing you encounter is your mom and dad, then the rest of your family. They can do you so much good, hold you, protect you, give you all the love you need in order to be happy.

GERION: Or they give you hell and destroy your life before it has even begun. But you are right; the family does constitute the first important stepping stone in your life. Other important institutions are kindergarten or school, and later on your workplace. where you interact with people who can either support you, or make your life miserable. But then, despite all these external factors, I suppose the individual is, to a great extent, responsible for the development of his own happiness. As you said, it starts in the mind. If you think positive, you will feel happy.

LISA: Right. Perhaps we should consider other factors which can make people feel happy. Often, it's little things, like listening to some good music, or performing music yourself. Or looking at wonderful pieces of art, or creating some yourself.

GERION: Absolutely. The ability to enjoy art in all its beauty is something that can relieve your mind and distract you from your sorrows. Like the blues, or watching a good play, or film. Comedy for instance, makes you laugh – and I should think that laughter, especially humour, is a vital part of happiness, so is catharsis, when at the end of Macbeth, or any other drama the world is put right again. All this does have a cleansing, a soothing effect on our minds and creates happiness in us.

LISA: That's a good point. Culture makes people happy, well, it makes us human, doesn't it? And you know what, when we did the theatre project in grade nine, you remember, writing our own script, our own music and so forth, and then performing it in front of a cheering crowd. I really did feel very happy, because I was part of a creative process.

GERION: Indeed. Being creative, and successful at that, must be a wonderful experience. I just wonder if artists, actors or musicians are coming close to perfect happiness.

LISA: I'm not too sure. I suppose fame has its price. You can't go shopping or anything like that, because the media, or your fans are there all the time. And if you look at how many superstars are suffering from depression, or drug addiction or died an early death, then I don't think that fame is necessarily a key to happiness.

Coming back to creativity, I suppose "happiness" boils down to having a fulfilled life, with things to do you really enjoy, a life where you have the opportunity to "go and create", as an advert once said.

GERION: I see, perhaps you don't need to be a genius artist then. I suppose you can find fulfillment in your job, because there, you can get things done. Or you can pursue a hobby to put your creativity into practice.

LISA: Yeah, that's the fascinating thing about happiness. It's up to the individual, because, as I said before, it happens in your mind, and it is up to you, how you live your life, how much you allow yourself to be happy. And of course, you must see there are always downfalls in everybody's life. Even if you're rich and powerful.

GERION: I suppose that's true. You just have to learn to take the rough with the smooth, as the saying goes.

LISA: True, well, as time is running, we should now discuss if happiness should become a subject taught at school all over Germany.

GERION: Spontaneously I would say yes, it should. Because happiness is such an important factor, not only for the individual, but also for our economy and for society at large. Just look at our culture of consumerism with the influence of the advertising industry, the film industry, the car industry just to name a few. They all claim to make us happy, in their own sweet way that is.

LISA: I agree. Happiness, as it is being treated in our society, is very important, also from a political point of view. Just remember, "the pursuit of happiness" is, as we all know from our English lessons, a vital part of the American dream, deeply rooted in the American constitution, so there is a political dimension to it as people's happiness relies on liberty and tolerance, specifically the absence of religious or political persecution and any form of discrimination. Now, practically speaking, the question is, how many lessons should be given to the subject of happiness, in which year or years should it be taught and who should teach it.

GERION: Good questions. I think happiness could be dealt with in religious and social studies, in history, in English, but also in biology and chemistry.

LISA: You mean looking at the effects of drugs and the function of chemicals on our frame of mind. That could be fascinating stuff indeed. I have just read recently that they treat depressed people with new medical drugs, and quite successfully, too, at least in some cases.

GERION: That issue alone could spark off a really good discussion. Do we have the right to make people happy, by meddling with their bodies? Or their brains? Can happiness be learned? Is it genetically determined? How much does nutrition contribute to happiness? Are we what we eat?

LISA: Some very interesting questions, indeed. It shows that the topic of happiness really needs a rather multi-disciplinary, cross-curricular approach, with perhaps several teachers working together.

GERION: There we are then; the topic should be incorporated into our lessons, as a cross-curricular project. But there is definitely no time for an extra subject, unless at the expense of another one. Well, Lisa you know that our timetable is full, and demands are high, so there is not really any space left for an extra subject. Unless you treat it as an optional subject.

LISA: I can't agree more. Perhaps we should look at the German states, how they have included happiness in their curriculum. Otherwise I would agree with you that we should integrate the topic of happiness into all the aforementioned curricula – as part of our cross-curricular teaching.

GERION: Agreed. And we should start early. Why not at elementary school and then proceed up to our final year.

LISA: Perfect. It's such a relevant and complex topic that it should be dealt with at all age levels.

(1214 words)

Prüfungsteilnehmer A

Topic: Characteristics of our times

At your school a cross-curricular project is being prepared that will include English and Social Studies. The topic is "Characteristics of our times" and you have been asked to give a presentation.

Comment on the cartoon.

"For the last time- will you please remove the parental lock!"

http://www.cartoonstock.com/cartoonview.asp?search=site&catref=than103&M
A_Category=&ANDkeyword=parental+lock&ORkeyword=&TITLEkeyword=&
NEGATIVEkeyword=

Together with your partner(s) discuss how you would define the times in which you live. Agree on what to include in your presentation and how to make it appealing.

Prüfungsteilnehmer B

Topic: Characteristics of our times

At your school a cross-curricular project is being prepared that will include English and Social Studies. The topic is "Characteristics of our times" and you have been asked to give a presentation.

Comment on the cartoon.

http://www.cartoonmovement.com/cartoon/924

Together with your partner(s) discuss how you would define the times in which you live. Agree on what to include in your presentation and how to make it appealing.

Prüfungsteilnehmer C

Topic: Characteristics of our times

At your school a cross-curricular project is being prepared that will include English and Social Studies. The topic is "Characteristics of our times" and you have been asked to give a presentation.

Comment on the cartoon.

Together with your partner(s) discuss how you would define the times in which you live. Agree on what to include in your presentation and how to make it appealing.

Lösungsvorschläge

Partner A: Ben

To start off our discussion on what characterizes our times, I was given a cartoon which depicts a situation all too familiar. We see a helpless parent who desperately asks his son, a child of about eight, to remove the parental lock from his computer. Either the father has installed it himself, and forgotten how to remove it, or the son has installed it in order to secure control of the computer. Be that as it may, the cartoon shows that even kids are nowadays outclassing their parents when it comes to modern information technology.

Well, there we are. This takes us right to the perhaps most striking characteristic of our times, the importance of media competence, and the generation gap that goes along with it. Just take my grandparents. They don't even possess a computer. My parents are somewhat more advanced. They use theirs as a typewriter and for emails. OK, they also consult the Internet for information, and last year they actually booked our holiday online. But compared to us, they are a bit like the parent in the cartoon, fairly ignorant of what else is out there. To my parents, Facebook is a mystery, unknown territory, dangerous, threatening and incomprehensible. My parents hardly know what an app is, and how and where you can download it, and what it is good for. They say "What do you need a smartphone for? Why can't you have an ordinary mobile, just for making phone calls?"

Now, just to get this right, I don't think my parents are stupid or anything, but our generation thinks differently about information technology and the development is so fast that older people are just left behind.

To put it in a nutshell, the digital revolution, together with the growing importance of the electronic media and the extent to which they are permeating our daily lives, is perhaps the most striking characteristic of our times. *(319 words)*

Partner B: Saskia

I would agree with that, although there are other issues that are equally important, for instance environmental protection or the use of our natural resources. You see, I was given a cartoon that depicts our throwaway society. There are two pictures. In the first you can see a private home and a repair shop with the home owner handing over an iron for repair. The second picture shows the same home, with lots of technical appliances being thrown out of the window and the repair shop having closed for good. I quite like the cartoon because it shows how little we care about our resources. When in the old days, things could be repaired, today they tell you that it needs to be replaced by a new device. No wonder our scrap yards are getting bigger and bigger. However, I suppose there is a new way of thinking about this, as our planet's natural resources become scarcer. This is shown by the growing importance of recycling, but really we are still miles away from a responsible, sustainable management of our resources. And this issue is important, even vital, because it is closely linked to the energy problem which affects us all. Everyone knows we are running out of oil, and what was, at least by some people, conceived as a "clean" alternative has been greatly discredited since the catastrophe of Fukushima. Now Germany is trying to find alternatives to nuclear energy, relying more on renewable forms of energy. But contrary to that, our neighbours, France and Poland (the latter is actually thinking of putting up their first nuclear plant) are still holding on to it. And so do many other countries.

Furthermore western industries find it hard to secure the supply of rare earth metals which are used in modern technological devices such as computers, or mobile phones, including your smartphone, Ben. This is why the cartoon depicts the madness of our society when it comes to using our resources meaningfully. Instead of using stuff again, you know, recycle it, we still throw tons of valuable materials away. *(352 words)*

Partner C: Klara

Well, we do live in a material world, don't we? The problem depicted in my cartoon is the impact of consumerism on our thinking. You can see a lady on a psychologist's couch. However, she apparently fails to communicate her problems, as her speech bubble is filled with the brand tags of fashion designers and textiles instead of meaningful language. So all she seems to be occupied with, or driven by, is fashion. This is highlighted by the fact that all her clothes have labels attached to them, which makes the woman herself resemble a shop window dummy rather than a human being. The self-indulgent smile on her face seems to suggest that she is quite content with what she is, a lifeless and somehow meaningless product of fashion and consumerism who has lost her human voice.

Indeed, in our society there are so many people obsessed with looking good and with buying the right things, either clothes or the latest electronic gadget, which after a short time land on the rubbish tip, like in Saskia's cartoon. I mean, philosophically speaking, our society is characterized by the predominance of consumer goods over substance, with social commitment or other pressing moral and political issues just fading into the background. Let's face it, we, as citizens of the richest societies the world has ever seen, do we actually care about what happens elsewhere? Many of us are just preoccupied with ourselves, buying things we don't really need.

(244 words)

Discussion

SASKIA: That's true. There are so many things you can buy, so many shops, so much ever more subtle advertising, and series like "Germany's Next Top Model", which suggest that looking good is the top priority when it comes to leading a happy life. And because of that you lose interest in more important things, like saving the environment.

BEN: I suppose that's true in a way, but you should not forget that many people do care. I mean in Germany, we have started to recycle electronic junk, and other valuable materials, for example copper cables and so forth. And many people have joined in and support recycling

KLARA: That's right, at least in Germany we are taking some steps in the right direction, but it's not enough, and we are running out of time. Just look at other areas where we squander the planet's resources, take fishing for instance. It's unbelievable that modern trawlers from Europe are now exploiting the fishing grounds of West Africa, after having annihilated most of the European fish population. In fact, some scientists warn that due to the extermination of certain fishes, e.g. tuna or sharks, the seas will soon be taken over by jellyfish. Yummy. And this of course would put a serious threat to world sustenance, endangering the eco-systems of our oceans.

BEN: I see your point, food and energy are problems. But I don't see it quite as problematic as you do. I mean there are lots of solutions to the problems you have mentioned. First of all there are people working on solutions to the energy problem by developing alternative energies. Solar power, for instance has come quite a long way and the car industries are working, quite successfully, on electric, environmentally friendly cars. And even when it comes to nature, environmental awareness has risen considerably and steps are being taken to alleviate the problems. There are now regulations as regards deep sea fishing and efforts are being made to create something like sustainable fishing practices in order to protect aquatic life throughout the world. It is even advertised on the labels of the fish you buy in shops. And efforts are being made to breed fish, like salmon, or tuna, so it can be harvested without endangering the fish population

KLARA: You are very optimistic, aren't you? You seem to believe that there is a solution to every problem

BEN: Right, I think there actually is. And this is what characterizes our times most, the advances in science. Never, at any given period in time, has mankind been so powerful, so much the master of their own destiny

SASKIA: Well, that's a very interesting proposition. OK, there are some efforts being taken to tackle (I wouldn't say solve) the aforementioned problems, but then, in spite of all the wonderful technologies at our disposal, the most basic need of human existence cannot be satisfied, as starvation is increasing, not decreasing. We have the Internet and are developing the most sophisticated technologies, but still people are starving to death, while developed countries do not only throw away their junk but also millions of tons of food, every day. That's the grim reality, and in that respect, the cartoon I was given is pretty harmless. There is a lot more at stake than just some repairmen's jobs.

KLARA: Absolutely. If we agree that technological progress characterizes our times, we should also include the gross injustice when it comes to the distribution of food and wealth – with all the political, ecological and economic problems that go with it.

BEN: Ok, you've got a point there, Saskia. There is indeed a huge contrast between our technological possibilities and our inability to provide even the most basic needs to a large part of the world's population

KLARA: Right. Contradiction and contrast should then be the keywords for our presentation. Just look at the west, there is (still) a climate of unprecedented liberalism. People are trying out new forms of living together, in communes, or patchwork families. And not only has overt discrimination of homosexuals diminished, there are even many countries now allowing homosexual marriages. What I want to say is that in western societies, people enjoy a great degree of personal freedom, never before seen in human history. But then, on the other hand, there are big areas elsewhere ridden by the political unrest, I mean civil wars, terrorism

BEN: And we shouldn't forget the dangers to our freedom posed by modern technologies, even in our western democracies. I just say "Big Brother is watching you" – which means that companies, all sorts of organizations and governments can follow people's electronic footprints. And they can spy on us by the most sophisticated means, without us knowing. And that's the dark side of modern technology.

SASKIA: That's a very important point, Ben. It should definitely be incorporated into our project, showing the contrast between modern information technology as liberating on the one hand, and seriously threatening our freedom on the other hand

KLARA: And we should not forget the great number of unsolved social problems like wide-spread unemployment, child labour, or even worse, child soldiers. You are right Saskia, there is a huge prosperity gap between the wealthy western nations and the poor rest. And like the lady in my cartoon, many of us are not even aware of that, because we are completely absorbed in fashion or going shopping. Many of us don't think "How can I make this world a better place?" But "What shall I buy next?"

SASKIA: Now Klara you are perhaps a bit too pessimistic here. I think a lot of people do care. They buy fair trade products for instance. And don't you think there are positive developments worldwide? Take countries that used to be fairly poor but which are now making good progress, for instance China or Brazil.

BEN: That's true, but whereas some countries have taken great leaps forward, others have fallen behind even more, like many countries in Africa, which are torn by civil wars or have even become what we call "failed states", like Somalia.

KLARA: Ok then, we agree. We should use the concept of contrast to present our findings to the class. I suggest we produce a great wall chart, with pictures, captions and short texts to capture our classmates' attention

BEN: Good idea, we could do it like a gallery walk, distribute different posters on the key issues in different places, so people do not get overwhelmed by the material, and have time to reflect on it while walking from poster to poster

SASKIA: I agree, there is so much to say, so many facts we could put forward, we must definitely limit ourselves to some basic ideas and concepts. I think we should aim at making people think, more than trying to provide them with lots of information

BEN: Good point, let's concentrate on three items then. Number one: "Information technology and its impact on society", focusing on the generation gap and the extent it is permeating modern life. And how it can be beneficial and dangerous to our freedom at the same time.

KLARA: Number two: Man and Nature, the contrast between technological possibilities and our present failure to preserve our planet. A suitable heading could be: "Killing off our Planet: Consumerism and the throwaway society."

BEN: But don't forget some of the efforts which have been made already. You know, I think we should not get too negative, or too pessimistic. All the moaning and groaning about environmental destruction and global warming, it's just not motivating.

SASKIA: OK, but then we don't need to look at the problem through rose-tinted glasses either. We should definitely point out the contrast between technological feasibility and reality. But of course we could give it a slightly hopeful and optimistic outlook by pointing out what we can actually do, like Obama said: "Yes, we can."

KLARA: Right, and last but not least, we should deal with the global prosperity gap. A title for a display could be: "Eat the rich? Eat the poor! Consumerism, hunger and poverty in the 21st century." We could try and show that it is partly due to our irresponsible behaviour that the fight against poverty hasn't been won, well, what do I say, hasn't even really started yet.

BEN: I like the heading, but we should be careful not to sound too biased or simplistic, as there are no easy solutions to any of those problems. These are all very complex issues, and if we want to make our classmates think, then we should refrain from offering easy solutions or blaming just one part of the world for everything.

KLARA: Ok, but then I think a bit of a provocation doesn't hurt either.   *(1466 words)*

Teil A: Text 1

We need an Academy of English to save our beautiful language

The attempt by the Queen's English Society to create an Academy of English, on the model of the Académie Française, is both welcome and long overdue. Authoritative bodies exist to maintain the purity of the French, Spanish and Italian languages, but English has been left to fend for itself at a time when it is under unprecedented attack.

5 Globalisation has meant that the predominance of English in computerised societies is making it more vulnerable to abuse than any other tongue. The advent of texting has had a disastrous effect on literacy and the mass media are complicit in bastardisation of language. Then there is the omnipresent, nightmarish gibberish of management jargon. The worst problem, however, is the collapse of literacy within our education system – the fo-
10 rum that should have been the sturdiest bastion of correct practice.

Instead, laissez-faire attitudes towards spelling, grammar and syntax, encouraged by trendy educationalists, have created a situation in which illiterate pupils have now been joined by a generation of largely illiterate teachers. The "inclusive" mania to embrace the lowest common denominator has left the language of Shakespeare fighting for survival.
15 The universal misuse of apostrophes recently provoked the writing of a best-selling book; its success suggests there is still a desire among the bulk of the population to understand and employ correct usage, but abuses are proliferating.

The inarticulacy of young people's speech is not something that will necessarily correct itself with maturity, as optimists rashly assume: where there is no understanding of the
20 basic structures of our language, self-improvement can only be a hit-or-miss effort. [...]

Aggravating the current crisis is state-sponsored illiteracy, with central and local government promoting politically correct Newspeak, such as "chair" for chairman, and innumerable hideous neologisms such as "spokesperson", which are additionally offensive in patronisingly attributing infantile insecurity to women. We live in an age of aggressive
25 Philistinism. Modern "art" is a sick joke, imposed on the public in the absence of courageous opponents denouncing the Emperor's new clothes; it is no coincidence that its iconic artefact was a urinal exhibited in 1917, as the old world that had produced so many glories of true art was dissolving.

In this climate of anti-aestheticism it is unsurprising that even an attempt to preserve the
30 beauty and coherence of the English language should meet with opposition by those who claim that it needs to "evolve" unimpeded. There is nothing wrong with a language evolving – English has always done so; but what is happening now is not evolution but nihilism. It must be resisted and the Queen's English Society is to be congratulated on its initiative. All champions of literacy will wish the society success in establishing a much-
35 needed Academy of English. *(459 words)*

Gerald Warner. "We need an Academy of English to save our beautiful language".
The Telegraph. 8 June 2010.
http://blogs.telegraph.co.uk/news/geraldwarner/100042575/we-need-an-academy-of-
english-to-save-our-beautiful-language/ [downloaded 8 August 2010]

Teil A: Text 2

Why proper English rules OK

"To be born an Englishman," Cecil Rhodes supposedly said, "is to win first prize in the lottery of life." But the old imperialist was wrong. What he should have said was, "To be born an English-speaker ..." The global rise of bad English is helping us native speakers rise.

40 I first realized our advantage at a conference last year. The speakers came from across northern Europe, but they all gave their talks in English – or a sort of English. Germans, Belgians and French people would stand up and, in monotones and distracting accents, read out speeches that sounded as if they'd been turned into English by computers. Sometimes the organisers begged them to speak their own languages, but they refused.
45 Meanwhile the conference interpreters sat idle in their booths.

Each new speaker lost the audience within a minute. Yet whenever a native English-speaker opened his mouth, the audience listened. The native speakers sounded conversational, and could make jokes, add nuance. They weren't more intelligent than the foreigners, but they sounded it, and so they were heard. Here, in microcosm, was a nascent inter-
50 national hierarchy: native English-speakers rule.

English has been invading international settings since at least 1919, when the Treaty of Versailles was written in English as well as French. Later leg-ups for the language include the rise of American multinationals, the fall of the Berlin Wall, the coming of the internet and the opening of China, says Nigel White, head of international training and
55 development at the Canning communications company.

Today about one in four humans speaks at least some English, according to the British Council. Many more want to learn it. Robert McCrum, co-author of *The Story of English*, hails "the apparent realisation of one of mankind's oldest dreams – the end of Babel".

Of course most of these new speakers don't speak proper English. They speak "Globish"
60 – a simple, dull, idiom-free version of English with a small vocabulary. Most Europeans at my conference, for instance, spoke Globish. Speakers of Globish often struggle to understand native English. They are confused by idioms, half-sentences, references to ancient TV programmes, or simply the British habit of not saying what you mean. [...]

Because English-Globish misunderstandings are common, experts often warn that native
65 English-speakers will suffer in this new world. However, native speakers simply need to learn Globish. White says a half-day course can teach native speakers to speak slowly, without irony, and to bin confusing verbs like "to put up with". [...]   *(414 words)*

Simon Kuper. "Why proper English rules OK". FT.com. (Financial Times). 8 Oct. 2010.
http://www.ft.com/cms/s/2/3ac0810e-d0f0-11df-a426-00144feabdc0.html#axzz1UQPI3aNu
[downloaded 8 August 2011]

Annotations:

l. 22:	Newspeak:	a fictional language in George Orwell's novel "1984"; a term used to refer to a deliberately impoverished language prompted by the state
l. 25:	Philistinism:	the state of being hostile or indifferent to culture or the arts
headline:	to rule OK:	*(coll.)* to be the best

A Text production

A1 Working with the text   25 BE

Analyse the two texts comparing what the authors say about the state of
English and how they present their topic.

Write a coherent text.

A2 Composition   25 BE

Choose <u>one</u> of the following tasks.

2.1 Comment on the message of the picture.

Funtoosh.com

2.2 In his article Simon Kuper focuses on non-native speakers' use of English.

Write a letter to the editor of the *Financial Times* defending the concept of
English as a lingua franca.

2.3 An international magazine calls for readers to send in articles or fictional
prose on the topic "We live in an age of …".

Write your text.

A1	Working with the text	Erreichbare BE-Anzahl (Summe A1 und A2):
		Inhaltliche Reichhaltigkeit und Textstruktur: 10 BE
		Sprachliche Korrektheit: 10 BE
		Ausdrucksvermögen und Textfluss: 5 BE
A2	Composition	Inhaltliche Reichhaltigkeit und Textstruktur: 10 BE
		Sprachliche Korrektheit: 10 BE
		Ausdrucksvermögen und Textfluss: 5 BE
		Gesamt: 50 BE

Teil B: Translation/Mediation

Choose <u>one</u> of the following tasks (B1 <u>or</u> B2).

B1 Translation

Stanley Wells: "Shakespeare, Sex and Love" (extract from a review)

If there is any one aspect of Shakespeare's work that singles him out from every other great writer, it is the astounding comprehensiveness of his treatment of love and sex. Not only do those great themes figure prominently in virtually every play he wrote, he explores, with detailed vividness, a range of sexual [...] experience that leaves Masters and
5 Johnson looking pretty skimpy. From the most exalted Petrarchan effusions to the basest bodily function, he covers the waterfront. [...]

Wells's concise and elegantly written book subtly and systematically illuminates Shakespeare's acknowledgment of the glory and the horror of what it is to be fully human, the unceasing contradictions, the inescapably oxymoronic nature of our life, especially in this
10 area of sex and love. It is his supremacy in this territory which makes him so much the greatest of writers, effortlessly eclipsing his closest rival for the crown, Charles Dickens.

Simon Callow. "Shakespeare, Sex & Love by Stanley Wells".   (*157 words*)
The Guardian. 24 April 2010.

20 BE

Annotations:

ll. 4/5:	Masters and Johnson:	research team that pioneered research into the nature of human sexual behaviour between the 1950s and 1990s
l. 5:	Petrarchan:	in the style of the Italian poet Petrarch (1304–1374)
l. 9:	oxymoronic:	an oxymoron is a phrase that combines two words that seem to be the opposite of each other

B2 Mediation

While dealing with Shakespeare in your course the following article on *Romeo and Juliet* has caught your attention. Sum up for your classmates what it says about the original work and its translations.

Love-Story mit Widerhaken:
Vom Gefloskel, Geferkel und Gewitzel in *Romeo und Julia*

Romeo und Julia ist ein Mythos. Jeder kennt ihn. Auch der, der das Stück nie gelesen oder gesehen hat.

Um so genauer Bescheid weiß natürlich derjenige, der dem Stück tatsächlich schon einmal in Schlegels Übersetzung begegnet ist. Romeo und Julia, die lyrische Liebestragödie:
5 eine idealische, hehre, reine Herzensliebe geht an den Widerständen der Welt so tragisch wie poetisch zugrunde. In hohem Ton und edler Bühnendiktion. Die Schlegelsche Übersetzung – in sich eine große, sprachschöpferische Leistung der deutschen Literatur – hat diesen getragen-lyrischen Ton geprägt und ihn im kollektiven kulturellen Unterbewußtsein so fest eingemeißelt, als wär's die Grabinschrift auf Julias Marmorsarg. (Daß Julia
10 aber zum Beispiel in einem Monolog ausführlich und handfest davon spricht, wie leidenschaftlich gern sie jetzt gleich mit Romeo ins Bett gehen wird, erfährt der deutsche Shakespeare-Leser aus dieser Übersetzung nicht.)

Wenn man aus guten Gründen meint, das jedermann bestens bekannte Stück *Romeo und Julia* anders übersetzen zu müssen denn als lyrisches Gedicht, so wird dies zumeist als
15 Kulturschande und Vergewaltigung des edlen Barden Shakespeare aufgefaßt – der Übersetzer spricht aus leidvoller Erfahrung. Da Shakespeares Text aber durch dieses tradierte

Vorverständnis einigermaßen beschädigt wird, bleibt dem Übersetzer nichts anderes üb-
rig, als an dieser Stelle Shakespeare gegen seine Verteidiger zu verteidigen.

Das genannte gängige *Romeo-und-Julia*-Verständnis begreift Shakespeares Text, als
20 wär's das Libretto der Westside-Story – als sentimentale Seelenoper, romantisch und
rührend, schön traurig und tränenselig. Shakespeares Love-Story ist aber widerborstiger,
welthaltiger und fragwürdiger komponiert: Sie ist ein üppig orchestriertes, wildes Kon-
zert realistischer Stimmen in den widersprüchlichsten und schrillsten Tonarten über das
Thema „Liebe" in allen Variationen und Facetten. Und einige dieser Tonlagen des Origi-
25 naltextes sind ungewohnt für den, dessen Ohr auf den Schlegel-Ton gestimmt ist.

Am auffälligsten ist zunächst einmal die gnadenlose Kalauerei, Wortspielerei, Wortverdre-
herei, die diese klassische Tragödie über lange Passagen in die Nähe einer Komödie rückt.

Ein Wortwitz, ein sogenannter „pun", war zu Shakespeares Zeiten ein seriöser literarischer Kunstgriff. Die Wortspielmode hatte ihren Nährboden in der Mehrdeutigkeit zahl-
30 loser englischer Wörter. Ein „pun" konnte ein derbes, deftiges Geblödel nach Stamm-
tischmanier sein, ein Kalauer oder genausogut ein phantasievolles Spiel mit der Sprache,
ein geistesschnelles Umdeuten der Wörter, ein „display of wits", ein Spazierenführen des
pfiffigen, gewitzten Geistes. Da mehrdeutige Wortspiele grundsätzlich die Mehrdeutigkeit der Welt spiegeln, sind sie keineswegs auf komische Situationen beschränkt: Shake-
35 speare verwendet Wortverdrehungen, also „puns and quibbles", mit Vorliebe auch in tief-
ernsten Situationen. Aus den schwimmenden Doppeldeutigkeiten der Sprache konkreten
Sinn zu schlagen galt zu seiner Zeit als seriöse Methode des Erkenntnisgewinns – eine
Tradition, die im deutschen Sprachraum nie bestand, wo Ernstes per definitionem ernst
zu sein hat und eben nicht Scherz, Satire, Ironie mit tieferer Bedeutung sein kann. Für
40 den exzessiven Gebrauch von „puns" selbst in Augenblicken höchster seelischer Erschüt-
terung der sprechenden Person wurde Shakespeare allerdings auch in England schon kurz
nach seinen Lebzeiten getadelt. [...]

Wie immer man nun Wortspiele wertet, ob man sie als albern und schäbig empfindet
oder als legitime Mittel zur Welterkenntnis – Shakespeare jedenfalls hat sie in *Romeo*
45 *und Julia* exzessiv verwendet. Der Versuch, sie in ihrer ganzen ungebärdigen Bandbreite
von grobschlächtig-derb bis raffiniert-subtil in einer Übersetzung wiederzugeben, steht
zwar in Widerspruch zum gepflegten deutschen Shakespeare-Verständnis, aber nicht in
Widerspruch zu Shakespeare.

Befremdlich ist zum anderen die beachtliche Menge an Verbalferkeleien, in denen das
50 Stück sich gefällt; *Romeo und Julia* ist durchaus nicht jugendfrei – was übrigens bis auf
den heutigen Tag zu einer Vielzahl gereinigter Ausgaben im prüden Amerika geführt hat;
da mußten „Stellen" getilgt werden. Der *Romeo-und-Julia*-Text ist – die Wissenschaft
hat's nachgezählt – im Gesamtkanon das Shakespeare-Stück mit den meisten Zoten. [...]

Kalkulierte Kontraste und Stilbrüche sind grundlegende Mittel der Shakespeareschen
55 dramatischen Kunst, die immer auf Wirkung aus war – und der Praktiker Shakespeare
wußte: Nichts wirkt fader als durchgehend empfindsames Gesäusel. Deftige, obszöne
Gossenkalauer als Einleitung zu einer seelisch hochgespannten, sensiblen Szene, in der
sich zaghaft und verwirrt zwei neuverliebte Kinder an das noch nie erlebte Gefühl der
Liebe herantasten – ein recht gutes Beispiel für die eigentliche Spannweite des so oft be-
60 schworenen „großen Shakespeareschen Atems". Mancher Shakespeare-Verehrer hätte
ihn gern etwas kurzatmiger. [...]   *(670 Wörter)*

Frank Günther. „Aus der Übersetzerwerkstatt". In: Shakespeare. Romeo und Julia.
Zweisprachige Ausgabe. Neu übersetzt und mit Anmerkungen versehen von Frank
Günther. dtv München, 7. Auflage, 2001, S. 245–249.

(Rechtschreibung und Zeichensetzung folgen der Vorlage.)   20 BE

Lösungsvorschlag

A Text production

A1 Working with the text

The key points are:
- *Differences between the two texts: biased, derisive, sarcastic, aggressive versus factual, mildly ironic, more relaxed*
- *Warner: English language is under attack by globalization and the failure of the British education system*
- *Kuper: only people whose mother tongue is English speak the language properly, English is not under threat*
- *Warner: uses war metaphors, and other stylistic devices*
- *Kuper: refers to facts, quotes experts, fewer rhetorical devices*

Gerald Warner claims that the global use of English – especially in "computerised societies" (l. 5) dominated by mass media – as well as recent developments in education ("laissez-faire attitudes", l. 11) and the rise of a "management jargon" (l. 8) are seriously undermining the English language. That is why he calls for the establishment of an Academy of English, similar to the Académie Française.

The tone of his text, which is a direct appeal for action, is subjective, biased, polemic, outraged, and even belligerent.

Beginning with the heading, Warner points out the vital importance of the issue by directly addressing the reader: "We need [...] to save our beautiful language". When in the opening paragraph he writes that the Academy of English "is both welcome and long overdue" (l. 2), he suggests that the establishment of such an academy is a general wish of society or at least of the readers.

To illustrate the urgency of the matter, the author constantly uses war metaphors, insinuating that the situation has become one of life and death, as the English language "is under unprecedented attack" (l. 4). The education system, which is supposed to be "the sturdiest bastion of correct practice" (l. 10), is failing to defend the English language. This development "has left the language of Shakespeare fighting for survival" (l. 14).

To show the reader who the enemy is, Warner is at pains to ridicule his opponents by employing expressions such as "hideous" (l. 23) and "infantile" (l. 24) (he refers to neologisms such as "spokesperson" (l. 23) here). One of his main targets is the educational system. To describe it he uses sarcasm and hyperbole, castigating the education system as consisting of "trendy educationalists [who have] created a situation, in which illiterate pupils have now been joined by a generation of largely illiterate teachers" (ll. 11–13).

To add further spice and colour to his arguments, Warner uses various rhetorical devices, for examples pejoratives such as "bastardisation" (l. 7) with its racist undertones alluding to racial impurity. The term "gibberish" (l. 8) is a strong onomatopoeic phrase and together with the comparison "nightmarish" (l. 8) it evokes darkness and destruction. It affects the reader on an emotional level and expresses the author's anger as well as his determination to fight. To strengthen the feelings the reader has for the English language Warner uses personification. The language "fend[s] for itself" (l. 4) and is "vulnerable" (l. 6). The reader is supposed to feel pity and to fight on the side of the language in danger.

The author's general criticism of the current political and educational system is stressed further by alliterations such as "the current crisis is state-sponsored" (l. 21, two alliterations) and "promoting politically correct Newspeak" (l. 22), the latter also being an allusion to George Orwell's *Nineteen Eighty-Four*, a novel dealing with the misuse and corruption of language by an all-powerful state. Here Warner reflects the general fear in the reader of the "Orwellian State" in which freedom of expression and political freedom are annihilated.

Similar to Gerald Warner, Simon Kuper points out the shortcomings of international English as used by non-native speakers when he describes native English as a superior variety in a globalised English-speaking world. This idea is already shown by the heading "Why proper English rules OK", a rather colloquial term, by which the author also demonstrates a certain ease regarding the topic. To him, international English does not pose a threat, and consequently, in contrast to the belligerent tone of Warner's text, Kuper employs only mild irony.

Furthermore, Kuper adds credibility to his argument by referring to facts and by quoting various linguistic experts. Overall, his style is simpler and more factual than the complex, more literary style used by Warner.

As the heading implies, Kuper believes that English has evolved as the dominant and all-pervasive language of the world with native speakers being at an advantage ("English rules"). According to Kuper, the English spoken by non-native speakers often represents a rather "simple, dull, idiom-free version of English with a small vocabulary" (l. 60) referred to as "Globish" (l. 59).

To Kuper, "Globish" fails to convey the irony, allusions and references contained in "proper English" (l. 59) therefore making it rather unattractive to listen to. However, in contrast to Warner, he does not see the English language as being under threat. On the contrary: the English language is spreading. Here it is Kuper who uses military language: "English has been invading international settings" (l. 51). In this image English is the aggressor rather than the victim. But its victory is for the benefit of all of us: quoting Robert McCrum, Kuper points out that the world-wide use of English might lead to better communication, to "the end of Babel" (l. 58).

So all in all, Kuper conceives a simplified global variety of English as a positive development. However, when he passes on Nigel White's advice that "a half-day course can teach native speakers to speak slowly, without irony, and to bin confusing verbs like to 'to put up with'" (ll. 66/67) the reader cannot help but note a certain ironic detachment as regards the linguistic value of "Globish". On the other hand, Kuper also employs some self-irony when it comes to taking one's native language all too seriously explaining that non-native speakers of English are confused by the "British habit of not saying what you mean" (l. 63).   *(905 words)*

A2 Composition

2.1 *The key points are:*
   – *Description, reference to the given photomontage*
   – *Different interpretations: change of eating habits, proliferation of American culture, exploitation of countries in the developing world*
   – *Support views by referring to facts: history, spread of American (western) culture, globalization, problems of developing countries*
   – *Neutral or personal style*

The photo, actually a photomontage, shows an African woman in traditional dress carrying a huge hamburger on her head and an oversized coke can in her hand. It looks as if the woman is walking through very dry, barren land, with the hamburger and coke replacing the fire-wood and water the woman might normally be carrying.

To me this image could contain several messages. First, it could stand for the proliferation of American fast food culture throughout the world, with the coke and burger symbolising western dominance and the attractiveness of western or American life styles.

Given the fact that companies such as McDonald's and Coca-Cola can in fact be found almost everywhere on this planet, even in the poorest developing countries, the picture makes the viewer reflect on why these American products are so successful. Why are burgers and coke so attractive that they find their way into virtually each and every culture?

To me, there is no easy answer to this. I suppose that all around the world people are attracted by the ease with which fast food can be consumed. No forks, no knives, and just throwing away the box the food is served in. It is somehow luxurious (though of course outrageous) to do so, something carefree, something most people would not do at home, especially when they happen to grow up in fairly poor societies. So eating out at a burger restaurant might mean a (temporary) place in the western throwaway society, representing an affluence which allows such a carefree treatment of natural resources.

Let me elaborate on this a little further: fast food is typical of the American life style, at least as depicted in commercials all around the world. And as regards the global competition of values and products, American values still rate very highly. America is still seen as the most powerful nation, a superpower representing freedom, affluence and individual opportunity as symbolized by the American dream. And in this respect, coke and burgers are the culinary and symbolic representatives of that dream, the part of America you can consume at your doorstep, together with American TV series, music and fashion – even if you live in an impoverished society as portrayed in the picture.

On the other hand, there is also a more sinister side as regards the global domination of American food culture. Consequently, the given image could also stand for the exploitation of the developing world by global western companies extracting the countries' natural resources but leaving the population with (almost) nothing in return. In this respect the oversized burger might also be interpreted as a burden the inhabitants of the developing countries have to carry.

Just look critically at the production of beef, the main ingredient of burgers. To secure supply for the western markets, cattle ranching has been introduced in many parts of the developing world, with great areas of the rainforests being chopped down to make way for cattle, or cattle feed which is imported to Europe or America. All this uses up a lot of water, water the indigenous population needs, especially in dry areas as shown in the picture.

Another example of western exploitation of developing countries in order to secure our food supply is the fishing industry. European trawlers, after having more or less wiped out the fish population around their owns coasts, are now invading west African fishing grounds. Shady deals with corrupt African governments make that possible, at the expense of the native fishermen who, with their traditional fishing methods, do not stand a chance against the modern fishing fleets.

And there are many more examples: take the establishment of huge plantations to produce palm oil or biofuel for the world, mainly western markets. The monocultures run by international companies destroy the natural habitat of many species and prevent the native population from establishing their own agricultural businesses.

To sum things up, to ensure that fast-food chains can offer cheap burgers and that we have enough fish up on our shelves, at a "reasonable" price of course, or that we can alleviate our environmental consciousness by putting biofuel into our tanks, we allow western companies to rob developing countries of their natural resources. And we don't mind, as long as things are cheap, as long as the price is right, or do we?

(721 words)

  - *Formal requirements of a letter to the editor:*
    - *Beginning: "Sir/Madam" or "Dear Editor" (US)*
    - *First sentence(s): reference to the article (e. g. author, date of publication, title) and the article's main message: Kuper's attitude towards "Globish", non-native speakers' use of English*
    - *End of the letter: name and where you come from (no "yours faithfully/ sincerely" necessary)*
  - *Commenting on the importance of English as a lingua franca*
  - *Stating your point of view: support, criticize, put into perspective*

Sir / Madam

I'm writing to you in response to the article by Simon Kuper from 8 October, which I consider fairly entertaining and, in part, a witty comment on the shortcomings of English as a lingua franca. However, being a non-native speaker of English myself, I do not quite appreciate Kuper's slightly condescending tone when it comes to the non-native's ability, or better, inability, to speak what he calls "proper English".

Sure, a native speaker has a lot more words and expressions at his disposal, he can crack jokes more easily, use puns, metaphoric language, in short more elevated language than we non-native speakers can. However, not all of us speak (or write) dull and boring English sounding as if it was generated by a computer. Neither do we all speak in monotonous and distracting accents. In fact, some British local accents sound at least as distracting, as even speakers of Standard English fail to understand them (fully). So Mr. Kuper should beware of such generalisations. He might come across a lot more arrogant and self-righteous than he intended to.

In his article, Kuper points out the importance of English as world language, and rightly so. English could indeed help to improve communication around the world, ushering in the "end of Babel" and consequently make our world a better place. Without a doubt the variety (or varieties) Kuper refers to as "Globish" (a term sounding rather unpleasant, if not derogative to me) acts as a lingua franca, but does that mean that it is just the cheap, debased and primitive off-spring of "proper English"?

One of the most famous writers in English literature is Joseph Conrad. He was born in Poland and learned English as a second language. This clearly shows that non-native speakers can master English to a very high degree, using metaphoric and idiomatic language. The same applies for the thousands of pop music bands worldwide, as well as filmmakers and artists, all of them communicating in English.

But you don't need to be a world-class writer or any other kind of artist in order to speak "proper" English. There are lots of scientists and other professionals who indeed communicate on a highly sophisticated level all around the globe, mastering technical terms which even a native speaker might not have heard of. Complicated machines like satellites are being operated, pilots of all nations land their planes safely only because they can communicate in English.

There are many more occasions where English serves as a lingua franca: e. g. tourism, a multi-billion dollar industry, or sports, which is just as important, economically and culturally. Both would not work without English as the one and only language (almost) everybody understands and can communicate in. International youth camps, furthering understanding between nations, would hardly work without English. Almost all international companies communicate in English as do important charity organizations operating on a world-wide scale. It does work, and that is what matters.

Furthermore, you cannot say that every version of English that is simplified or contains grammatical "mistakes" is "improper". Because English is a lingua franca, several varieties of English referred to as Pidgin or Creoles have developed around the world, e. g. in the Caribbean. Would you really denounce Bob Marley's lyrics (and music) as "improper"? I guess you wouldn't.

English has a great potential and the fact that the community of speakers and users is growing steadily (currently, some billion people are able to speak English) will surely enrich the language rather than create just a dull and impoverished version of it.

In fact, as a native speaker of English, Mr. Kuper should take pride in the fact that the world revolves around English and that the language is bringing people together on a global scale and perhaps, as I have already said, helps to make our world a better place.

Tobias (18), Dresden (Germany)   *(647 words)*

2.3 *The key points are:*
 – *Write __either__ an article __or__ fictional prose.*
 – *Article: (mainly) formal style; should contain a headline; typical stylistic devices (e. g. rhetorical questions, comparisons, allusions, idioms ...)*
 – *Prose fiction: literary devices like interior monologue, stream of consciousness, elliptic sentences, allusions, quotations, formal and informal language, rhythmic elements, imagery, narrative perspective, setting*
 – *Concentrate on a (self-chosen) theme: e. g. age of uncertainty and contradiction, age of technology, age of transparency, age of crisis ...*
 – *Include plausible arguments, facts, developments etc. to support the theme (This applies not only to the article, but to the fictional text as well. It makes your text more convincing.)*

Just another Monday in the age of uncertainty and contradiction
Henry woke up early. He didn't even have to set his alarm clock. He knew he was supposed to be up at least an hour earlier than normal.

But what is normal these days? Are there any certainties these days? Not really. Not anymore.

Ok, there must have been long and hard winters before. But this one? Quite unusual. Result of the climate change? Global warming? But Europe was getting colder, not warmer. To hell with all the sensationalist loudmouths, or scientists coming up with new theories every day, and politicians paying lip service as regards climate change. Nothing is certain. Explosion of facts and figures. But no certainty.

The global economic crisis, the financial crisis. Where is the difference? How did it happen? Who could foresee it? Nobody. Even the experts don't have a clue. Age of uncertainty.

The strain on the European Union. Will it break apart? (Who are the Europeans anyway? Ex-colonial powers, once ruling the world, imperialists, makers of the industrial revolution, but now being obliterated by the USA and China.) Losing our grip, losing power, losing coherence ... things are falling apart.

Henry was worried. And confused. He was worrying about things all the time. Politics, the economy, the climate, the social coherence of society, the food people eat, the media, the health system ... absolutely everything. What is right, and what is wrong?

A fast world, a changing world where you don't know what might happen next, where things are uncertain, where old alliances and securities have become null and void, where you might have a job today and join the dole queue tomorrow.

Henry put on his coat, boots and woolly cap. This winter was the coldest, and snowiest and longest in donkey's years. Time to clear the pedestrian way. At least he would get some exercise. Important, very important these days.

Be fit, look fit, feel fit: fit for life, fit for fun, fit for winter (sports). Body consciousness, good looks are important. Be strong. Work out in the gym, washboard stomach, six pack, biceps and triceps in perfect harmony, proper nutrition, protein, low-carb shakes. Well, the pressure is on. Constantly. The health craze, the food craze ("Go organic, take your supplements: you are what you eat."). – On the other hand: sharply rising figures of obese people, not caring at all. Not having the time to care, not having the money, the education? Confusing contradiction: Nutritional deprivation in the land of plenty. – On the other hand: we have never had it so good. But which direction are we heading? A healthy society? Or a society of the sick?

Henry had cleared away most of the snow by then. The newspaper boy (actually an elderly man trying to supplement his meagre pension) said hello. As a matter of fact, Henry felt a bit of a cultural conservative: he was still reading newspapers, printed matter that is, and real books, like his parents.

Of course he was on the internet every day, writing emails or looking things up, or just watching weird things on YouTube.

He was not on Facebook … yet.

I could live on Facebook, like so many others. Why go out into the real world? I could have a thousand friends on Facebook. Or be what I want to be, create my own identity. Unlimited freedom.

But then: Computer games, the surrogate of reality. People don't go out anymore. Stay indoors, in their own self-chosen private prison cells.

Others do the exact opposite: Engage in extreme sports, go on survival trips in South America. Outdoor activities being a craze, too. At least according to the media. Contradiction again. The real world? Where or what is it?

Uncertainty. How should I live? Are there only the extremes left?

What should I do? What is the right thing to do?

The net. Endless freedom, but under close surveillance. Leaving my electronic fingerprint everywhere. For all eternity. Because the net never forgets. But then, we all leave our tracks, don't we. Uncertainty. Should I be using the net at all?

I can be tracked down at any time by Big Brother. But they say we don't need to worry. We live in a democracy, don't we. So don't you worry. You've got nothing to hide, have you? And these cameras in public, and not so public places, closed-circuit TV. It's good for you. Guarantees your personal security. Helps to fight crime and terrorism. We can't do without. And you have got nothing to hide, … or have you? Give up your freedom to be free.

A contradiction in terms: "Freedom is slavery." Orwell.

Henry went back in and put on the kettle. Time for a cuppa. Time to get moving. Time for school. Start into a new week. Get ready for the real world.

Becoming an adult.

Learning to live with contradictions and uncertainties.

Learning to live.

Your life.   *(825 words)*

B Translation/Mediation

B1 Translation

Stanley Wells: „Shakespeare, Sex und Liebe" (Ausschnitt aus einer Rezension)

Wenn es irgendeinen besonderen Aspekt in Shakespeares Werk gibt, der ihn gegenüber jedem anderen großen Schriftsteller auszeichnet, so ist es die erstaunliche Bandbreite seiner Auseinandersetzung mit Liebe und Sex. Diese großen Themen spielen nicht nur in praktisch jedem Theaterstück, das er geschrieben hat, eine herausragende Rolle, er behandelt darüber hinaus mit großer Freude am Detail ein solches Spektrum sexueller Erfahrungen, dass er Masters und Johnson geradezu armselig aussehen lässt. Von den überschwänglichsten Gefühlsausbrüchen im Stile Petrarcas bis hin zu den niedrigsten Körperfunktionen deckt er alles nur Erdenkliche ab. [...]

Wells prägnantes und elegant geschriebenes Buch beleuchtet hintersinnig und systematisch Shakespeares Anerkennung dessen, was es bedeutet ganz und gar menschlich zu sein, samt allen Höhen und Tiefen sowie[1] der unvermeidbar widersprüchlichen Natur unserer Existenz, besonders in Hinsicht auf die Thematik Sex und Liebe.

Es ist seine Überlegenheit auf diesem Gebiet, die ihn so sehr zum größten aller Schriftsteller macht, dass er seinen ärgsten Rivalen beim Kampf um die Dichterkrone[2], Charles Dickens, mühelos in den Schatten stellt.

Anmerkungen
1 Das „sowie" dient der besseren Lesbarkeit. (Stil)
2 Die Krone muss hier in Ihrem übertragenen Sinne gesehen werden. Der Begriff Dichterkrone trifft die Bedeutung im Originaltext am besten.

B2 Mediation

The text is written in a high brow-style. Probably you will have to read the text several times before you understand it properly. Then you have to break down what Günther says for your classmates. After you have identified the most important aspects of the text try to express them in a simple way.

The key points are:
– in Schlegel's translation: love between Romeo and Juliet = spiritual rather than physical
– Frank Günther made a translation of the play himself (cf. source)
– original play contains several sexual connotations
– German audience = strongly influenced by Schlegel's translation → rejects translations that contain sexual aspects.
– many puns (often dirty and rather colloquial) = symbolize that many aspects in life can be interpreted on several levels and are deliberately used to create contrast
– play is written for adults
– to do Shakespeare justice and to get the full literary effect of his work, all aspects of the play have to be translated

Frank Günther, who produced a new translation of Shakespeare's *Romeo and Juliet* himself, writes that in Germany, even those who have not seen the play on stage, or have not read it yet, are still deeply influenced by traditional, bowdlerized translations which have failed to come to terms with the diversity of Shakespeare's language.

He accuses especially Schlegel's translation of having removed many passages he considered improper or offensive, thereby turning *Romeo and Juliet* into a harmless, sentimental lyrical ballad. However, these cleaned-up translations still exert a considerable influence on the German audience and, as a result, more appropriate translations are often seen as a violation of Shakespeare's work.

Günther goes on to point out that Schlegel has not only obliterated the apparent sexual innuendos, but has also failed to do justice to one of Shakespeare's most remarkable literary techniques, the skilful and entertaining employment of puns and quibbles. It is for that reason that Schlegel's translation misses out on Shakespeare's display of wit and deliberate change in style. Günther claims that the rather saucy, wild and provocative statements add realistic and lively colour to Shakespeare's work and therefore must not be omitted.

Günther comes to the conclusion that *Romeo and Juliet* is indeed a piece intended for an adult audience and therefore any translation should try to include Shakespeare's complete stylistic scope, without making any concessions to "good taste" or public morals. *(233 words)*

Prüfungsteilnehmer A

Topic: School in Society

Your headmaster has called for students to contribute ideas towards promoting cooperation between your school and external partners.

Comment on the notices.

> Watercolour pictures, linocut prints and collages by A-level Art students re-exhibited in the local hospital from November 10th to December 10th.

> A-level language students have prepared topical city tours in English, French and Russian. The City Council welcomes this idea as a good example of cooperation.

Together with your partner discuss the mutual benefits of cooperation between schools and external partners. Try to develop realistic suggestions for your school.

Prüfungsteilnehmer B

Topic: School in Society

Your headmaster has called for students to contribute ideas towards promoting cooperation between your school and external partners.

Comment on the notices.

> Local firm advises students on running their own company at school and acts as main sponsor.

> A-level student writing research paper in Biology on the composition of blood, assisted by specialists from the local hospital where he is doing practical research.

Together with your partner discuss the mutual benefits of cooperation between schools and external partners. Try to develop realistic suggestions for your school.

Lösungsvorschläge

School in Society

JEREMIAS: Our topic is "School in Society", and we are supposed to contribute some realistic ideas about how our school could cooperate with external partners and to what extent our school could benefit from such a cooperation.

Now I have been given two notices about two projects where students have worked with external partners. The first one is a notice advertising an exhibition in which A-level art students show their work in a local hospital.

I should think this is quite interesting, because as an artist you do rely on an audience. If you paint, you don't just do so for yourself: you want to have people look at your work, be delighted, and – at least if you want to turn professional – you want people to buy it. So any exhibition which allows people to look at your products is helpful, and why not use a hospital as a venue? I can see the mutual benefit here. Hospitals are, more often than not, fairly dreary places. People are sick, they don't feel well, and as regards interior design, most hospitals look quite uninspiring, to say the least. Therefore, some lively art, made by young people, and hopefully not too depressive, might cheer people up. Give them something beautiful to look at. Why not create some art for hospitals, art that gives you a good feeling, keeps your mind busy, but on a positive plane. You know what I mean? That would be a real challenge and a good deed, too.

ANNALENA: I get your idea, but perhaps you should not really impose any restrictions on those students. As you know, the beauty of things lies in the eye of the beholder. What you might conceive as depressive, might just be a good and realistic representation of other people's feelings.

JEREMIAS: Yeah, perhaps you are right. But as a patient, I would rather look at something colourful, something positive, and anyway, why shouldn't artists be considering a specific audience, or place? Not just "l'art pour l'art", but art to achieve a certain effect such as the use of art in advertising or industrial design. It would open up some art students' perspective, you know, so that they could get a well-paying job with a company later on.

By the way, that connects nicely with the other notice I have been given. It's about making yourself useful, and perhaps even making some money, by using your language skills. You see, it's about A-level students working for the city council, offering topical city tours in different foreign languages. I think that's great, as you can practice your foreign language in a realistic, truly communicative setting. You don't speak to be graded by your teacher as we are doing right now, but to really inform people who have a genuine interest in what you have to say. Again, you use your skills to do something useful for others, namely the city council and the tourist, as well as for yourself. Even if you don't take up the job as a tourist guide for the rest of your life, you could still do that on the side, for instance when you go to university. And I guess it could be fun. If you are good and well prepared, you would get positive feedback in a real life situation, and when working out a tour, you might get to know your own town a lot better.

ANNALENA: Perhaps that is the major point here. Mutual benefit. Doing something for others and getting something in return. One of my notices says that there is a company that advises students on running their own company at school, and not only that, it also acts as main sponsor. It does not say what kind of company they have in mind, but I could think of a catering firm, providing sandwiches, drinks and so forth. You know, the typical "Schülerfirma", a students' company.

JEREMIAS: Sounds intriguing. These are things that school does not really prepare us for: the economy, economic thinking, thinking up strategies of how to sell your services, or your skills, or products like in my art project, on the market, how to earn a living, real life.

ANNALENA: Or just how to make things work. How to get yourself organized in a commercial context.

The other note I got is equally interesting. It's not so much about the economy, but finding a job in science, of finding out why the stuff you learn at school in the natural sciences might prove useful and rewarding. You see, the note is about an A-level student writing a research paper in biology on the composition of blood. He is assisted by specialists from the local hospital where he's doing practical research. Sounds like a BELL[1] to me, our "special project" we can do to replace one of our orals. So that one is quite practical, catching two birds with one stone, so to speak. As a future scientist, or medical doctor, you get some good insight into practical research, and as a student, you can hope for a good grade. And on top of that, your research might indeed be more than just a little exercise, it might in fact be relevant, if it is imbedded in a greater project. As far as I know, research on blood cells or other biological items is almost always done in research groups, often spanning the entire world. So in this context, such work might prove to be very fruitful to the student. It might even open the doors to something greater, helping to establish some useful contact with other scientists, or sponsors. You never know.

JEREMIAS: And for the other side it might be good because they can recruit some new scientific talent, junior scientific staff.

So we both agree that such projects with external partners, commercial or non-commercial, are of mutual benefit to all partners involved.

Now, how about some more realistic suggestions for our school. What other projects could we think of, which are both beneficial and realistic?

ANNALENA: How about our musicians performing in homes for the elderly, or the local hospice. Music is great for bringing happiness to those with a hard life. And our musical people would have the chance of playing for a real audience, ...

JEREMIAS: ... and experience the great benefit and joy music might bring, apart from the usual critical listeners such as teachers, fellow musicians, or parents who expect, or at least hope for, top performances.

ANNALENA: Right, it would be playing without the pressure, just to be enjoyed by others. In a real context, with a real, grateful audience.

JEREMIAS: It could be done either as charity, for free, or they could charge a little money from the institutions, or pass the hat around after the performance. And some students could start organising this on a more professional basis, with various groups, from solos, to duos, trios, up to an entire orchestra, playing in all sorts of places, perhaps even commercial ones, like restaurants, or at weddings, where you would earn some money.

ANNALENA: Good thinking. I believe it is important to look at the commercial side of things like how you can make money, because that is what makes the world go round. You cannot live on charity projects for the rest of your life. If you want to become a musician, you need to find a way to make ends meet.

JEREMIAS: Sure, but using your talent for charity does not hurt either. Still, you do have a point, "mutual benefit" could well mean that things also pay off financially.

Our musicians could perhaps also give lessons. Why not found our own music school, using the classrooms for giving lessons in the afternoon? Or during the lunch break? That would be great for students who think of taking up an instrument, but do not really want to attend a professional music school. They could try themselves out, at low cost ... or at no cost at all, if we could find a commercial sponsor, or at least students whose parents have a small income could get lessons for free. But finding such a sponsor might prove difficult ...

ANNALENA: But not impossible. Maybe we could find some more parents to act as sponsors. Anyway, I was thinking of a student firm which could run an extra tuition network, where, for a modest fee, they organize student tuition, with older or more advanced students helping those who need "a little help from a friend". Something that would be useful for those in need of extra tuition, and fruitful for those who run such a service. I mean, education is big business, and there are lots of commercial companies out there offering support for students. A student firm like this would prepare you to think in economic terms, think about supply and demand, think about qualifications. Perhaps you could even organize some training for your student teachers. Here the teachers of our school could come in. The school would benefit in terms of better students, better results, and less stress for the teachers. Of course it would be great if the teachers would get paid to train us. That's why a sponsor would come in handy. We could then perhaps offer something more substantial, more professional, and make it a real success.

JEREMIAS: I agree. All these projects should be supported by a professional external partner to help with money, and most of all, expertise.

ANNALENA: Or just providing facilities, like rooms, or equipment, like computers, projectors, teaching materials, or musical instruments ...

JEREMIAS: But they should not just be asked to give something to us. We need to think of something we could give back in return.

ANNALENA: Right, but difficult to do since students cannot really act professionally, nor can they really produce anything that meets professional standards. We would need some good will on behalf of the companies in the first place, but as we have pointed out, they might profit in the long term.

JEREMIAS: Like boosting up their reputation, or finding recruits for their own company. But you are right: it's finding sponsors or partners who would be prepared to make a financial commitment, which is the difficult part.

ANNALENA: Yeah, that would be the first task on the list. Find out who could sponsor what, and I suppose at the end of the day it would be a matter of trial and error. We would have to send mails, try and establish contact.

JEREMIAS: That's right and find out about networks of support. Perhaps asking the parents might be useful because at least in principal, they should have a genuine interest in helping.

ANNALENA: Or they might know somebody who knows ... It would definitely be worth a try.

(1804 words)

Anmerkung
1 *Besondere Lernleistung*

Prüfungsteilnehmer A

Topic: Equality

As an assignment in your English class you are expected to write and deliver a speech on the topic "Equality".

Comment on the results of this survey.

Earnings by degree and sex (for women and men in the US, ages 30–44, in 2007)

Degree	Median weekly earnings, women	Median weekly earnings, men
Doctoral	$ 1,243	$ 1,754
Master's	$ 1,126	$ 1,458
Bachelor's	$ 891	$ 1,200
High school graduate, no college	$ 542	$ 716

Age Groups	Women's % of Men's Earnings
20–24	92.9 %
25–34	88.7 %
35–44	77.4 %
45–54	73.6 %
55–64	75.3 %
65+	76.1 %

Data based on U. S. Bureau of Labor Statistics: Current Population Survey.
Median Weekly Earnings of Full-time Wage and Salary Workers by
Selected Characteristics, 2007.

Together with your partner(s) discuss the topic "Equality". Refer to different spheres of life. Plan a convincing speech.

Prüfungsteilnehmer B

Topic: Equality

As an assignment in your English class you are expected to write and deliver a speech on the topic "Equality".

Comment on the results of this survey.

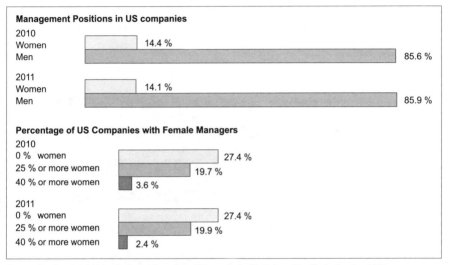

Source: Catalyst Quick Take: Statistical Overview of Women in the Workplace. New York: Catalyst, 2012.

Together with your partner(s) discuss the topic "Equality". Refer to different spheres of life. Plan a convincing speech.

Prüfungsteilnehmer C

Topic: Equality

At an assignment in your English class you are expected to write and deliver a speech on the topic "Equality".

Comment on the results of this survey.

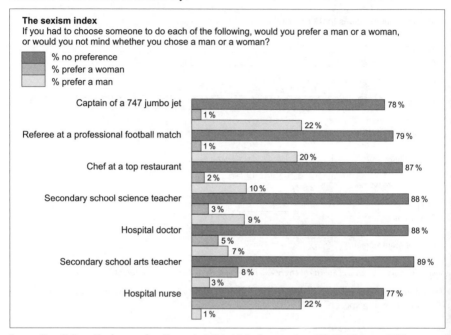

Source: Peter Kellner: Number cruncher: How sexist is Britain? In: Prospect, Issue 180, 23rd February 2011.

Together with your partner(s) discuss the topic "Equality". Refer to different spheres of life. Plan a convincing speech.

Lösungsvorschläge

Equality

The representation of the values in the diagram for Test Participant C is distorted. This distortion can be included in the analysis.

Partner A: Alina

Right, here we go. We are supposed to write a speech on the topic "Equality" and deliver it as an assignment in our English class. Now, I have been given some statistics from 2007 about earnings by degree and sex for men and women aged 30 to 44 in the US. You will hardly find it surprising that academics with doctoral degrees are the top earners, closely followed by people holding a master's degree. Then come people with a Bachelor's degree. At the bottom of the table are people without a college education.

It also comes as no surprise that women earn considerably less for obviously doing the same job. The differences in weekly earning amounts to more than 500 dollars as regards people with a doctoral degree, which, if my calculation is correct, results in men getting almost 40 percent more pay than women. This more or less accounts for the other groups as well.

Another table shows the differences between the earnings of women related to that of their male counterparts in relationship to their respective age group.

Here it becomes obvious that young women, aged 20 to 24 receive about 93 percent of the men's earnings. However, this number gets smaller the older the women are. Funnily enough, with 73.6 percent the difference in the age group of the 45 to 54 year-olds is the greatest.

So this leaves us with two messages. Number one: the bad news, which is: women earn considerably less than men. Number two: there is hope, as the income gap, with "only" about 7 percent, doesn't seem to be quite so big as regards the younger generation, which is encouraging for the people who have just started a career.

Anyway, what matters is that women do not get the same pay for doing the same work. That's not fair and must not be tolerated. So that is definitely a point to be mentioned in our speech: the inequality as regards pay, which is one of the most significant forms of sexual discrimination, and I really wonder how companies and employers can get away with it.   *(353 words)*

Partner B: Zita

I can't agree more. It is a scandal. But the facts you have just mentioned fit nicely into the statistics I have been given. They show that in US companies, in 2010 and 2011, management positions in companies were largely held by men, with 85.6 percent in 2010 and even more – 85.9 in 2011. So there has even been a slight dwindling in numbers of women in management. The same is true for the number of companies with 40 percent or more women as managers. In fact this number fell from 3.6 percent in 2010 to 2.4 percent in 2011. Quite a significant decline, which might allow the speculation that for whatever reason women find it harder to become managers these days. Although, of course, we do not have sufficient data, for example the numbers for 2012, to prove that this is a general development.

On the other hand, to me it is significant that companies with no female managers at all remained at a steady percentage of 27.4 percent. That's almost a third of all American companies.

To sum up, women are still largely underrepresented when it comes to managerial positions, or any of the top jobs in the economy. And that's of course true for every country on this planet, also for Germany where they have been discussing affirmative action to change things for the better.

So affirmative action as a tool against discrimination ought to be discussed in our speech. It's not enough to go on moaning and groaning about inequality. We should try to show a way out.   *(262 words)*

Partner C: Luca

Well, I don't know if affirmative action is the right way, but I agree, the current state of affairs is not satisfactory, especially if you take into account that by now, in most western countries, if not all, women have at least as many academic degrees as men, and that they are as well qualified. The question I ask myself is: Why do they often apply for what are typically "female" jobs, if I may say so.

You see, my statistics, referred to as "The sexism index", show that, when it comes to jobs traditionally regarded as "a man's job" like flying a plane, or being a ref at a football match, significantly more people would prefer a man to a woman. It is the other way round, when referring to a job traditionally associated with women. The classic one being that of a hospital nurse. I mean, as far as I know, there isn't even a proper word for a male nurse. It's just "male nurse". Well, there we are then … Anyway, the good news is that the great majority of people, between 89 and 77 percent, do not have any preference.

For our speech I would suggest that we should also consider traditional role models and expectations when it comes to women's position in society, and also discuss if there are genuine differences between men and women as regards job preferences.   *(234 words)*

Discussion

ALINA: What do you mean?

LUCA: What I mean is that if you look at job preferences you still find rather few women taking degrees in technology, or engineering, or maths, or physics. Isn't that so?

ZITA: So you mean, that it is a man's world out there. I suppose numerically, you are right, but perhaps we should ask ourselves the question why that is so.

ALINA: I know that in other countries, there aren't such great differences. Perhaps our school system does not do enough to encourage girls to take up sciences and maths?

LUCA: I don't know. As far as I know there have been attempts to involve more girls in this field, by establishing extra natural science and maths classes for girls.

ALINA: Be that as it may, it is fact that nowadays, apart from some fields where women are underrepresented, women are as well qualified as men, but still earn less and do not get into the top jobs.

ZITA: True, that cannot be denied. And that's what we should focus on in our speech. Because that can and that must be changed.

ALINA: To quote Obama: "Yes, we can!"

LUCA : Only if we really want to. But I assume, men are not really willing to make way for women, that is, to give up their dominant position in society.

ZITA: That's why we need affirmative action. A law that forces companies to make a change.

LUCA: I don't agree. For the same reason, laws like this have not yet been implemented, or only partly. It must be up to the companies to decide who is running them. In a free economy, politics must not interfere with entrepreneurial decision making.

ZITA: I see, you are a real liberal then.

LUCA: Well, I don't know about that. But perhaps we can agree on other measures, like making it easier for women to reach top positions in society.

ALINA: Now, wait a minute. First we should agree that there must be equal pay, no matter what. That to me is not negotiable.

LUCA: We are in agreement. Equal pay is a must for any democratic society, and that can be enforced by law, or at least it should be. Equal pay for equal work.

ZITA: Right. Unequal pay is discrimination on the grounds of sex. And that's illegal. So that would be our starting point.

ALINA: And then, we have to talk about ways in which society can enable more women to reach top positions, as Luca has rightly suggested. How to make it possible to have a family and a good job.

JUCA: Something they seem to manage in France, or Scandinavian countries.

ZITA: Yes, we could point out some facts about countries where things are better than in Germany. By putting forward some convincing arguments we could show that things could work a lot better.

ALINA: Like hinting at the fact that Germany will soon face a shortage of qualified workers, so it would be indeed wise to improve working conditions for women.

LUCA: Good point. And closing the income gap would mean that more women would be motivated to find a job, and have a family as well.

ZITA: And men taking paternity leave, as younger men apparently do in growing numbers. By the way, would you, Luca?

LUCA: I would indeed. No problem, at least not for me. We could show that in the new generation, both men and women want to have a good life, that they are not prepared to sacrifice everything just for the sake of their jobs, and that this development is a positive one.

ALINA: I read about this tendency in young people as well. This might indeed be a great step forward towards equality, if both, men and women, concentrate on what is really important for them, not just on working as hard as they possibly can in order to earn as much as possible.

ZITA: Talking about a great step forward – why don't we include some of the historical landmarks as regards the development of sexual equality in order to show how far we have progressed on the one hand, and how far we are still lagging behind on the other hand. Did you know, for instance, that some 50 years ago, women in West Germany needed their husband's written consent to take on a job? Or he could go and terminate his wife's employment, if he wanted to.

ALINA: Sounds absolutely absurd to me.

ZITA: As absurd as receiving 30 percent less pay for doing the same job?

LUCA: True. That's a very good strategy, juxtaposing the "good old times", with all its overt sexism and discrimination with the injustices applying to today's situation.

ALINA: Yep. First we should make people think: Oh, yes, those were terrible times, but now ... And then they realize that things are still absurdly bad, for instance when it comes to equal pay.

ZITA: And equal opportunity.

ALINA: And preconceived notions of what is a man's or a woman's job. *(841 words)*

Teil A: Text 1

Food for thought

Walking through the park on my way to work, I pause to admire a bag lady feeding the pigeons. A few have perched on her arms, a few in her lap, and she chatters with them while scattering seed. One bird tells another, more birds join, until finally, there are too many birds. Overwhelmed by flapping, clawing, pecking, and scratching birds; the old
5 lady becomes a blurred confusion of feathers and beaks and claws and beady black eyes.

I have just told Mum a truth that will change the rest of my life. "Mum, are you ok?" I ask. At the other end of the phone, I hear her lighter flick flick, a crackle of burning tobacco, a sharp inhalation, then a release of tension in a long, sighing exhale. "It's going to be ok. It's going to be ok. No matter what happens, we'll always love you," says Mum. "I know."
10 "I have to go now, ok." "Go." "I'll pick you up tomorrow darling," click, then silence.

Lying on the couch, thumbing through a magazine, my ears prick to a familiar sound: the raspy exhaust note of Mum's car as it drives up my street. "Your Mum's here," says Pete, my flatmate, "she's out by her car, but she won't come in. Christ, she looked at me like I'm some kind of axe murderer." "Sorry," I reply while peering through the blinds; Mum
15 is waiting by the car with a face like thunder. My stomach starts churning, my heart starts racing, and I want to run away, out the back door to anywhere but here. We drive to Bunbury in silence, it has been raining hard for a week; we rush by wet paddocks, full creeks, and fat cows. I can't get comfortable, I wriggle and fidget; with the seat, the radio, the air-conditioning, "Would-you-just-sit-still," demands Mum through clenched teeth. We
20 are home now, Mum is on the opposite end of the couch from me, smoothing the black couch fabric with her left hand, cigarette in her right, her face lost in a layer of smoke. "When did you know? You know … that you were gay?" Mum asks. "I don't know. I thought you knew." "I suspected, but, then there was that girl …" "Mary?" "Yes." Sounds of Dad cooking come from the kitchen: pots rattle, knives chop, and pans sizzle –
25 the everyday noise comforts the tense house. "Did you tell Dad?" I ask. "Yes." "And?"

"You have no idea how difficult this is for him, for someone of his generation." "And it's not difficult for me?" "Well, that's your choice." "No. The only choice I had, was to live the rest of my life a lie, or to tell the truth." The smells of pancetta and garlic frying mix with the kitchen clatter; Dad is cooking my favourite – Spaghetti Carbonara. A quiet
30 man, Dad is most comfortable in the kitchen, he talks to us through his love of food. Nothing more is said, Mum and I set the table together, TV off, music on. Dad brings us our meals. He passes mine to me, this steaming, heaped bowl says for him: you are my only son, and right now I am mourning for the life you will not lead, the grandchildren I will probably never have, but, I love you and nothing you do will ever take that away. He
35 avoids my eye but halfway through dinner I look at him, he has stopped eating, and a tear slips down the angles of his face, dropping into the last of his pasta. He says nothing, leans over and squeezes my hand.

As quickly as they came, the pigeons are gone, as if by some silent agreement they take to the air as one, flying up into the sky through the arching fig trees. Together, the old
40 lady and me, we watch them fly, she catches my eye, and we both laugh. *(657 words)*

Myles Formby: Food for thought. 23/06/2004.
URL: http://www.abc.net.au/shortstories/stories/s1138797.htm

Teil A: Text 2

I look at the world

> I look at the world
> From awakening eyes in a black face
> And this is what I see:
> This fenced-off narrow space
> 5   Assigned to me.
>
> I look then at the silly walls
> Through dark eyes in a dark face
> And this is what I know:
> That all these walls oppression builds
> 10   Will have to go!
>
> I look at my own body
> With eyes no longer blind
> And I see that my own hands can make
> The world that's in my mind.
> 15   Then let us hurry, comrades,
>
> The road to find.   *(95 words)*

Langston Hughes: I look at the world. In: Langston Hughes: The Poems 1921–1940.
Edited by Arnold Rampersad. Columbia: University of Missouri Press 2001. © 2001 by
Ramona Bass and Arnold Rampersad, Administrators of the Estate of Langston Hughes.

A Text production

A1 Working with the text   25 BE

Examine how both authors present the topic *Being Different* and explain how each text appeals to its reader.

Write a coherent text.

A2 Composition   25 BE

Choose <u>one</u> of the following tasks.

2.1 You are attending a public speaking workshop during which you are expected to deliver a motivational speech for your peers with the title *Dare to Be Different*.

Write your speech.

2.2 "Lies that build are better than truths that destroy."
Discuss this proverb referring to different spheres of life.

2.3 "We hold these truths to be self-evident, that all men are created equal, that they are endowed by their Creator with certain unalienable Rights, that among these are Life, Liberty and the pursuit of Happiness."

Comment on how these ideals from the Declaration of Independence (1776) have stood the test of time in the United States.

		Erreichbare BE-Anzahl (Summe A1 und A2):
A1	Working with the text	Inhaltliche Reichhaltigkeit und Textstruktur: 10 BE
		Sprachliche Korrektheit: 10 BE
		Ausdrucksvermögen und Textfluss: 5 BE
A2	Composition	Inhaltliche Reichhaltigkeit und Textstruktur: 10 BE
		Sprachliche Korrektheit: 10 BE
		Ausdrucksvermögen und Textfluss: 5 BE
		Gesamt: 50 BE

Teil B: Mediation

Gemeinsam mit einer englischen Schule nehmen Sie an einem internationalen Projekt zum Thema „The Technology of Tomorrow, Today" teil.
Ihre Aufgabe besteht darin, auf der Grundlage des folgenden Textes einen englischsprachigen Artikel für den Internetauftritt des Projekts zu verfassen. Darin beschreiben Sie die Funktionsweise des autonomen Autos und stellen die möglichen Auswirkungen seiner Nutzung dar.

Computer am Steuer ist noch ungeheuer

Die Geisterhand sitzt oben auf dem Autodach, eingezwängt in eine Büchse aus Metall. Das Konstrukt sieht seltsam aus – wie eine fahrende Kaffeemühle. Tatsächlich aber handelt es sich um ein Hightech-System, das den Straßenverkehr revolutionieren könnte: Die Metallbüchse soll Autos ohne Fahrer ans Ziel bringen, vorbei an Staus und Unfallstellen,
5 sicher, pünktlich, spritsparend. Wie von Geisterhand geführt.

Das „autonome Auto", wie es in Fachkreisen genannt wird, klingt nach Science-Fiction, doch auf den Straßen von Nevada ist es schon Realität. Seit ein paar Wochen dürfen die Bordcomputer dort das Steuer übernehmen, nicht nur auf einer Teststrecke, sondern im normalen Berufsverkehr. Der Führerschein für die Geisterhand ist ein Novum in der ame-
10 rikanischen Verkehrsgeschichte. Einzige Bedingung der Behörden Nevadas ist die Präsenz eines menschlichen Beifahrers, der einspringen soll, falls die Systeme verrücktspielen. Ein Tritt auf die Bremse oder eine Bewegung des Lenkrads genügen, um den Autopiloten auszuschalten.

Hinter dem Projekt stehen Ingenieure aus dem Hause Google, allen voran der deutsche
15 Computerwissenschaftler Sebastian Thrun. Als 18-Jähriger verlor Thrun seinen besten Freund bei einem Autounfall. Er entschloss sich, den Rest seines Lebens darauf zu verwenden, gegen den tödlichen Alltag auf den Straßen anzukämpfen. Thrun studierte in Hildesheim und Bonn, dann wanderte er nach Kalifornien aus. Dort lehrt er an der Universität Stanford und widmet sich als Google-Fellow den Forschungsarbeiten am autono-
20 men Auto.

Acht Prototypen aus den Laboratorien des Technologiekonzerns haben nun in Nevada eine Zulassung erhalten. Sechs Toyota Prius, ein Audi TT und ein Lexus RX 450h. In allen Fahrzeugen übernehmen Lasersysteme und GPS-Ortung die Rolle der menschlichen Sinnesorgane. Computerprogramme verarbeiten die Datenströme und lenken die Google-
25 Mobile durch den Wüstenstaat [...].

Sogar ein eigenes Kennzeichen für die autonomen Autos gibt es in Nevada schon. Eine liegende Acht, das Symbol für Unendlichkeit, auf einem roten Hintergrund, dazu der Schriftzug: „Autonomous Vehicle". Bruce Breslow, der Chef von Nevadas Zulassungsbehörde, findet das Unendlichkeitssymbol würde am besten passen zum „Auto der Zu-
30 kunft". Aber macht sie wirklich das Auto der Zukunft aus, die auf dem Dach aufmontierte Geisterhand?

Es ist kaum vorstellbar, dass Autokäufer in ein paar Jahren bereit wären, auf computergesteuerte Autos umzusteigen. Viele Menschen beschleicht ein ungutes Gefühl, wenn die eigene Möglichkeit zur Kontrolle der versprochenen Sicherheit eines IT-Systems ge-
35 opfert wird. Und selbstverständlich verlöre Autofahren die emotionale Qualität, auf die Konzerne in ihrer aufwendig produzierten Werbung so gerne abheben.

Solche Fragen beschäftigen Thrun nicht. Für ihn geht es vor allem um eines: die Sicherheit. Im Autoland Amerika sterben jedes Jahr 30 000 Menschen im Straßenverkehr. Und menschliches Versagen ist mit großem Abstand die Unfallursache Nummer eins. [...]

40 Die Akzeptanzprobleme sind [jedoch] gewaltig. Menschen vertrauen eben lieber ihren eigenen Fähigkeiten; das Gefühl, sich einem Computersystem auszuliefern, schürt hingegen Angst. [...]

Eine vielleicht noch wichtigere Hürde für die Einführung der neuen Technologie als die psychologischen Vorbehalte gegen Computer ist der Einwand, dass führerlose Fahrzeuge 45 im Straßenverkehr enorme Verwirrung stiften würden. Beispielsweise an Kreuzungen, an denen Menschen ihr Fahrverhalten oftmals nach Zeichen anderer Fahrer richten.

Sie geben einander Signale, eine Handbewegung, ein Blick in die Augen reicht zur Verständigung. Menschen wissen, wie sich andere Menschen orientieren. Was in einem Computer vor sich geht, wissen sie nicht. Dieses Problem ließe sich nur lösen, wenn alle 50 Autos auf Autopilot umstellen würden – was einstweilen noch vollkommen unrealistisch erscheint. Doch vielleicht werden die Vorteile autonomer Verkehrsmittel die Skeptiker irgendwann überzeugen, schließlich gehen sie über den Sicherheitsaspekt hinaus. Computersysteme im Auto dienen schließlich auch dem Umweltschutz. Die Programme lassen sich so einstellen, dass sie den Spritverbrauch minimieren. Anders als mancher 55 menschliche Fahrer haben die Bordcomputer keine Freude an heulenden Motoren und quietschenden Reifen. Und auch darum geht es: um verlorene Zeit. Staus sind eine massive Produktivitätsbremse in modernen Volkswirtschaften. Stunden, die für die Arbeit genutzt werden können, verstreichen mit stumpfsinnigem Warten, wenn mal wieder eine Unfallstelle die Autobahn blockiert.

60 [...] Zwar sind die Aussichten gering, dass das autonome Google-Mobil demnächst in Serienproduktion geht. Der Computerkonzern kann aber darauf hoffen, Technologien und Patente an Autohersteller zu verkaufen. *(656 Wörter)*

Moritz Koch. Computer am Steuer ist noch ungeheuer. Süddeutsche Online.
12. Juni 2012. http://www.sueddeutsche.de/auto/fahren-ohne-fahrer-computer-am-
steuer-ist-noch-ungeheuer-1.1380556 [downloaded 12 September 2013]

20 BE

Lösungsvorschlag

A Text production

A1 Working with the text

The key points are:
- *Presentation of the topic of being different in the texts (text forms, tension, stylistic devices, content)*
- *How the texts appeal to the reader (suspense, use of language, creation of images, appeal to emotions)*
- *Short story: typical narrative features (direct opening, short episode, rise of action/ building up/ creation of suspense, open ending) and stylistic devices*
- *Poem: imagery, development of conscience, extra line in third stanza*

Both the given texts are works of fiction which deal with the topic of being different and changing one's life. "Food for thought" is a short story and "I look at the world" is a poem, literary genres that are well suited to appeal to the reader's emotions.

Myles Formby's short story "Food for thought", which appeared in 2004, is about a homosexual man recalling the moment when he told his parents about his sexual orientation. The story centres on the feelings and fears the narrator has as he is trying to come to terms with the anticipated reactions of his parents.

The dense emotional atmosphere is created by the story being told by a first-person narrator in the present tense, using direct speech and imagery as to give the reader a first-hand, direct insight into the protagonist's thoughts and feelings.

Formby starts his story with an element of suspense, depicting a homeless woman ("bag lady", l. 1) feeding pigeons in a park the narrator is crossing on his way to work. The seemingly harmless situation turns out to become a gruesome incident, with the homeless woman seemingly being attacked by the birds: "Overwhelmed by flapping, clawing, pecking, and scratching birds" (l. 4) she "becomes a blurred confusion of feathers and beaks and claws and beady black eyes." (l. 5) Here, the usage of enumerations and alliterations consisting of menacing expressions such as "clawing", "pecking" and "scratching" evokes the sense of immediate danger.

The tension is enhanced by the narrator breaking off his narrative abruptly. The reader's curiosity as to whether the woman will come out of this situation unscathed is not satisfied.

Formby then introduces a new moment of suspense as he leads over to the sentence in which the narrator tells the reader that he has "just told [his] Mum a truth that will change the rest of [his] life." (l. 6) Again, the reader is left to speculate, this time about the "truth", which causes him to go on reading and which makes the whole text appeal to our sense of suspense.

The reader knows, by the reaction of the narrator's mother, that the "truth" must be of a substantial, even devastating nature, which is shown by the mother's repetition of the sentence "It's going to be ok." (ll. 8/9) and is further enhanced by the usage of onomatopoeia such as "flick flick," (l. 7) creating a direct sensual impression on the reader as to the mother's irritation.

When his mother comes to pick the narrator up, we, as readers, still do not know what the problem is, but when we learn that, wearing a "face like thunder" (l. 15), the mother refuses to enter the narrator's flat and looks at his flatmate as if he was "some kind of axe murderer" (l. 14), these drastic metaphoric expressions make us speculate about the gross nature of the conflict.

The tense atmosphere is perpetuated when the narrator's inability to come to terms with the situation is described in detail, including the narrator's physical reactions of panic and fear ("My stomach starts churning, my heart starts racing," ll. 15/16) and his mother telling him off as if he was a little child ("Would-you-just-sit-still," l. 19). The fact that she is sitting on the opposite side of the couch with "clenched teeth" (l. 19) shows both emotional detachment and distress.

The tenseness is finally dissolved when we gradually learn that the father has prepared the narrator's favourite dish. The cooking noise "comforts the tense house" (l. 25) and the father passes the food to his son, a symbol of togetherness. Together with the word "love" (l. 30) the atmosphere of tension and insecurity is replaced with that of peace and forgiveness. The fact that the father "talks to [his family] through his love of food" (l. 30) could also stand as a symbol of intuition, transcending words and language, literally a "gut reaction" as to the importance of family ties over sexual and social conventions.

The other, second moment of denouement is the outcome of the pigeon episode from the beginning. Just as the narrator's coming out ends in a peaceful note of compassion and understanding, the pigeons prove to be harmless, as harmless as they should be as symbols of peace, with the narrator and the homeless woman connecting in communal laughter. On a symbolic plane, both, parents and pigeons, have finally emerged as what they should be, caring and peaceful.

This positive outcome leaves the reader with a feeling of relief and hope as to the future of the narrator and his relationship with his parents.

In his poem "I look at the world" from 1930 Langston Hughes, like Myles Formby, uses the present tense to draw the reader directly into the train of thought in which the lyrical I develops a political consciousness to wake up to the reality of racial oppression in the United States in the 1930s and take political action.

The development of the speaker's consciousness is described in three stages which correspond to the three stanzas of the poem.

In the first stanza, the lyrical I depicts how he discovers ("I see", l. 3) that he is living in a society which excludes him from full participation because he is black: "This fenced-off narrow space / Assigned to me."(ll. 4/5)

In the following stanza, the experience of being discriminated against is enhanced by the transition from the "awakening eyes" (l. 2) in the first stanza, to the "dark eyes" (l. 7) in the second one, symbolizing anger and frustration. Furthermore, the speaker does not only "see" (l. 3) the injustice as stated in the first stanza, he now "know[s]" (l. 8) about it which means that he has started to understand the underlying mechanisms of political and racial oppression. More intensity to the poem is added by the fact that, for the speaker, the "fenced-off narrow space" (l. 4) from the first stanza has now grown into "walls [of] oppression" (l. 9) which "[w]ill have to go" (l. 10), which indicates the need for direct involvement.

The last stanza finally dissolves into a straightforward call for action. The speaker has now come to a full understanding of his situation ("no longer blind" l. 12), is reassured as regards to taking an active role ("my own hands can make" l. 13) and even calls for immediate collective action, by transcending his own individual politicisation to promoting communal action ("let us hurry", l. 15), with the ensuing term "comrades" (l. 15) evoking an outspokenly radical political movement, perhaps even with strong left-wing leanings (as the poem was written during the Great Depression).

The importance of political action is further enhanced by the fact that in the last stanza the rhyme scheme is broken up by adding a sixth line, emphasizing the message that black people in the USA have to find a "road" (l. 16) to emancipation.   *(1,156 words)*

A2 Composition

The key points are:
- *Motivational speech: You favour and promote difference/diversity*
- *Reflect on individuality and conformity*
- *Use rhetoric devices typical of speeches to appeal to and persuade the listener, e. g. repetition, alliteration, antithesis, metaphors, similes ...*
- *Incorporate facts and examples of non-conformist behaviour/life-styles*

Dare to be different.

Dare to be different. Well, first of all, why should it be so daring to be different today?

Do we not live in an age of diversity, tolerance and – as my mum puts is – unlimited individualism? "People today are ever so open-minded, you can have tattoos all over, listen to all kinds of music, wear fancy clothes, nobody cares. Right then, deary, why should you then give a speech on difference?"

Well, that's my mum. And I do agree to some point. Yes, Germany has become a fairly liberal place. Tolerant to a great degree. But we shouldn't take that for granted.

In fact, my dad – whose head now looks like a bowling ball, smooth and clean, no hair whatsoever – once looked like a hippie, and he really got a lot of stick from his teachers, parents, but most of all on the football ground. "Hairy ape", "caveman", "loafer", "beatnik", "bum" ... were the more friendly expressions attributed to him. And of course he was accused of being a "homosexual". Now, my dad stood his ground. He did not choose the easy way out. He did not get a "decent hair cut". When I asked him how he could find the strength to see it through, he said that he gained the necessary confidence because there were always people who liked him for what he was.

Anyway, that's the seventies, you say, a long time ago, and times are different today. But not quite.

Let's look at today's professional footballers. You know what I'm driving at. If, as a professional player, you admitted to being gay, you've had it. End of story. At least that's what managers say, well, and the players themselves: Here, being different would make a huge difference indeed as it would mean the end of a player's career.

So what should we, as ardent football supporters, say to a homosexual footballer?

Well, we should encourage him. We should tell him that we love him for what he is. A player in our team, regardless of his sexual orientation.

We should point out examples of people who had their doubts about their coming out. Like Freddy Mercury, lead singer of the great glam rock band Queen, in case you didn't know. He had been hiding in the closet for years before he finally decided to come out. And it did him a good turn. Far from leaving him, his fans loved him even more, and they stood by him, even when it became known that he was suffering from AIDS.

Look at German politicians like the mayor of Berlin, Klaus Wowereit, or our ex-foreign secretary. Their coming out didn't mean the end of their careers either. On the contrary, to many people they came across as authentic, which perhaps made them more popular than before.

Anyway, standing by what you are, saying yes to being different will make your life better. Hiding from the truth, building a world of lies around you and trying to adapt to a way of life that is not at all yours will only get you depressed. Yes, conformity can be depressing.

So listen to the good news. Looking at the aforementioned examples, we can conclude that people are not as dumb or intolerant as we might think.

Let's now turn away from the football stadiums, concert halls and parliaments to the classroom. It's a place that in some respect requires a lot of conformity, where it is not always easy to be different. As we all know, status symbols are important. People without smart phones for instance are often mocked. Now, I don't have a smart phone myself, so I'm somewhat different, but then I dare to be different. You know why? Because I know there are quite a few others like me out there. And that helps. Seeing that you are not alone.

Because, and that's my message today, people might differ in some way like a hairstyle, whether or not they have a smart phone, or their sexual orientation, but they normally have a lot more to share with each other.

So don't be afraid. Be yourself. Be different.

(693 words)

2.2 *The key points are:*
  – *Introduction: explanation of the proverb*
  – *Discussion: pros and cons of lying/telling the truth*
  – *Different spheres of life (e. g. on a personal level, in business or in politics)*
  – *Final statement*

To begin with, lies are generally regarded as deceptive acts, as immoral, and religiously speaking, as sin. That's why people feel, by and large, committed to the truth. But when is a lie really a breach of confidence?

A famous proverb says: "Lies that build are better than truths that destroy." Sometimes the truth is painful; it can disrupt a relationship or hurt someone's feelings. In this case it may be better to tell a lie. However, we ought to draw a line between lies that under certain circumstances are acceptable and even necessary and truths, which – as painful as they might be – must be told.

Medical doctors can serve as good examples of people who have to tell patients unsettling truths. If a patient is fatally ill, for example, he must be told. There is no holding back, or is there? In the case of people being expected to die soon, this will, without a doubt, have a devastating effect on their psyche. Moreover, apart from making the patients' life miserable, their family and friends are also deeply affected. So in this respect, telling the truth does indeed have a destructive effect. But would it be better to hold back? There is no easy answer to this. Doctors are bound by oath to tell their patients what is wrong with them. However, they can choose not to tell the whole truth. They can remain vague when it comes to certain information, or just withhold it (if not directly asked). They can keep up hopes by telling the patient that there have always been exceptions. So there is room for interpretation, room for leaving things unsaid without telling downright lies.

Telling somebody the truth can also have a destructive effect when it comes to people's hopes and aspirations. If a violin player asks his or her teacher if they could embark on a professional career, being told that their talent would not suffice will undoubtedly cause frustration and may have a negative effect on their self-esteem. But clearly, not telling them the truth means shunning one's responsibility, as it can mean years of investment in something that cannot be achieved, thereby increasing the level of frustration and the student losing money and missing out on other career opportunities.

There are, however, spheres of life, where a straight lie might be acceptable. For example when it comes to war casualties, the army might tell the family of the deceased soldier that their child died "a clean death", that he or she didn't suffer, instead of giving the gruesome details. Here a lie might indeed alleviate a little bit of the pain instead of causing even more grief.

In the private sphere, a lie might, a least in some situations, be a good choice in order to spare your partner or your family the harsh consequences of the truth. People having an affair outside their relationship might choose not to tell their partners, as confessing the truth might be extremely painful to their partner and would put the whole family at risk, maybe for something that is not worth it.

There has also been substantial evidence that at the workplace, or at school, lies have a beneficial effect on employees and students. Following a culture of appraisal, people are often praised for just making an effort, even if they haven't accomplished anything substantial yet. Here, the praise (which could be taken as a friendly lie) helps to build up confidence and therefore turns out to be motivating, helping the pupils or employees to improve their performance.

However, in many cases the truth will be revealed at one point or other, so in conclusion, people should be very careful if they choose to tell a deliberate lie. Normally, the alternative to telling a lie is careful diplomacy including the use of euphemism as an attempt to make even bad news sound somewhat positive and constructive by either adding a pinch of hope or hinting at a solution. *(664 words)*

2.3 *The key points are:*
   - *Historical and political background of the Declaration of Independence*
   - *Examples of how the ideals are put into practice (democracy, voting rights, checks and balances, fewer social class barriers, freedom of expression, freedom of religion, free enterprise)*
   - *Examples of how the ideals have been violated throughout history: slavery, Native Americans*
   - *American Dream: land of opportunity, rags to riches, shortcomings*
   - *Current situation: gap between rich and poor, war on terrorism, spying on citizens (NSA affair)*

When the American colonies proposed their Declaration of Independence, they were at the starting point of creating a new society that would differ from that of Europe's. First of all, they wanted to be independent from the British Empire which suppressed its American subjects by imposing unfair taxes, by putting up trade barriers and – most of all – by not allowing the colonists any substantial political participation in their own affairs. The slogan "No taxation without representation" was a clear message to the British rulers that they wanted to be the masters of their own destiny.

Thus, the liberty not only of a new nation but also of the individual became the central point of the American constitution. There were no traditional ruling classes like the nobility or other set class boundaries. Free elections were introduced and a complex system of checks and balances was established to ensure that political power was not concentrated in the hands of a few.

Furthermore, there was freedom of religion which included the separation of church and state to avoid any substantial political influence by religious groups on the government. The freedom of expression ensured that people could speak their mind, and there was also the freedom of enterprise. People could pursue their happiness by setting up businesses without the state interfering. This triggered the myth of the American Dream, the idea of the self-made man who can achieve anything by working hard. In this respect, the USA became, and still is the most popular country in the world when it comes to attracting immigrants.

However, there have always been considerable dents in the American Dream, and serious doubts as to what extent the ideals of the Declaration of Independence have been achieved.

First of all, many of the Founding Fathers, including Washington and Jefferson, were themselves slave owners, and even though some of them seemed to oppose slavery or principle, they did not abolish it. So their ideals of equality did not apply to thousands of African Americans, who neither came to America of their own free will, nor were they granted the right to pursue their happiness. On the contrary: they were not ever conceived as individual human beings but as property. And the mistreatment of African Americans did not stop after the American Civil War. Segregation and discrimi nation went on for at least another hundred years and continues today. Although the United States now has an African American president, race is still a controversial issue. The second group that was excluded from the American ideals of the Constitution were the Native Americans. As the slaves were regarded as property, the "Indians" were seen as an inferior race that had to be civilised and assimilated. They were murdered, driven from their land and forced to live a life of degradation on reservations. Only in the last decades has their situation gradually improved, but it can be questioned as to whether they have really found their place in American society.

Apart from the planned and wilful exclusion of certain parts of the population, it should also be stated that the idea of the self-made man rising from rags to riches has not become true for everyone. In fact, the gap between the haves and the have-nots seems to be wider than in other industrialised nations.

Another controversial development is the intensifying intrusion on people's privacy in the USA and elsewhere by the NSA and other government institutions in the cause of the War on Terrorism, which has triggered worldwide discussion as to the right balance between individual liberty and the necessity of comprehensive surveillance.

To sum up, it is evident, that in spite of the USA having failed to live up to the ideals set out in the Declaration of Independence in some areas, some of its ideals have indeed stood the test of time, as millions of immigrants have found their way to America to set up a new and better existence for themselves, thereby helping to build a country that is still the economically, technologically and militarily most advanced nation in the world. *(681 words)*

B Mediation

The key points are:
– *Text form: article: heading, introduction, clear structure, conclusion*
– *Style: neutral, informative, aimed at a young readership (so it does not need to be too formal)*
– *Computer system replaces human driver*
– *Advantages: prevention of (fatal) accidents, environmentally friendly, helps to avoid traffic jams*
– *Disadvantages: lack of trust in a machine, less fun when driving, difficulties in communicating with other road users*
– *Conclusion: no immediate wide-scale introduction of autonomous cars*

The Autonomous Car: Opportunities and Shortcomings

When looking at the great number of fatal car accidents worldwide, it seems a proper solution to invent a car that drives people safely through ever growing traffic.

That is why Google has set out to build the car of the future, a so-called autonomous car that is navigated by a computer placed on its roof. Laser systems and GPS replace the human driver. In fact, prototypes are already driving through the state of Nevada (USA) – under the condition that a human driver is present who can take over if necessary.

The advantages of a computer driven car are obvious:

First, there is the prevention of (fatal) accidents, as we all know that the great majority of accidents are indeed caused by human error. Second, the autonomous car saves energy and thus helps to reduce pollution. Third, computer-driven cars can help to cut down on traffic jams, an economic problem which accounts for huge losses in terms of working hours spent on the road.

However, the self-driving car also has its shortcomings. Despite the improvement on safety most people still feel very reluctant when it comes to fully trusting in a machine to drive their cars. Apart from that, many automobile enthusiasts would dearly miss the excitement and the fun of doing the driving themselves. The human factor also plays an important role when it comes to communicating with other drivers. In fact, safe and moving traffic would require all motor vehicles to be controlled by computers, a rather unthinkable scenario at the moment.

All in all, research into autonomous cars will be continued, but mass production is still a thing of the distant future. *(281 words)*

Prüfungsteilnehmer A

Topic: Germany Today

You are taking part in a student exchange with your partner school and plan to give a presentation on your home country.

Comment on the chart.

In 2012 Britons were asked what they liked best about their country (selected results)

Countryside	65 %
History / National pride	51 %
Monarchy / Queen	42 %
Being an island	29 %
Diversity / Multiculturalism	15 %
Weather / Climate	6 %
Sense of community	6 %

From: Kellner, Peter: What do you want?
PROSPECT, June 2012 (Issue 195), p. 38.

Together with your partner speculate about what a similar question might reveal about the Germans' likes and dislikes concerning their home country. Plan the presentation.

Prüfungsteilnehmer B

Topic: Germany Today

You are taking part in a student exchange with your partner school and plan to give a presentation on your home country.

Comment on the chart.

In 2012 Britons were asked what they liked least about their country (selected results)

Anti-social behaviour / Crime	49 %
Lack of respect	43 %
Economic weakness / Unemployment	43 %
Being part of the EU	30 %
Poverty / Inequality	30 %
Bureaucracy	23 %
Class system	17 %

From: Kellner, Peter: What do you want?
PROSPECT, June 2012 (Issue 195), p. 38.

Together with your partner speculate about what a similar question might reveal about the Germans' likes and dislikes concerning their home country. Plan the presentation.

Lösungsvorschläge

Germany Today

HANS: Now, we are supposed to give a presentation on our home country for our British partner school. I have been given the results of quite an interesting survey from 2012 in which Britons were asked what they liked best about their country. As we are asked to speculate about the Germans' likes and dislikes in order to prepare our presentation, I would like to tell you what it says in this survey. Apparently, Britons really love their countryside a lot, which in fact leads the table I was given at 65 per cent. Furthermore, they seem to be attached to their history and hold their monarchy dear. Almost a third of those questioned describe Britain's being an island as something positive. Being a multicultural society on the other hand has only 15 per cent. The weather – hardly surprising – as well as the sense of community rates relatively low, at only 6 per cent.

Now I was wondering, as to whether our countryside would rate so highly with Germans. On the one hand, we do have fantastic scenery and landscapes: the Alps, the Black Forest, the Rhine valley – all of which are known all over the world being popular tourist destinations – the coast with two very different seas, the Baltic Sea for a quiet time, and the North Sea if you want something adventurous.

TALILE: Well, I should think that we do like our countryside. That's why most Germans spend their holidays in their own country. And as you have just pointed out, our countryside is very diverse, there are places for everyone.

HANS: True, so we should include this in our presentation then and illustrate it with some good images.

TALILE: Absolutely. Show that Germany is indeed a beautiful country. And in addition to the mountains we should also have some German "Wälder", German forests, like the Black Forest, because they don't really have any big forests in Britain, or do they?

HANS: Not really. I think they cut them all down for making ships, some hundred years ago. Well, there we are then. The pride Britons take in their own history. Chopping down their woods in order to become the world's greatest naval power. The decisive step towards creating an empire …

TALILE: … on which the sun never sets. You are right, most British have indeed a positive perception when it comes to their history. Empire builders, making English the lingua franca of the planet, mother of modern democracy and coming out the winner of both the First and Second World War.

HANS: So there is a big difference to Germany, is there? Compared to Britain, Germany looks like a loser, losing two world wars, and far from being the cradle of democracy, the Nazis established one of the worst dictatorships the world has ever seen, murdering millions of innocent people. Absolutely nothing one could be proud of.

TALILE: You are right, we still do have our problems when it boils down to our history, and if you look at British television, it's exactly the cliché of the brutal Nazi still dominating the scene.

HANS: Quite disturbing, isn't it. But then, on the other hand, lots of Britons know differently. They are aware of the fact that Germany has become a democratic and civilised country, and that is what we should show in our presentation.

TALILE: True, perhaps we could show some images of the football world championship in 2006, when Germany presented itself as a modern, tolerant and cheerful society, threatening nobody but being a fantastic host to the world. That brings me to the question you mentioned earlier, about the apparently fairly low sense of community in Great Britain. Do you think that in Germany there is more social cohesion?

HANS: There definitely was in 2006, but that was just a couple of weeks. All in all, I think there are still some problems when it comes to forming something like a German communal spirit. One legacy of totalitarianism: there still is the division between eastern and western Germany.

TALILE: Come on, that's our parents, or some people from the older generation. But it's not really true for us, is it? Do we, as Saxons, really care about being "eastern Germans"? Do young people in the East and West really differ that much? As far as my own experiences are concerned, this is no big deal anymore. But it should definitely be an issue we should talk about in our presentation.

HANS: Absolutely, lots of people abroad know about the Berlin Wall, so German reunification and its aftermath should have a place in our presentation. However, we should definitely conclude with a current outlook on things from our generation's point of view.

TALILE: You mean saying that young people are more tolerant? Now what about the neo-Nazis, especially, I'm afraid to say, here in eastern Germany. In the lovely countryside, there are definitely too many of them.

HANS: We surely cannot deny that problem. People will ask us about it anyway, also because of the Nazi legacy and the international media coverage. But we should point out that in Germany right wing tendencies are probably not more pronounced than in any other parts of Europe. Well, hopefully, they aren't.

TALILE: I guess we should do some serious research then, just to get the facts and figures right. It's a very sensitive subject, so we should have some solid facts to back us up.

HANS: I couldn't agree more. We really need to be careful about this topic. On the other hand, we should also point out that Germany has changed into a multi-cultural society. That migrant workers have become German nationals and that integration has come a long way. That people with Turkish or African roots are now playing for the German national team, or have great careers as actors or comedians, like Bülent Ceylan, or Kaya Yanar.

TALILE: That's something we should point out in our presentation, and as comedy plays such an important role in British life, showing how a full football stadium is cheering on a German-Turkish comedian might provide a good image of the new Germany.

HANS: Yep, there definitely is a distinct German-Turkish culture. However, we should also look on the other side, and mention the fact that not all immigrants have integrated or are accepted.

TALILE: You mean radical Muslims, who refuse to integrate, forming what the Germans refer to as "parallel societies" – and who are therefore considered a threat, or at least a nuisance.

HANS: So the multicultural society is also put into question, at least by some people.

TALILE: Well, to put it this way. There are problems which still need to be solved, but by and large, I think most Germans are generally open-minded people, who have come to terms with living in a multi-cultural and diverse society. And we get on well with our neighbours, like France and the Netherlands, even our relationship with Poland has improved. That's why I think most Germans feel quite comfortable living right in the centre of Europe.

HANS: I would agree. There definitely is a strong interest in foreign cultures, as the Germans are referred to as the world champions in terms of travel, and we eat lots of foreign food, mainly Italian, Turkish and Chinese.

TALILE: Yes, travelling abroad and foreign cuisine, these are definite German likes.

HANS: But what are our dislikes? What is it that gives Germans the creeps?

TALILE: Well, I suppose we share a lot with the British. According to the survey given to me Britons deeply dislike anti-social behaviour and crime. Well, who doesn't. And German.

definitely do. On the other hand, at least as far as I know, most of us feel quite secure, apart from in some distressed inner city areas. The second item on the list is lack of respect. I don't know ... that sounds like my grandma, like "people knew how to behave in the good old days". Ok, there is a lot of vandalism, and some inner city schools seem to be battlefields rather than places of learning, but then, I don't know if there is a widespread moral panic as regards social standards.

Another problem mentioned in the survey is economic weakness and unemployment. Of course these two things are connected. A weak economy results in greater unemployment. And as Germany is doing fairly well at the moment, with the numbers of unemployed people currently on the decline, I should think that Germans in general might not be that worried about this issue. On the other hand, you never know.

Inequality and social injustice are also factors Britons look at critically, and these are issues people in Germany also argue about. I mean there are people in this country working themselves to the bone and still they can't make ends meet and are forced to claim social benefits. No wonder the government has introduced a minimum wage.

Another aspect we could mention when it comes to inequality is directly related to social class. When I read about chances in education the other day, it appears that Germany is still quite a class ridden society. Which means that your success at school is very much dependent on your parents' income, as well as their educational background. And class also still seems to be an issue in Great Britain, even if at 17 per cent, it does not rank that highly.

One point, which accounts for 23 per cent in the British survey, might be considered even more controversial in Germany: Bureaucracy. I should think that this is an issue Germans really feel strongly about. What do you think, Hans?

HANS: I agree, bureaucracy is indeed a problem: Look at the federal structure of Germany, just from our point of view. Sixteen different states, sixteen different school systems. You try and move to another state, and school will be totally different from what you know. The same confusion applies to policing, financing and what have you. It's ever so complicated.

Another great example of German bureaucracy is taxation. My parents get really upset when they have to do their annual tax declaration. "Exceptions and loopholes all over the place. And it's ever so time consuming." I hear them say. Now, Germans are supposed to be bureaucratic by nature, but I think enough is enough.

TALILE: So we should include the topic bureaucracy in our presentation, especially when talking about the European Union. That's why the British have invented the wonderful word "Eurocrats". As we all know, being part of the EU is a really controversial issue in Great Britain, a fact that is also reflected in my survey, with Euroscepticism ranking highly at 30 per cent.

HANS: But then, as far as I know, the Germans have quite a different perspective on this. Down in their hearts, most Germans see themselves as Europeans, even if there are some doubts and criticism, especially when Germany has to pay billions in order to support countries like Greece. But at the end of the day, we know that we profit a lot from being part of the Union.

TALILE: To sum up, in our presentation we will include our relationship with our history including the Nazi legacy and German reunification, but also point out that Germany has become a modern, democratic and multi-cultural society, and that we are, by and large, committed to the European Union.

HANS: And that we are fond of our countryside, but all the same love travelling abroad and enjoy foreign food a lot, and that, like everybody else, we don't like crime. And we should show that Germany is a fairly safe and stable place, socially and economically, well, at least for the time being. Touch wood!   *(1,961 words)*

Prüfungsteilnehmer A

Topic: Prohibition

Life is full of situations in which certain objects or activities are not allowed.

Comment on the cartoon.

'Trust me. If they do ban mobile phones in schools, you will gradually learn to speak without one.'

© *Daily Mail*

Together with your partner(s) find examples where bans have been imposed and talk about the intended effects. Discuss if prohibiting something makes sense.

Topic: Prohibition

Life is full of situations in which certain objects or activities are not allowed.

Comment on the cartoon.

Steve Delmonte / cartoonstock.com

"We'd like a book that's been banned
in 23 countries, please!"

Together with your partner(s) find examples where bans have been imposed and talk about
the intended effects. Discuss if prohibiting something makes sense.

Topic: Prohibition

Life is full of situations in which certain objects or activities are not allowed.

Comment on the cartoon.

Annotation:
Mayor Bloomberg: mayor of New York (2001–2013) who tried to ban the sale of big-sized sweetened drinks

Together with your partner(s) find examples where bans have been imposed and talk about the intended effects. Discuss if prohibiting something makes sense.

Lösungsvorschläge

Prohibition

HENRIK: As you can all see, the topic we are asked to discuss is prohibition. We are supposed to find out where bans have been imposed and talk about the intended effects, and of course, whether these bans have been successful or not. Finally, we shall discuss whether prohibiting things makes sense in general or not. Okay then, let's start with the cartoon I have been given along with the task. It shows a school girl on the psychiatrist's couch, trembling all over because of an impending ban on mobile phones in schools. Apparently, for her the only way to communicate with others is via her phone, which she is actually holding to her ear at that very moment, even when speaking to the psychiatrist. The latter – holding a phone himself – seems to be at pains as to how to ease her fears, saying that she will gradually learn to speak without a mobile.

Now, this cartoon is obviously making fun of young people's dependency on modern communication technology which – up to a certain extent – has replaced what we consider normal face to face communication. And honestly, some kids, well, and adults, seem to be clinging to their phones the whole day. Of course, it is not quite as bad as portrayed in the given cartoon, but all the same, a ban on mobile phones is not exactly popular, as it really intervenes with many people's way of communicating with others. Like writing and reading text messages, checking things on Facebook and what have you.

As you all know, our school did in fact impose a ban on mobile phones for pedagogical reasons, as they said. So what were these reasons? If I remember correctly, the teachers, together with some eager anti-mobile-phone parents, had invited a psychologist from the local hospital, just to give a talk on the effects of mobile phones in the classroom. The outcome was, as you know, that playing videogames or texting just after you have done Maths or other demanding cognitive activities, wipes away all you have learned, or a lot of it anyway, from your brain. To cut a long story short, the argument went that the usage of mobile phones hampers the learning process, hinders you from getting smarter, well, to put it in a nutshell: Mobile phones make you dumb. So lots of our parents jumped to the occasion and, together with most of our teachers, promoted a general ban on mobile phones, which was then implemented.

ROBERT: For quite a good reason, I think. I mean there are exceptions, for instance if you want to do some research on the Net, like checking vocabulary. You can ask the teacher, and normally, they don't mind if you check it on your mobile. But remember, people were on the phone during the breaks, or even playing games in the lesson, not to speak of phones ringing all the time. That's why I think, as a school community, the ban did us a good turn – as even the teachers must now refrain from making phone calls during lessons or checking text messages.

PHILLIP: Well, maybe, but look at people running off to the toilet to send messages, or just retreating into some remote corner of the school to do some gaming. It is exactly what such bans provoke. Doing exactly the same thing – secretly.

HENRIK: Okay, that is a problem with all bans. But perhaps we should discuss that later. Now, Robert what kind of cartoon have you been given?

ROBERT: Well, it depicts a scene in a library, with two teenagers eager to borrow a book, quote, "that's been banned in 23 countries", unquote. This is what Phillip has just said. You ban it, and it becomes even more attractive, a must-have. Like when bands are banned for their outrageous shows or lyrics. It's the best incentive for fans to ask for more, as the forbidden fruit tastes the sweetest. In many cases, I believe record companies or book sellers deliberately stage such scandals, as they know a ban on their product is most probably going to boost sales.

The same is true for smoking, at least for some people, as we all know. Parents and teachers, and a whole lot of health experts tell you that it is ever so harmful, but maybe it is exactly that. If the adults, or experts, say it's bad for you, you enjoy it even more, or you do it just in order to oppose the authorities, the "system".

An even more telling example is drugs. Why do people take drugs? I have no idea, really. Everyone knows it is bad for you, that it might kill you in the end, or turn you into a nervous wreck, but all the same, people do it, whatever the consequences. I mean, in some countries you get shot just for the possession of the stuff. Even here, in Europe, you can face a stiff sentence if you are caught, but to no avail. So in this respect, prohibition does not really work, does it? I think we should look into this and try to find out why so many people choose to disobey the law and hurt themselves so much.

PHILLIP: Now, Robert, I suppose when people take drugs, they don't really think about the long term consequences. They think of what they gain at that very moment. Pleasure, distraction and a good feeling, like being able to dance all through the night without tiring. They do not feel powerless then, on the contrary, they feel as if they are on top of things.

I mean, people, from all walks of life, don't like to be told what to do. Like being told what to eat. You remember when the German Greens suggested the Germans take one day a week as a veggie day. There was quite an uproar in the media, coming even from people who would normally sympathise with green ideas. Now, talking about food. I have been given a cartoon showing a big, bloated, overweight American, holding a ridiculously small drink in his left and a supersized fast food meal in his right. He asks the then Mayor of New York when, as a consequence of the latter's attempt to ban the sale of oversized sweetened drinks, his weight would start coming off. The discrepancy is obvious. What does it help to ban sweetened drinks, if the fatty fast food is still consumed in such vast amounts as shown in the cartoon. It is simply ridiculous, and does not have any positive effect on people's health. Perhaps, a broader campaign for a "healthy America" could bring some change, but that has to be carefully planned as a change in diet must be accepted by the people themselves. It cannot just be imposed by the state, not in America, not anywhere. Your body belongs to you, and most people consider their bodies and their health a very private matter. So if you can't convince them to eat healthier, there is not much you can do.

ROBERT: You could impose a tax on unhealthy food, like they do with cigarettes. In fact, that does have an effect, as tobacco has become so expensive, people do not smoke as much as they used to.

PHILIPP: But you can easily lose the next election if you overdo it. An extra tax on fast food will probably be a very unpopular decision, especially in America. So you really have to think of how far you can go.

HENRIK: Talking about America: You remember the Prohibition. Forbidding people to drink alcohol. What was the outcome? A rise in organised crime most of all, as people like Al Capone and other bootleggers got filthy rich, and powerful. And millions drinking perhaps even more, secretly in illegal bars, called speakeasies, and in private. No wonder the American state gave up after about 13 years. They just couldn't follow through, with millions of Americans resisting it.

ROBERT: Reminds me of the Puritans who established a dictatorship in England during the 17th century. Not only did they want to ban alcohol, they also closed down the theatres, forbade music and even the celebration of Christmas. Just because they thought it would distract people from what they considered to be a godly life. Anyway, it didn't work. They could only impose it in part, by establishing a police state. After they had been driven from power, people livened it up all the more.

PHILLIP: We definitely have some examples here, where prohibition did not work. People just did not obey. I suppose they didn't see any sense in it.

HENRIK: Indeed, that seems to be the point. I mean everybody in his right mind agrees that children should not work in factories. Interestingly enough, people in Europe thought otherwise just some 150 years ago. But at the moment, we all agree that child labour should be prohibited. And people in Europe obey the law, because they accept it. Because they see that sending their kids to school makes much more sense.

ROBERT: Good point. Education is widely accepted as something positive, and child labour isn't. Another example is making fire in the wood when it is hot, and especially when there is a drought. Only idiots disobey orders prohibiting the making of fires or having a barbecue in the forest at that time.

PHILLIP: So as a conclusion, we can probably agree that in order to have a far-reaching effect, bans have to strike people as meaningful, as something worthwhile. Otherwise they will do almost anything to evade them. *(1,601 words)*

Erfolgreich durchs Abitur mit den STARK-Reihen

Abitur-Prüfungsaufgaben

Anhand von Original-Aufgaben die Prüfungssituation trainieren. Schülergerechte Lösungen helfen bei der Leistungskontrolle.

Abitur-Training

Prüfungsrelevantes Wissen schülergerecht präsentiert. Übungsaufgaben mit Lösungen sichern den Lernerfolg.

Klausuren

Durch gezieltes Klausurentraining die Grundlagen schaffen für eine gute Abinote.

Kompakt-Wissen

Kompakte Darstellung des prüfungsrelevanten Wissens zum schnellen Nachschlagen und Wiederholen.

Interpretationen

Perfekte Hilfe beim Verständnis literarischer Werke.

(Bitte blättern Sie um)